Palmiro & Metaphysics
Contemplating Everyday Mystery
by
Alain Marie Sauret
Copyright © 2018 Alain Marie Sauret

Designed by James Kent Ridley
Published by Goodbooks Media
Printed in the U.S.A

ISBN-13: 978-1725609624
ISBN-10: 1725609622

This is a draft version of a work in progress,
printed in its present form as a required text for students
of philosophy at the
Franciscan University of Steubenville.

goodbook
GOODBOOKS MEDIA
3453 Aransas
Corpus Christi, Texas, 78411
www.goodbookmedia.com

PALMIRO
&
Metaphysics

Contemplating
Everyday Mystery

PROLOGUE
Who is Palmiro?!

Palmiro lives in Glasgow. He's my brother in law. He was named after his grand-dad, Palmiro Foresi, the father of Pasquale Foresi who was one of the cofounders, with Chiara Lubich, of the Focolare Movement, alias "The Work of Mary", a dynamic wave of spirituality, focused on the intimacy with Jesus and Mary in daily life. The name of "Palmiro" comes actually to "*Palma*" the foliage people use on Palm Sunday to celebrate the Lord. It is actually symbolic to use the name Palmiro to indicate the one who brings the Palms to celebrate the truth, which is one of the main metaphysical issues…

Together, Palmiro and I, we often meet over the phone. Many are the topics of our conversations, as it is usual between relatives. Slowly, but consistently we started enjoying talking philosophy together, particularly metaphysics issues.

The conversation on the topic took by surprise both of us. It was a remarkable involvement. He called me one afternoon to say hello to his sister, Chiara, who is my wife. Then, while expecting to talk to her over the phone Palmiro asked me what I was doing.

- I am grading philosophy papers. I said
- *I wonder how you can be teaching such boring stuff?*
- Philosophy is tiresome only for those who do not trust it.
- *How that?* He insisted.
- Pythagoras called "philosophy" the expertise of those who love wisdom. I replied.
- *What do you mean by wisdom?*
- Wisdom is intimacy with truth!
- *You're kidding me, right!? Can you explain that in plain English?* (Actually we were talking in Italian)
- According to Aquinas, truth is when what you say corresponds to the facts. In its original version in Latin the words are: "*Veritas sequitur esse rerum*". Then, the degrees of truth belong to the field of metaphysics. It can be seen under diverse perspectives.
- *I was told that metaphysics does not exist anymore.* Palmiro argued
- On the tracks of Immanuel Kant many people, especially scholars, believe today that there is no room any more for metaphysics.
- *Why?* He did insist.
- Because Kant believes that there exists only what we know. He makes reality dependant on knowledge. Therefore there is not such thing as a "being", which is the main topic of metaphysics. When we believe that reality does not exist outside of our mind, no metaphysics is available.
- *Is that possible?*
- Well, let us proceed by steps
- (short silence)
- Many people today do not believe that truth really does exist. They resemble the Sophists, whom Socrates opposed.
- *Is that metaphysics?* He asked.
- Yes, it is (…) The name was given to certain works of

Aristotle that his followers did not know how to put together, not being sure of what they were dealing with: those books, 14 actually, were dealing with problems of physics but addressing facts which are beyond physics...

- *So, what is metaphysics?* was the last question he asked and the one I do now intend to address.

Palmiro died on Sat. Nov 15, 2014. His presence is still alive in my heart. Through the following pages, our conversation continues...

Metaphysics

GREETINGS

WELCOME ABOARD,
AS WE EMBARK ON OUR JOURNEY INTO THE WONDROUS VASTS OF THE UNIVERSE OF METAPHYSICS!

Hello Everyone,

Hello to everyone who wants to become familiar with Metaphysics. Studying Metaphysics is a serious endeavor, full of interesting discoveries, which involves a specific behavior which slowly but surely will change us into true philosophers. The process starts with course reading; notwithstanding, as the Gospel says, all those who listen to the word are already pruned. The enlightening process does start here and never ends. It can become the amazing adventure of our entire life.

We are supposed to address together during the reading the issues which make the facts consistent, and cause them to be what they are. Metaphysics addresses what stands beyond ("*meta*")what physical things are, which they depend on. Our study will promote the capacity to see. It is simple but not obvious. All people look around but only a few can see. Metaphysics trains us to watch at what fundamentally stands below the evidence of facts. Such ability to see requires an enlightenment that all true philosophers address and acquire sometimes under diverse perspectives: it will be our concern to investigate their suggestions and methods.

Metaphysics expands in the meanders of the universe of culture, history, and people. It is an open inquiry, which may be frought with difficulties at the beginning, because of the new perspectives that it includes and the necessity to think 'out of the box,' as many previous students liked to stress. They agreed to say that, little by little, philosophy becomes more and more insightful, as soon as we accept to look at the facts for what they really are.

As a result, there is some hardship while we start. It is part of the game. Search is a process of suffering to delivering acknowledgment. The faster we address the difficult beginning, the faster we will move forward, and the earlier we will enjoy the new neighborhood of knowledge and wisdom that metaphysics is. We will improve together in the management of the secret of life and the way love gives consistency to knowledge. We need to become familiar with the proper interaction of things... It is a natural process. There is nothing mysterious. Metaphysics investigates what the world is, what other people are, what we personally are, where we come from and wherever we move to. Somehow we roughly know that already... Following the tracks of great philosophers, a course of metaphysics is supposed to induce us to **deliver** what we deeply know inside but are not yet aware of. Socrates defined it as a process of "*maieutics*," of "delivery", as by a midwife. Delivery, indeed!

μαιευτική
(midwifery)

At the source of our study there is the experience that J. Maritain calls "Intuition of Being", which M.-D. Philippe explains as "Judgment of existence", and previously Aquinas indicated as "The act of Being"… His coeval Bonaventure sees as a process of enlightenment, and John Duns Scotus as sharing of God's love in the whole of nature, which allowed Maritain to define such expertise as "Philosophy of Existence"… The diverse approaches refer to the same genuine fact that Heidegger pointed out as "why there is something instead of nothing." Such connection between life and understanding is typical of Franciscan tradition.

Metaphysics uses a specific language that brings its own acquaintance. It must be grasped from inside. Then its understanding grows up and produces our blossoming with it. Ultimately it becomes a magnificent endeavor. Everyone will be going through before we know it!

Expect to encounter two challenges at the outset of our endeavor. First of all there is the need of sharing, which is necessary to philosophy as much as air is needed for our lungs. Sharing is the way students overcome the gap between their own awareness and true knowledge. Do not hesitate to ask questions, to yourself first, then among friends. Every concern is an occasion to improve. As far as your inquiry fits text topics your inquiry makes the reading interactive. Sharing and communicating to one another, we get acquainted, we memorize, we read, we think, we speak, we understand, we know, in one word, we increase in knowledge and wisdom far beyond what at first we were expecting. This is the reason why a philosophy journey is personal but not individual. Then, the second challenge is trying to anticipate the contents of the following chapter; here is the manner to check your advancement in study. The good news is that every challenge is ultimately a time of improvement. They make the learning consistent. Such improvement leads students towards the awareness of what things are. It is a smooth enlightenment.

Each coming chapter deals with a specific aspect of metaphysics. While reading it, somehow it is going to change our life. Each one is a diverse enlightening, leading us to addressing everything with the awareness that, slowly but surely, unveils the amazing surrounding reality. So let's start of our splendid journey together.

Most of us are familiar with the place of wisdom, sharing and reflection located at Taizé, near Lyon, France. Brother Roger Schutz, founder of Taizé community, who died on Aug.14, 2005, is considered as a prophet among the people of our days, just because he lived in simplicity of heart and clearness of mind. He never planned to do anything special but; nonetheless, his consistent life and behaviors made him create a very strong community of prayer, meditation, and dialog, which looks like an example of how to promote a new society, which may improve our civilization towards the globalization process. He made true the words of Pope St. John XXIII to which Brother Roger was fond of referring:

"Be joyful, seek the best, and let the sparrows chirp".

That could be our motto, too, at the start of the semester together.

Congratulations

Hello everyone!

After offering the contents of "Greetings" note, during a university course, the insights on "Welcome aboard a Metaphysics Journey", provoked a vivid discussion in class; If reading it made such an enlightenment for you, felicitations are in order. I congratulate you for the good insights you got, showing that you are able to listen and understand... That reminds me of the experience I got when observing in the eyes of many the enthusiasm of getting the truth, the enjoyment of grasping here and there pieces of wisdom. Nonetheless, during the following thirty minutes, when the discourse became more speculative, I also could recognize the concern appearing on the faces of most of the people in attendance. It's ok! Don't be uneasy. We will return more systematically to the issue of **being** when dealing with ontology. Don't worry with the necessary hardship at the beginning of the course.

Among the few issues we started with, we saw the different kinds of language: **equivocality** in daily conversation, **univocity** in science, and **analogy** in philosophy and, particularly, in metaphysics. Allow me to make here an analogy, too, as an example. While teaching in class we need to use the blackboard; and in order to write properly on the blackboard we need to have it clean. In the same manner to get the proper context when we share issues in metaphysics we need a warm neighborhood, a milieu of friendship, an atmosphere of peace. Friendship and peace of heart are the necessary context we need to develop, for addressing and properly studying metaphysics. It may seem surprising for some. Let me explain better.

A few mornings ago, in the liturgy of the Mass, the Responsorial Acclamation to psalm 85 was: "**Kindness and truth shall meet**." According to a very old tradition with which Aristotle agreed, and after him almost all great thinkers walked in his tracks, like Augustine, Aquinas, Bonaventure, and recently Maritain: people get the truth with the heart but then, they need the head to understand it in a manner that allows them to share what they received. Kindness is the behavior of heart, the proper way to get the truth which, later, blossoms in the head. In other words, we grasp the entity of facts with the heart, and later we understand them with the head. Here is why Augustine and Anselm said that we need to believe in order to understand. This fits with the words of Pascal that "The heart has reasons that reason disregards". Nonetheless, heart and head need to interact; Kindness and truth shall meet. Jean Daujat referred several times the words of Gandhi that "Being kind is more important than being right", which Mother Theresa stressed, saying that "Kind words can be short and easy to speak but their echoes are truly endless." I posit that everyone who reads these pages knows by experience how much these words are true.

There is more to say. **First of all**, contrarily to common opinion, in the process of knowledge the heart is first,

knowledge is second. In their teaching Thomas Philippe, O.P. and Marie-Dominique Philippe, O.P., spoke about what they call affective knowledge which precedes speculative knowledge. I was not sure on that issue until I experienced directly when I discovered how this is true by looking on my grandkids that I had the chance to watch home while they are growing. Yes, it is true! We grasp the facts around with our heart before we understand everything with the head. Young kids know first what they want, a walk, a hug, a selection of food… Later, when language emerges, they start understanding and they can express and say what they want and tell you why.

Also, **Second of all**, the logic of life is richer than rational logic which suggests first to observe, to see, to understand and then to decide. We properly proceed according to the opposite manner. St. Bonaventure suggests that when we do not live the way we believe we soon end up thinking the way we live. The gospel suggests the same. According to the Gospel of John, the Lord encourages us to first live His Word, which is the Truth, for "Those who live the truth go the light" (Jn 3:21) and "the truth makes them free" (Jn 8:32), which stresses both the priority of truth and then that it is experiencing it that makes us understand.

Maritain said that most of the time in philosophy there is more to contemplate than to understand. It means that the truth has to become a way of life before becoming a way of understanding. Here is why he suggested that every class must be a time of contemplation. We must do our best to make it happening in our reading during our philosophy journey, while addressing the four main fields of first philosophy that metaphysics are, i.e. ontology, peratology, critique and natural theology. According to what has been previously said: Metaphysics must become our way of living, before being our way of thinking. Intimacy with truth will change our life and will promote us towards a better understanding.

Along the journey, do not try to check all what you learned; more important is to enjoy familiarity with the whole field of philosophy, in what some thinkers call the no man lands where philosophy does grow, between common sense, science and theology. Remember, when you have a question, let it grow in your mind and continue the reading with confidence: as the question rose up, the answer will pop up in your mind while proceeding ahead the journey.

During the reading, underline the issues that speak highly to you and your meditation will make slowly the truth more evident.

STARTING METAPHYSICS

BREAKING ICE

There are many ways to enter the field of metaphysics. As soon as you have your foot inside you have entered. When you want to take a piece of paper, it does not matter what section of it you seize in your hand. Whatever is the section of it that you hold, you have it all. It is the same with metaphysics: as far as we deal with some metaphysics issue, wherever we start with it, it works well. It is a way to repeat the medieval popular motto "All roads lead to Rome." It would be like saying: "whatever you do, when you seek the truth, you will find it".

Addressing metaphysics is not like moving on a map from one city to another. It is not the process of gathering information as it is in many fields of study, when quantity of knowledge provides expertise... Metaphysics is a process of growing into wisdom. Famous are the words of Heraclitus (Pre-Socratic +475 BC) "A lot of knowledge does not provide wisdom." Such improvement requires a particular capacity to see in order to get a better level of understanding. It is more likely similar to the process of swimming: it does not matter how you do move or where you do go through the water but how much you get the capacity to float and breathe in the air while moving in the water.

Let us begin with a short account.

(I) Anecdote of Two Leaders: Raïssa & Jacques Maritain

A. **Going across Saint-James Street.**

• Sorbonne students, Raïssa & Jacques, pathes crossed during October 1901. She is a Jew, born in Marioupol on the Don, Ukraine, who flew to Paris with her family to avoid the pogroms of persecution. He is a Calvinist. Both are seeking the truth. Because of this common fervor, their friendship surprisingly deepens.

• Both are disappointed with the positivism prevailing in Sorbonne, which leaves no room beyond sensorial activity for spiritual issues. Sorbonne professors teach that Kant has concluded any philosophic endeavor. They teach that philosophy is over and science has replaced philosophy (See later Jean-François Revel). Common friends, like Louis Massignon, witness how dramatically they undertake the endeavor.

• Jul.1903, in the botanical garden, they despair for not being able to find the truth. Their souls are starving for the Absolute, as Raïssa wrote:

Before leaving the "Jardin des Plantes" we reached a solemn decision which brought us some peace: to look sternly in the face, even to the ultimate consequence — insofar as it would be in our power — the fact of that unhappy and cruel universe, wherein the sole light was the philosophy of skepticism and relativism.

We would accept no concealment, no cajolery from persons of consequence, asleep in their false security. The Epicureanism they proposed was a snare, just as was sad Stoicism; and estheticism — that was mere amusement. Neither did we wish, because the Sorbonne had spoken, to consider that the last word had been said. The French university world was then so hermetically sealed within itself that by the very thinking of this simple thought we showed some little merit.

Thus we decided for some time longer to have confidence in the unknown; we would extend credit to existence, look upon it as an experiment to be made, in the hope that to our ardent plea, the meaning of life would reveal itself, that new values would stand forth so clearly that they would enlist our total allegiance, and deliver us from the nightmare of a sinister and useless world.

But if the experiment should not be successful, the solution would be suicide; suicide before the years had accumulated their dust, before our youthful strength was spent. We wanted to die by a free act if it were impossible to live according to the truth."

(Raïssa Maritain, *We Have Been Friends Together*, Longmans, NY 1942, Ch.III, p. 77-78.)

- Charles Péguy leads them to Henri Bergson at the Collège de France, across rue Saint-Jacques. Going across Saint-James St. is the paradigm of transcendence: the truth is always near to us, nearer than any place we go and look for it. Transcendence is a way of the heart, a way of the soul, not a mere speculative endeavor as Nietzsche said: "there is no road for the Hyperborean."

- Henri Bergson is stressing the faculty of intuition which allows every human being to get the truth through and beyond sensorial experience. Raïssa and Jacques start a new endeavor. They finally understand that there is a way towards the truth beyond science.

- Doing metaphysics is striking the distance between what we do (existentially) and what we are (ontologically). Doing metaphysics is overcoming the barriers that we address and that actually are more ghosts than real difficulties. In other words, doing metaphysics is going across Saint James Street.

B. Conversion and consistent behavior

- 25 June 1905, they encounter Léon Bloy (Role of N.D. de La Salette).

• 11 June 1906, baptism of Jacques and Raïssa, 3 Aug. 1st Communion.

• Consistent with a Faith that they believe is not compatible with Philosophy, (1) Jacques refuses to teach and accept every job opportunity (2) they leave for Heidelberg, Germany to a specialization in biology.

C. Meeting Aquinas provokes a new endeavor

• 1908, back to Paris (rue Jussieu); disease of Raïssa; suggestions of Fr. Humbert Clérissac, O.P. to read Aquinas… It was a sudden illumination. On the track of Aquinas they discovered that "*Every philosopher is a contemplative.*" (Pierre-Thomas Dehau, *Des Fleuves d'Eau vive*) or to say it with the words of Marie-Dominique Philippe, the founder of the brothers of Saint John: "*The art of a philosopher consists in putting intelligence at the service of heart.*" (Marie-Dominique Philippe, *Cours de Métaphysique*)

• Reading Saint Thomas they find the long tradition of philosophy from Socrates to Aristotle and later: they discover **Critical Realism**, and enter into a spiritual and intellectual engagement.

• Later, applying Aristotle's method, they started a circle of contemplation and updated the Aquinas' doctrine, addressing all current issues, even the most burning of the days with a full wisdom, according to Bonaventure words: "*Live as you must and you will think as you hope to*", which fit with Gospel words: "*The one who lives the truth gets the light and the light makes free*" (cf. Jn 8:32) and "*The truth will set you free*" — Ibid.

• The life of Maritain is the growing life of those who seek the truth all along their life and exert the process of moving near to the truth, to the One who is the truth as described in. St. Francis said: "*Conversion is a growing *capacity of suffering"*

Actually, Maritain himself describes the life of a philosopher as a Christian life: "*The life of a philosopher consists in the painful paradox of a total fidelity to eternal values in a tight connection with the most attentive understanding of the anguishes of the times, in order to bring the world back to the Truth*" (Jacques Maritain, *Carnet de notes*)

- At the end of his life, Maritain left us the wisdom of great endeavor, of familiarity with the truth. The day after Maritain died, Pope Paul VI wanted to show his great esteem and did testify from his window on St. Peter Square, saying "*a voice has ceased to cry this week in the south of France, it is the one of Jacques Maritain, who was really a great thinker in our time, a master in the art of thinking, living and praying. He died alone and poor, associated with the "Petits Frères" of Father Charles de Foucauld. His voice and his stature will remain great in the tradition of philosophical thought and catholic meditation.*" (Paul VI, *Angelus in St. Peter's Square, 28 April 1973*)

- Somehow Jacques Maritain helped me to rediscover Franciscan tradition, when life is the key of understanding…

Bl. Charles de Foucauld

(II) Philosophy and Contemplation

Allow me to introduce the issue of what metaphysics is with the words of Maritain, (the numeration was put by Maritain in his work on *The Degrees of Knowledge*, Chapter 8). He wrote…

(10) For St. John of the Cross, as for St. Thomas Aquinas and the whole Christian tradition, the final end of human life is transformation in God, "to become God by participation", which is fully achieved in heaven by the beatific vision and beatific love, and fulfilled here below, in faith, by love. The supernatural love of charity, by which we love God and creatures with a properly divine love, makes us one with God and causes us to be one same spirit with Him. *Qui adhaeret Deo, unus spiritus est.* "The end of all actions and human affections," writes St. Thomas, "is the love of God, that is why there is no measure regulating that love; it is itself the measure and measures everything else, and can never be too great. The interior act of charity has the *ratio* of an end because the highest good of man is that the soul adhere to God, in accordance with the words of the Psalmist, "it is good to cling to God…" and St. John of the Cross writes, "As love is union of the Father and the Son, even so also is it union of the soul with God."

St. John of the Cross

Perfection consists in charity, says St. Thomas again. The perfection of divine love is commanded of all, undoubtedly not as a term to be immediately attained, but at least as the end to which everyone must tend each according to his condition. *Estote perfecti* — seek the perfection of charity which is a perfection of heaven, the *raison d'être* of our life. "At eventide they will examine thee in love", cries St. John of the Cross. And again: "After all, it was for the goal of this love that we were created." It is our supreme reward on this earth; for love confers no payment save of itself." — "The soul that loves God must not claim or hope for aught else from Him save the perfection of love." Before seeing God in heaven as he sees us, the highest achievement of our life here below is to love God "as much as He loves us." Despite human frailty, such is the state of souls who have attained to spiritual marriage, attaining during their moral life — I mean in a state of increasingly rapid motion and progress — that equality of love with God which is consummated in the blessed, these souls truly unite heaven and earth within themselves. "*Le amara tanto como es amada.*" (She will love him as much as she is loved). No stronger words have been spoken, illumining our darkness as with a lightning flash, because — as is the wont of John of the Cross — they unveil in a concrete way the highest goal accessible to us here on earth, before the dissolution of this poor flesh. They show us, if I may so speak, our penultimate end, our end on earth, and the end of this perishable existence itself.

(11) In beatitude we shall be deified by intellection. But this very vision will be the crowning effect of love, the hand by which it will grasp its good,

and in the delights of exultant love this vision will blossom. Furthermore, here below, where we do not know God by His essence but by His effects, no pure knowledge is able to unite us to God immediately and without an intervening distance. But love, on the contrary, can. "God, who in this world cannot be known by himself, can be loved by himself" and "immediately", as the Angelic Doctor profoundly remarks. And again: "The love of charity has for its object that which is already possessed," to wit, he who has already given himself by grace. And what does the Catholic faith say? That God is love, as St. John proclaimed. *Oti Qeos agaph estin*. We are to understand that, even though god has many proper names, and though to Moses as *Thought of Thoughts*, the Gospel reveals to us an even more secret name, by showing us that He is subsistent Love. As love He transforms us into Himself; this is the name that holds all His secrets with us. These truths which we stammer out were the very breath of life to St. John of the Cross. That is why he said "there is no better or more necessary work than love."— "God is pleased with naught save love." That is why the idea that pure knowledge or pure understanding could be the means proportionate to union with God, seemed to him to be absurdity itself. That is why he is convinced, with all Christianity, that **contemplation** is not its own end but remain a means (the most excellent of means and already united to the end), for the union of love with God and that it is itself a knowledge of love, a "loving attentiveness to God."

We are here at the antipodes of neo-Platonic intellectualism. And we are here at the very heart of the theology of St. Thomas. We must add, we are also very far from certain modern interpretation of St. John of the Cross. This doctrine is a commentary on a Canticle because it explains the moments in a dialogue of love, at whose end the lover and the beloved are but one voice, truly one in a unity not of substance but of love: "Two natures in one spirit and love".

Jacques Maritain, *The Degrees of Knowledge*, Scribner's Sons, NY 1959, Ch. VIII, pp.320-24.

(III) Critical Realism

A. Critical Realism is the so-called method of inquiry started by Socrates (*Maieutics*), and then developed by Aristotle, Aquinas, Maritain, Gilson, Guitton, Daujat, Garrigou-Lagrange, Sertillanges – to name just a few among Aquinas disciples. C.R.. is based first on facts and second using knowledge (information sources) and intelligence (critical reasoning) to understand the facts. Critical realism accepts the priority of reality on knowledge.

Such a method suggests that every philosophical inquiry must consider the facts, pay attention to possible pieces of information, perceive comments about, and examine related discourses... even those we dislike. In other words: observe everything and then reflect personally on collected data... We must go beyond the trap of the words in order to discover the solution through contemplation and meditation on the mystery of facts. While idealism accepts only what I know, Critical Realism agrees with the fact that even if I do not know you, you may exist...

B. Critical Realism addresses the whole of reality; it must not be confused with many pseudorealisms which stress only a part of the whole. Briefly stated :

Critical realism is not **Naïve Realism**, (See Maritain's

Degrees of Knowledge) for it rejects the view of naïve realism that the external world is as it is perceived.

In the same way, Critical realism **Does Not Correspond** to any of the following theories, which make an improper use of "realism" like :

Metaphysical Realism, which holds that there exists a mind, as independent reality;

Scientific Realism, stating that reality is the material world and mathematic formulae, for scientific realism puts the focus is on propositions and include unobservable entities;

Theological Realism, consider reality the material world as it is given under God's perspective;

Semantic Realism holds that science and theology contain propositions, that are statements capable of being true or false in the sense of correspondence to the reality to which they refer;

Epistemic realism, which holds that it is possible to put forward propositions that are approximately true, that some propositions actually are approximately true, and that belief in their approximate truth can be justified. In scientific realism this applies primarily to theories and theoretical propositions about unobservable entities; in theology it applies to propositions and theories about God.

All these partial realisms differ from true position of critical realism which does not make any previous discrimination on the world to address. Critical Realism observes everything, gather all available information, and then reflects personally on collected data... We must go beyond the trap of the words in order to discover the solution inside of the contemplation of the mystery of reality.

Critical realism teaches that reality is first, knowledge comes afterwards: it agrees with Shakespeare, "there is more in the world than in my mind," Such a fact is true for every kind of knowledge and especially for spiritual topics which are beyond sensorial experience.

It does proceed by steps....

C. To say it succinctly:

(1) C.R. is looking first to the facts, with the best and simplest way we can,

(2) Getting all possible information and considering every eventual connected discourse,

(3) Then reflecting personally on all collected data,

(4) Avoiding the trap of the words to discover the solution in the mystery of reality (Reality overcomes Logic). This is why for John Duns Scotus, "Univocity" is not the same in logic and in metaphysics.

John Duns Scotus

(5) When facing some aporetical question, we must look at it from the highest view point.

(6) Critical Realism is the typical method started with Socrates (Maieutics) then followed and improved by Aristotle and Aquinas, which leads to a doctrine and never to a system - A philosophy system does not address the whole of reality.

(7) While Maieutics was a method of teaching, C.R. is a method of inquiry.

(8) CR is able to get the best of every philosophy thinker: it never rejects anyone or even does not decide on a first glance among opposed statements of them which of these is right and the one is wrong. The attitude of CR is another: it

seeks what is consistent in every thinker.

(9) While a philosophy system rejects systematically what does not comply with it, C.R. does address every philosophy with a favorable approach and does not stop before it gets what really a philosopher did express. In other words, while every system rejects anything else C.R. is able to deal with every one else. It is the only method which is consistent.

(10) While C.R. is able to understand and get the positive in every philosophy waves, the diverse philosophy waves are handicapped in their analysis of the facts and are not able to understand properly the doctrine of Thomism.

(11) Those who consider that Aquinas' doctrine is a system (ambiguity of the word "Thomism") and go with the conclusions of St. Thomas study are not thomist because they do not use C.R. even with the thoughts of St. Thomas in order to understand what Aquinas would say if he was living today among us, dealing with the issues that we have to address.

D. As a result :

(a) While dealing with the many contradictivel theories which ragged among the Pre-Socratic thinkers, Aristotle said that "there is no stupid idea that has not had some philosopher to promote and defend it". The same was said by Descartes in his *Meditations*. But there is a huge difference between the two philosophers: while Descartes reject all through a sort of cleaning history from every mistake, Aristotle showed why someone promoted some statement in opposition to another: typical is his reflection on Parmenides

René Descartes

Heraclitus

Parmenides

and Heraclitus, who lived in the same period at almost a 1000 miles distance from one another. While the first affirmed in *Magna Graecia* the permanency of the being, the other stated in Asia Minor the "*Logos*" as the universal experience of change… We know then that they addressed the same issue under opposite perspectives: permanency shows identity of concepts (mental being), while change stresses the experience of change (real being).

(b) Philosophy addresses reality as a whole. Oppositely to science, it barely addresses a question with a YES/NO answer. It is more likely a structural answer which is proper. As an example, between TRUTH and SEARCH for truth, what is first? A philosopher seeks the truth. He is aware of the existential priority of search and the ontological priority of truth. Truth and search are both first under a diverse perspective. The whole picture is said in Augustine's words, "Our heart is restless until it rests in you" (*Confessions* §1), or paraphrasing Pascal's words: "You did not find me if I was not looking for you." While science addresses properly entire sections of reality, philosophy addresses the whole as such in a continuous interaction.

(c) There are human experiences which go far beyond words. During our study we occasionally see that prayer is an intimate relationship that goes beyond words like love between people. Sometimes love is being silent together as prayer does together with God. Such a silent behavior is an even more intense relationship than intimate conversation...

(d) When you are really facing some aporetic (tending to doubt) question or contradictorily statement, please search for a higher level of experience, which offers a more homogeneous perspective, a more insightful sight on it. Never answer a question at the same level the question is asked. Get a better point of view.

(e) **First Philosophy** is the nickname of metaphysics. It is the branch of philosophy that examines the fundamental issues on the nature of reality, beyond (meta-) the regular perspective (-physics) of things. Metaphysics is traditionally divided on Ontology (being as such: nature of being, substance and accident), Peratology (actual or precarious being: form & matter, causality & changes), Critique (basic relationship between mind and matter, between the subject, who knows, and the object, which is known — Critique does include both Gnoseology or else Theory of Knowledge, and basic elements of Epistemology, which refers to the meaning, the nature and the purpose of Science) and finally Natural Theology (ultimate causes and existence of God — It is important to notice that Natural Theology is not Theology in its strict sense. Natural theology appropriately belongs to philosophy as its natural way of investigating on God. Such a study opens the way to Theology, which is the specific study of revelation — a good philosophy makes possible any appropriate Theology).

(IV) What Is a Being?

"The being can be said in many ways."
                    (Aristotle, Book "G")

1. **BEING** refers to whatever exists. A being is something that exists. A "being" is "everything which is". It can exist outside of our knowledge (real being) or just in our thoughts (mental being). As far as it exists somehow and somewhere, it is properly a "being."

2. **Real being** — refers to every being whose existence does not depend on my knowledge. It refers to every being belonging to the world. When we adopt the idealism position that only what we know may exist, it means that we consider that nobody existed in the class before we knew each other, which is an absurdity. Every real being is in act (every real being in act of what it is and it is in potency of any possible change). Then, when we talk about Being in act or **Actual Being** — we refer to any being in its actual existence.

3. Yes a **BEING** does consist in something that exists. And as such, the being may show up under diverse aspects, with a different consistency. Aristotle affirms that "the being can be said in many ways." We may deal with a Real being, which is a being whose existence does not depend of my knowledge. It is a being belonging to the world. Every real being is in act, Actual Being, or being in act, which is every being in its actual existence. Each being in act is in potency of any possible change. Potential being is something that can develop or become actual. It refers to every possibility an actual being has to change. Mental being is a being existing only in my mind and not in the reality surrounding me. Mental being usually refers to universal concepts (e.g. nothingness, essence, value). It is also known as "rational being," which must not be confused with Intentional being,

which is the kind of being which refers to a real being when it is present to my mind in the process of knowledge. It refers to an event. It is no more material and not yet mental. However it is consistent. Aristotle calls it intentional. Additionally we must recall that Aristotle classifies the Real Being in ten categories, the Substance and nine Accidents. Here it is said, in a very rough synthesis on the description of the being the whole panorama of ontology and peratology.

4. Since the onset of philosophy up to our days there is a Common Misunderstanding on the Being. The main confusion about the being is to put together mental being (that which exists only in our mind) and real being (that which exists in reality, independently of the fact that I know it or not). The distinction was made by Aristotle, to resolve the huge confusion made by Heraclitus (whom, such confusion induced to deny consistency of things and to state that everything is change — such a permanent change was called *logos* = Logos) and by Parmenides (whom such a confusion induced to deny any change and to affirm that everything is permanency and the same: If the being is, it is what it is, therefore no change is possible, and any change is only illusional).

5. Today such a confusion continues to induce philosophers to deny after Hegel (and the Rationalists) the consistency of reality, or after Marx and Foucault the consistency of individuals, culture, and values, or after Kant (and the Idealists) and Derrida (and the Structuralists) to disregard the existence of things, or after Hume (and empiricists) ito state the incapacity of people to know facts and address reality. Such a variety of interpretations should not discourage the neo-philosopher that every student is, but conversely encourage him or her to investigate more closely the events, in order to get the full understanding of them.

Hegel

Marx

Foucault

Kant

Derrida

Hume

6. The solution suggested by Socrates, Aristotle, Aquinas and their followers is that every Being is real in its existence. A being cannot be considered as a mere concept (it would only be an essence, which as such the being is not). As a concept the being would indicate the mental characteristics of it. Every real being exists right now and it is what it is, with a consistency that even includes changes. Under the pole of being (ontological pole) every being is something (what it is

= whatness = essence), contemporaneously, under the pole of facts (existential pole) every being is supposed to change, so it is pregnant of its future changes (it holds the capability of the changes it is supposed to get further...). Such a capacity is called its potential of change. So the being is said to be IN ACT or what it is now, and to be IN POTENCY of every eventual changes. Such a capacity to think a being as existing simultaneously in act and in potency is typical of Aristotle.

7. With such a reflection, Aristotle included the whole capacity of understanding things (their essence) inside of their real actuality (their existence). Such a distinction is the key for addressing the question of Universals. He was able to put together theory and praxis, rationalism (idealism) and existentialism. He gave the proper suggestion to address together opposed theories, and to show that every theory usually indicates just a part of reality, as a picture indicates only a side, a perspective on a place. Philosophy, according to Aristotle, must restore the knowledge of the whole face of reality.

(V) The Intuition of the Being

(1) Critical Realism leads to the fundamental experience of the being. A "being" is whatever does exists. A "being" is "everything which is". It can exist outside of our knowledge (real being) or just in our thoughts (mental being), or even in our imagination and in the movies (virtual being). As far as it exists somehow and somewhere, it is properly a "being." Nonetheless, metaphysics is focused on real being: what belongs to the facts. According to J. Maritain, addressing real being is more an action of contemplation than of study.

Nobody can become familiar with the truth if she/he does not experience such intuition of being, which is the perception of existing, i.e. of being out of nothingness. Metaphysics starts here. It includes the amazing awareness of the precariousness of our existence and the mystery of it, together with the fact that such existence is so rich that no explanation can be sufficient to say why. The "intuition of the being" includes the perspective of a continuous miracle of the emergence of the being out of nothing....

The intuition of the being is not mere intuition… It is the capacity to enter in the mystery of existence and investigate in it as an endless endeavor. While science addresses problems, philosophy deals with mystery.

Metaphysics is not only the study of the being, but it is so under the perspective of the mystery of existence.

We grasp the heart of the whole of metaphysical field, addressing the topic of **Intuition of Being**. The experience which Jacques Maritain gave the name of "Intuition of Being" is a cornerstone of every philosophy endeavor. Here below are gathered a few quotations intended to introduce us into the "mystery of reality" through the figure of Maritain, (A) as a Philosopher, (B) as a Searcher of the Truth, (C) as a Contemplative, and finally (D) as a Mystic. What Maritain called the "Intuition of Being", is the same that Marie-Dominique Philippe used to call "Judgment of Existence". It is the same experience that Aristotle called simply "BEING" and Aquinas identified as "The act of being". In *Brief Treatise of the Existence and the Existent*, Maritain indentifies the doctrine of St. Thomas as a "Philosophy of Existence". The great intuition of Aquinas was the awareness of the "Being in Act" which is the true answer to contemporaneous existentialism. It stresses existence without denying essence.

(2.) Experiencing the emergence of the being was typical of Augustine, Bonaventure and Duns Scotus. The expression of "Intuition of the being" that we are familiar with Maritain was previously used by John Duns Scotus as the verbalization of the synthetic experience of intellect, reason and intuition in front of the fact that something does exist. Such amazing discovery led him to affirm it as a univocal concept. We will address the issue while dealing with the way language does address the truth.

(3) "The German philosopher, Heidegger, assures us that no man can become a metaphysician who has not first experienced anguish, this anguish being understood not only psychologically but also as metaphysically as possible. It is the feeling at once keen and lacerating of all that is precarious and imperiled in our existence, in human existence. As the effect of this feeling, of this anguish, our existence loses its commonplace and acquires a unique value, its unique value. It confronts us as something saved from nothingness, snatched from nonentity. Certainly such a dramatic experience of nothingness may serve as an introduction to the intuition of being, provided it is taken as no more than an introduction." (Jacques Maritain, *A Preface to Metaphysics*, Mentor Omega Bks, 1962, Lect.3 §.5, p.54)

Heidegger

(4) In his *Brief Treatise*, Jacques Maritain "places the intellectual intuition of that mysterious reality disguised under the most commonplace and commonly used word in the language, the word to be; a reality revealed to us as the uncircumscribable subject of a science which the gods

begrudge us when we release, in the values that appertain to it, the act of existing which is exercised by the humblest thing — that victorious thrust by which it triumphs over nothingness," The awareness of it corresponds to what he properly called "The Intuition of Being" that he understood as an experience which stands at the root of metaphysical knowledge,

A philosopher is not a philosopher if he is not a metaphysician. And it is the intuition of being — even when it is distorted by the error of a system, as in Plato or Spinoza – that makes the metaphysician. I mean the intuition of being in its pure and all-pervasive properties, in its typical and primordial intelligible density; the intuition of being secundum quod est ens. Being, seen in this light, is neither the vague being of common sense, nor the particularized being of the sciences and of the philosophy of nature, nor the de-realised being of logic, nor the pseudo-being of dialectics mistaken for philosophy. It is being disengaged for its own sake, in the values and resources appertaining to its own intelligibility and reality; which is to say, in that richness, that analogical and transcendental amplitude which is inviscerated in the imperfect and multiple unity of its concept and which allows it to cover the infinitude of its analogates and causes it to overflow or surabound in transcendental values and in dynamic values of propensity through which the idea of being transgress itself. It is being, attained or perceived at the summit of an abstractive intellection, of an eidetic or intensive visualization which owes its purity and power of illumination only to the fact that the intellect, one day, was stirred to its depths and trans-illuminated by the impact of the act of existing apprehended in things, and because it was quickened to the point of receiving this act, or harkening to it, within itself, in the intelligible and super-intelligible integrity of the tone peculiar to it.

There are diverse ways and paths leading towards the attainment of this intuition. None is traced in advance, none is more legitimate than another — precisely because here there is no question of rational analysis or of an inductive or a deductive procedure, or of a syllogistic construction, but only of an intuition which is primarily fact. The senses, and what St. Thomas calls the "judgment of sense," the blind existential perception exercised by the senses, play here a primordial and indispensable part. But this is no more than a prerequisite; the eyes of him who was blind must be opened; the touch of the spiritual virtues of the intellect must release into intelligible light this act of existing which sense attains without discovering it and touches without perceiving it. (…) what counts is to take the leap, to release, in one authentic intellectual intuition, the sense of being, the sense of the value of the implication that lie in the act of existing. What counts is to have seen that existence is not a simple empiritical fact but a primitive datum for the mind itself — in a word, the primary and super-intelligible source of intelligibility.

It is not enough to teach philosophy, even Thomist philosophy, in order to possess this intuition. Let us call it a matter of luck, a boon, perhaps a kind of docility to the light. Without it man will always have an opining, precarious and sterile knowledge, however freighted with erudition it may be; a knowledge about. He will go round and round the flame without ever going through it. With it, even though he stray from the path, he will always go farther than he can advance by years of mere dialectical exercise, critical reflection or conceptual dissection of phenomena; and he will have the added privilege of solitude and melancoholy. If the poet can be called a seer, the philosopher is no less entitled to this name, though in his own way... At times he will know the joy of discovery... and will remained enraptured with being." (Jacques Maritain in "Existence and the Existent", Image Book, 1987, p.28-31)

(5) During the years 80' I was accustomed to meet in Rome Fr. Marie-Dominique Philippe, who used to come on the Tuesday after Easter with the novices of the Brothers of Saint-John to introduce them to Pope John-Paul II. Some of his followers were studying theology at the Angelicum in Rome and spent often the time of an evening or a dinner to my place of Via dell'Orso near Piazza Navona and sometimes they did criticize Maritain and his "Intuition of the Being" to the point that I was considering to stop teaching Maritain at the Gregorian. One day Marie-Dominique Philippe organized a meeting in my place with some friends of his community in Rome, I took this occasion to offert to stop teaching Maritain if he believed it was a good decision: "Not at all" was his answer. "My uncle, Fr. Thomas Dehaut was the spiritual director of the Maritains and it would be a shame if you stopped teaching him. I surely do not intend to criticize Jacques Maritain when I say to the Brothers that I like to call "Judgment of Existence" what Maritain names "Intuition of Being". But it is the same. And I am surely not suggesting you to stop teaching Maritain, on the opposite I suggest you to do so and I hope you will continue to do so as long as you can". It was one of the last times I met him, and that meeting was a sort of goodwill he left me. I am pleased to refer to that event at the onset of our journey together as a stress of how the Intuition of the Being" is a particular experience, typical of philosophy tradition and also, for what I late unerstood, typical of Franciscan tradition and charism, too.

Fr. Marie-Dominique Philippe

(6) The words of "Intuition of the Being" are not always easy to grasp, because metaphysical experience is difficult to get, especially from the ones who look at things superficially, under logical approach or under scientific perspective. It is sometimes almost impossible to tell it to those who did not get it yet. Nonetheless, such awareness, such "wisdom is waiting at the door of our heart" (Wisdom 2:15). Wisdom "comes to the ones who love her, and reveals herself to the ones who want her" (Wisdom 2:13-14). It is more a question of docility, than of violent research. It consists of a true desire of uprightness and blossoming. Such enlightenment is easier to experience than to describe. We must leave our heart to be open to wisdom and wisdom will come and will deal in us… It is a kind of conversion of our heart to the truth we are made for. In such an adventure we are not alone: wisdom wants to meet us even more than we look for her. It may happen very fast. It only depends on a internal decision of our heart.

Seat of Wisdom

(7) Philosophy improves with the discovery that truth is not just investigating for something, but getting the real consistency of the whole of reality we live in. So truth is the awareness of reality that we are supposed to grow in intimacy with. Scientific expertise tends to state that if we cannot get the whole truth right away we only get doubts… Philosophy behave differently, True philosopher does not refuse to humbly recognize all the rainbow colors of reality.

It is not sufficient to accomplish the blossoming of people and society. "More spiritual values are needed. In modern society, technology is usually assumed to be a good think; technology is usually seen as a boon, not a detriment. But our technological capabilities are mostly a result of influences of the material pole of every person; it is purely of the physical, and not spiritual. The continuously accelerating pace at which technology advances spontaneously forces more and more of the focus on the material, and not the spiritual. As stated by Nietzsche, Heidegger, Lubac, Daniélou, Daujat, Guitton and others, our spirituality has not advanced with technology. Guitton and Foresi affirmed that it may have advanced in spite of it.

(8) Among scientist of the XX century, there was the habit, if not the certainty, that science has nothing to do with faith and must develop not just autonomously, which would be legitimate, but out of it. Maritain refers in his historical survey how the scientists of the XIX and XX centuries used to leave out of their laboratory they hats, their umbrellas, their coats, and their faith. There is no reason now to be surprised that science developed with the wrong belief that faith is not grounded and that science is not compatible with an experience of faith…

Lubac

Daniélou

Daujat

Guitton

Foresi

The great technological boom of the last century unfortunately has been generally accompanied by an increased secularization of society. Arguably, this has led many to a spiritual decline, which in turn leads to moral decline and societal erosion and decay. For true progress must serve the human person and the human person must grow; we must grow in love and humanity as well as materially. This means wisdom. Fortunately human people are made for the truth. Historically, when they look more lost, that is the time when usually they find a shortway towards her.

(9) Being an optimist is not an option, it follows the facts. Philosophy is the amazing endeavor of meeting the truth which calls us, leads us, and supports us towards her – even if most of the time we feel to be the only ones who solely look for her. Ultimately, as Pasquale Foresi said, "Every true metaphysician endures the tragic dilemma of the awareness of belonging to the being without covering fully its identity". Here is the true dilemma of every philosopher, understanding that we want the being, we are made for it and we are truly aware that we are not the being." Such dilemma is the sign of a call from above. Those who feel the call are true philosophers.

As a first conclusion, every course of philosophy is the wish to all student for starting an amazing journey because as philosophers (as Aristotle says everyone is a philosopher) we are part of a great endeavor. Teaching philosophy means wishing you all a great endeavor!

(VI) Philosophy and Common Sense

As a first conclusion, every course of philosophy is the wish to all student for starting an amazing journey because as philosophers (as Aristotle says: everyone is a philosopher), we are part of a great endeavor. Teaching philosophy means wishing you all a great endeavor!

Common sense is defined as the "usual thinking of Common people" or more restrictively "what should be proper to think and common people would agree with" – Common sense is a fact not a mere concept... It is the basic natural capacity of people to behave, associate, speak and think.

Common sense is the field of opinions. Philosophy leads people from opinions to reasonable truth. In other words philosophy moves people from usual thinking to what is proper to think.

Common sense and philosophy interact: philosophy leads to a better wisdom that helps common sense to improve.

    a. Common sense shows simplicity and proper disposition towards the truth — B. Montazel

    b. Common sense disagrees with any unnecessary sophistication — G. Trivié

    c. Philosophy improves common sense and common sense checks philosophy — J. Daujat

    d. Common sense may evaluate the consistency of philosophy conclusions.

See more below in section in J. Maritain, *Introduction to Philosophy*, Part One, Chapter VIII.

(VII) Philosophy and Positive Science

Let us stress a few points to show the relationship between philosophy and positive science:

    a. Philosophy deals with reality as a whole while each positive science studies a section of facts;

    b. Sciences investigate on material things and lead to "Command nature obeying its laws" (F. Bacon) which is ultimately power. On the opposite, Philosophy deals with everything concerning human life, without discrimination, seeking wisdom;

c. Sciences put intelligence at the service of knowledge, but Philosophy puts intelligence at the service of people, putting head at the service of heart;

d. Science works by tentative (hypothesis) and verifications (experimentation), then builds theories; oppositely, Philosophy works by degrees of abstraction, which also are progressive syntheses;

e. Science ignores individuals and the real world, focusing on "theory-experimentation-formula", while Philosophy addresses primarily facts and the real world, without discrimination.

f. Science trains intelligence up to a certain degree of abstraction (language, numbers, formulae), whereas, Philosophy incites people to exert a higher degree of abstraction up to the absolute.

g. Science uses observation (physics), imagination (math), while Philosophy exerts intelligence.

h. Science deals with Generality; Philosophy deals with Universality.

i. Science offers a field of investigations and basic information which is essential for philosophers, as a proper context of reflection; Philosophy offers proper directions to scientific investigations: "philosophy governs science" (Shawn) — See also JP2, *Faith and Reason*;

j. Philosophy is more consistent, more actual, more perceptive, more real than any other science.

See more in J. Maritain, *Introduction to Philosophy*, Part One, Chapter VII

(VIII) Philosophy and Theology

While Philosophy is the natural knowledge on the whole of reality, theology provides the same knowledge on everything that philosophy investigates on, but from the teaching and perspective of God... especially reading the Scriptures. Specifically:

a. Philosophy deals with earthly reality with full human capability, supported by all knowledge areas, when Theology addresses earthly reality according to the perspective of the teaching of God as expressed in Revelation: Holy Scriptures, Patrimony of Tradition, Magisterium teaching, examples of Saints, and personal experience of faith (we need familiarity with the Holy spirit to understand what the Holy spirit is teaching in each of these kinds of teaching).

b. Philosophy opens widely the way to theology, providing a good use of intelligence and reasoning, while Theology improves the usage of intelligence with the understanding of eternal words.

c. Philosophy investigates on the righteousness of theology topics, when Theology completes Philosophy investigation with additional enlightening (see *Faith and Reason*, JP II)

d. If you want to understand the relationship between philosophy and theology look at the relationship between Mary and Jesus " (paraphrasing JP2 in Faith and Reason, §103-108). Like Mary delivered Jesus (the Truth), philosophy introduces and makes the ground of theology.

e. "Actually each one, theology and philosophy, needs the other to properly perform the way it is.

See more in J. Maritain, *Introduction to Philosophy*, Part One, Chapter VI

Important Note:

Be sure no one makes any confusion between Theology

and Metaphysics. The fields of metaphysics are Ontology, Peratology, Critique (Gnoseology) and Natural Theology. Occasionally Theology (study from Revelation) can be referred to, but only as an additional comment of those topics never as the foundation of these because theology belongs to a field of knowledge diverse and complementing of the field of our course, which in turn is necessary for theology.

All fields of Theology (liturgy, dogmatic, tradition, worship, sacraments, ecumenism, and more) are intrinsically extraneous to metaphysics. They belong to the patrimony of knowledge that philosophy may interact with, according to the words of Seneca "I disregard nothing among the experience of people".

From the beginning of its elaboration by Aristotle, Metaphysics is the best expression of "human knowledge" or, if you wish, the best exertion of "natural reason," as the scholastics used to say.

Concerning the term of "Faith" it is often used in philosophy with the assertion of "true conviction". This is why we talk about the faith of Marxists, existentialists, or rationalists or even positivists. It never includes the faith that theologians refer to, when they indicate that we cannot be a theologian if we do not believe that Revelation comes from God; here is why Augustine used to say that we need to believe in order to understand the contents of Revelation. Analogically, you cannot be a philosopher without the intuition of being.

St. Bernard

According to St. Bernard, in his 24th homely to *The Song of the Songs*, "Faith is necessary to please God, but it is not sufficient for becoming a saint". Additionally,

"Love" is required. Actually "Loving the other as ourselves" is part of the main commandment of "loving God". It is the achievement of the new Commandment of the Gospel, "Love one another", because "whatever you do to one of these you do to me". I wish us a full exertion of it in our life.

The whole issue is so simple that it takes time for everyone to get it clearly: "many listen but only a few understand." More will be said in class.

(IX) Philosophy and Mystical Knowledge

Above theology there is another field of knowledge that every true philosopher does consider. It depends fist on the human capacity to be open and silent towards the transcendent and second on the free action of God: nothing in that relation can be organize as an automatic process... There are, nonetheless, a few considerations that we may observe among the mystics.

Mystical experience explodes in the free relationship between people and God: Freedom of people and free grace of God. Both are first in their own perspective. If one of the two is absolutely first, we have some sort of heresy: Pelagianism when human activity is put first, Predetermination when God's Grace is put first: "God does not know what we will do tomorrow because he does not live in time, he is eternal, and creates us now. So we only can say that God knows what we are doing tomorrow." God knows in the same way our present, our past, our future, he does know all better than we do.

    a. Beyond the study of God and revelation, there emerges the experience of God... in "apophatic" experience that, through sharing, people translate later in "cataphatic" explanation.

b. In all the previous fields of knowledge human intelligence is first and understanding requires abstraction… At the mystical level God is first (Cf. *Union with God* as the last spiritual step of San Juan de Yepes) and requires silence, transparency and human sharing, in order to put in language what is above any discourse.

(X) Philosophy and… Every Human Activity

Sociology, Psychology, History, Geography, Literature, Education, Politics, Marketing, Business, Ethology, Medicine, Poetry, Music, Tourism, etc. are the fields of human activity, which feeds philosophy reflection.

All knowledge areas enter at any time in philosophy investigation: when one is missing, its reflection is defective. All fields of human experience permanently interact together and with philosophy

    a. They all express some human endeavor.

    b. Philosophy, always deals with Human Nature and its values.

    c. There is a need for a common understanding between all (see *Faith and Reason*, JP II)

(XI) What Is Philosophy?

This short recap refers to Jacques Maritain when addressing in Introduction to Philosophy (Part One, Chapters V, VI, VII, VIII, pp.60-92) the identity of philosophy in relation to the other fields of human knowledge. It eventually completes the teaching of Jacques Maritain it does not replace it.

1. Philosophy is more than…

    a. "Unintelligible answers to insoluble problems" -

Henry B. Adams

    b. "A blind man in the dark looking at a black hat which is not there" – Stalin, Marxist Motto

    c. "A philosopher can only do one thing, and that is to contradict others philosophers" - W. James

    d. "Skepticism is the first step on the road to philosophy"- Denis Diderot.

    e. Science address facts, philosophy deals with opinions – Honoré de Balzac

    f. Philosophy is the consolation of the benighted – Lenin

    g. "There is nothing so absurd that did not received the support of some philosopher" – Aristotle, Cicero, Descartes

2. Philosophy starts with...

    h. Philosophy accepts reality as such and investigating on it without discrimination and taking what is consistent (Aristotle, Aquinas. Daujat). It offers a knowledge of facts consistent like every positive science (MD. Philippe). Ultimately philosophy is the art of explaining what things are...

    i. Every discourse belongs to a specific neighborhood (Aristotle, Freud) which includes: the background which a discourse is raised from (Merleau-Ponty), the context in which a discourse is spoken (Foucault) and the impact of the people and culture to which a discourse is spoken (Dehau), so every Philosophy is the expression of a typical human experience (Heidegger) and above all particular perspectives there is perennial philosophy (Lacombe)

    j. Learning to philosophize is already a philosophical discourse (I. Kant) - It has a strong impact on the whole civilization: ideas move the whole world (Hegel)

    k, There is no stupid question in philosophy – Every concern must be checked.

3. Philosophy is…

l. Etymology of the word "philosophy" - "Friend of Wisdom" – (in reference to Pythagoras)

m. Philosophy is the First Science: it is above positive sciences.

n. Philosophy is a training of the entire person (Socrates, Plato, Aristotle). It requires intelligence, will, love, sensitiveness, memory, imagination, creativity, Intersubjectivity, language, culture, friendship, relationship... All human faculties are involved in this art. Therefore everything is supposed to be used in a philosophy investigation: material sources, objective ones, opinion, feeling, psychological insight, ethical measure, ontological issue, metaphysical one, theological perspectives, spiritual experience, and even surrounding quests.

o. Philosophy is the typical process of human beings; it starts with the consciousness of what and who we are (Socrates), enlightened by the wisdom of being aware of the extent of our ignorance (Socrates). The whole process is pulled by the truth: "Philosophy is going to the truth with all our soul" (Plato, Augustine).

p. Philosophy is the art of putting intelligence at the service of love (M.-D. Philippe), which includes to coordinate every human expertise at the service of mankind: "Through philosophy, people blossom in what they are." (Cf. Aristotle)

q. Philosophy is so much in love of truth that it moves the world back to it (Dehau). Remember the words of Saint Paul to the Colossians, "Everything belongs to us, but we belong to Christ, and Christ belongs to God" (1Cor 3:23). See also the definition of a Christian by J. Maritain and the paradigm of the cross..

4. Conclusion…

r. As a first conclusion, every course of philosophy

produces the wish of students for starting an amazing journey of reflection, meditation, and ultimately contemplation.

s. Aristotle stated that "Everyone is a philosopher', for everyone seeks the truth. As philosophers we take part of an amazing endeavor. Teaching philosophy means wishing you all such a great endeavor!

(See J. Maritain, *Introduction to Philosophy*, Part One, esp. Chapter V)

(XII) What Is Metaphysics?

Inside of philosophy there is a science which in itself is even more philosophy... It refers to that knowledge which the followers of Aristotle could not name properly, but they put its notes after the books of physics (meta => after). This being put aside became allegorical, "after-physics" became not pseudo-physics", but beyond physics.

Metaphysics is the heart of philosophy. According to Jacques Maritain, when a thinker is not a metaphysician he/she cannot be a true philosopher: he/she eventually is an expert of philosophy history, logic, ethics theories, politics movements, knowledge theories, or other philosophy areas, but he/she will never be a true philosopher. Metaphysics is the enlightenment of philosophy. (Cf. Maritain)

Some reflections can be roughly made to indicate the location, role and nature of Metaphysics:

a. Etymology of the word "metaphysics":

1. Chronologically after, following, subsequent to physics

2. Ontologically beyond, above, greater, superior to physics.

b. Subordination of Metaphysics to the other fields of knowledge in order to improve them

1. The background of the other sciences is needed to

metaphysics to properly investigate on.

2. The field of metaphysics is necessary to enlighten a proper philosophical discernment.

3. Metaphysics helps philosophy to determinate the proper specificity and human usefulness of each science

4. See the role of metaphysics according to Faith and Reason.

   c. Primacy of Metaphysics or First Philosophy

1. Philosophy starts with metaphysics and irradiates from it.

2. Then philosophy is the human field where all sciences meet and find their own identity

3. Metaphysics is the center of gravity of human knowledge (Cf. Faith and Reason, JP2)

   d. Sections of Metaphysics

1. Ontology I ("logos" (= discourse on) "ontos" (the being as such)

2. Peratology - also said Ontology II - Peratology. is discourse (logos) on "peratos" (limited being).

3. Critique (gnoseology, epistemology)

4. Natural Theology (discourse on God before God's Revelation)

(XIII) What Is a Philosopher

As a result of the above reflection, no one is a philosopher when he/she is not a metaphysician. Expertise, i.e. knowledge of philosophy, its history, its questions does not suffice as far as there is not yet the intuition of the being, (Maritain), i.e. the judgment of existence (Fr. M.Do Philippe), the contemplation of the being (Aquinas).

In other words:

   a. Everyone is a philosopher (Aristotle) because each human being wants the truth. Actually every person is made (created) for the truth: "You made me for you, Oh! Lord! And my heart is restless until it rests in you" (Augustine).

b. "The life of a philosopher consists in the painful paradox of a total fidelity to eternal values in a tight connection with the understanding of the anguishes of the times, in order to bring the world back to the Truth" (J. Maritain).

c. A philosopher is a contemplative… who stand in society at the heart of action…. (P.-Th. Dehau).

d. To be a philosopher we need (1) humility (reality) comes before knowledge), (2) Curiosity (appropriate information) (2) Friendship (sharing and checking information with other people) (3) Simplicity (sound reflection), (4) Courage (to express personal views) (Marcel Clément).

e. As philosophers, we take responsibility of what we are (Sartre).

f. "If you want to enter in the intimacy of metaphysics become familiar with Mary" (paraphrasing JP2 in *Faith and Reason*, §108).

g. "O metaphysics, my friend, jumps on me!" (Paraphrasing Nietzsche's *Oh Eternity!*).

h. Paraphrasing Pasquale Foresi: "Metaphysics is the fantastic endeavor of getting the being, knowing that we are made for the being, with the terrible awareness that we are not the being yet."

(XIV) References

Raissa Maritain, *We Have Been Friends Together*,
Jacques Maritain, *The Degrees of Knowledge*,
   Metaphysics
   Confession of Faith
Science inflates with pride, charity builds
(St. Paul, 1 Co 8:1).

 Long after their experience in the botanic garden with Raissa (See "Crossing St. James Street"), Jacques Maritain made a short survey on the main steps of his own conversion and discovery of Metaphysics.

We let him speak:

During my childhood I had been educated inside of the liberal Protestantism. Then I met the different waves of secular thinking. At the Sorbonne the scientist and phenomenist philosophy of my masters led me to the point to despair about reason. For a while I thought that I could find total certainness in sciences. Even Félix Le Dantec believed that my fiancée and I could become the followers of his biologic materialism. However, the really best I got from the Sorbonne studies is to have come across Raissa, who so happily has been near to me in all my works in such a perfect and blessed communion. Then Bergson was the first to properly answer the deep inquiry of both of us on metaphysical truth. He released our desire of absolute.

Before being caught by St. Thomas Aquinas, the main influences that affected me are the ones of Charles Péguy, Bergson, and Léon Bloy. One year after Raissa and I came across to Bloy, and just after we chose him as our godfather, we received the baptism from the Catholic Church.

I had been traveling with such a passion amongst the whole of the philosophic doctrines, which belong to the modern philosophers, never being able to find nothing but disappointment and large uncertainness. After my conversion to the Catholic

Church, I discovered Thomas Aquinas. It was like a sudden illumination of my reason. All my philosophic vocation was back to me in fullness. In these days, I wrote in one of my books: Woe to me if I do not Thomismize. Then, after thirty years of works and battles, I am still walking in the same track, bearing the same awareness that the more I am connected with the enlightening coming from the wisdom which has been elaborated through centuries and which resists to the fluctuations of times, and the more I share it, the deeper I am able to sympathize with the researches, the discoveries, the anxieties of modern thoughts.

To go ahead in that track, we must constantly join extremes bounds, which are considerably distant with each other (for no solution to our problems can be found already done in the heritage of the Ancients). We also must make a difficult beginning between the pure substance of the truths, which many "modern" thinkers reject as a disgusting garbage coming out of past opinions, prejudices, obsolete images, arbitrary constructions, and which many "traditional" thinkers confuse with what really deserves intelligent veneration.

I spoke about the different situations I had been passing through, for they gave me an occasion to experience personally the positions first of an idealist free-thinker, then of an inexpert newly converted, and finally of a Christian who - the more his/her faith is taking better roots – is having a better awareness of the purifications he/she must go through. I also could get a practical idea of the consistency of the party of antireligious and of the so-called well-thinkers. No one of both is worth anything. The worst disgrace of the second wave is that the innocent and even persecuted Church can be damaged and compromised. The Church is the mystical body of Christ, whose the essential life, sine macula sine ruga, consist in Truth and Saints, and walks towards its fullness through the weakness of its memebers and the ferocity of the world. I see that God lead and form us through our deceptions and mistakes, in order we finally understand that we must believe only on him and no more in human beings. That helps to be amazed for all the good that emerges over all, and for the good they do in spite of themselves.

I finally got the conclusion that there are only two ways to properly know everything. For there are only two kinds of wisdom. Both are insane, even if in an opposite way. First is the wisdom of sinners who, embracing everything to fully taste its nothingnessly savor, make a full experience of this world, knowing the evil of it more than its good. The second is the wisdom of Saints who, adhering with the subsistent goodness, who created everything, receives a full experience of God and of the out-of-love creation. The Saints pay for everyone through their own compassion and suffering. Well really! If they are not damaged by any pride and remain loyal to their own experience, it is obvious hoping that the followers of the vain wisdom will be finally saved "from the fire" by the ones who belong to the true wisdom. If they convert before they die, they happen to be even more demanding to the ones of their brothers who remained in the night. So, after having been a long time enjoying the delights of the world and having been vain, sometimes up to the last moment, they will get in an instant the delights of their virtues before they enter in eternity.

Jacques Maritain

Jacques Maritain *Confession de foi*, Editions de la Maison Française, New York, 1941 - Cf. *Numéro spécial pour le centenaire de J. Maritain* -Notes et documents #27, Institut International J. Maritain, Rome - The Text either in French and in English is from J. Maritain with some personal adaptations for the English version.

READING ARISTOTLE'S METAPHYSICS

GENERAL INTRODUCTION

1. A too sophisticated mind would not be able to grasp the real endeavor of the facts: reading Aristotle's *Metaphysics* requires an attitude of sincerity, fairness, flexibility, even curiosity and naivety. In other words it requires simplicity of life; it is not a slip of the tongue: good life is the best preparation to understand good words... Good behavior increases attention and quality of intelligence breathing.

   a. There is no mystery to discover under the words which are given.

   b. Metaphysics needs an effort of intelligence more than imagination.

   c. The context is new and demands a particular asceticism or proper exercise of intelligence.

2. Aristotle's style is simple, analogous, addressing the

facts. A similar behavior is needed to address properly his writing. Reading Aristotle is a serious engagement and a proper discernment: absolute must be distinguished from other beings, e.g. God/gods. The same has to be said between universal concepts, general ideas, and singular facts, e.g. Truth/rules and principles/examples.

3. Philosophers deal with reality itself, scientists deal with some accidents and concepts of it, opinions deal with its first experience of it. As a reminder, the univocity of meanings is for a positively scientific discourse, as scientists and mathematicians are used to. Also opinions belong to an equivocal speaking. Words are behind the facts: do not try to define your words, try to define the reality you are supposed to deal with.

4. We must be ready to approach the reading with some flexibility. It is necessary to be familiar with the usage of analogy in every philosophical discourse. Philosophers always speak by analogy. They constantly are addressing realities that are richer than the used words. Our understanding is under the constant invitation to overcome the borders of the words to enter the hidden blossoming of facts.

5. After Aristotle, philosophy is said to be the first science and as such it is not less grounded than science is. In other words, philosophy is an accurate reflection, a consistent reasoning, leading to an objective — or universal — statement. Philosophy is the art of introducing a universal and valid truth, which is acceptable for everybody who is supposed to reflect on it. It is a good exercise to be prepared for teaching, preaching, and helping people to understand better everything they have to deal with.

6. During the reading, our reflection must focus on positive perspectives. Stressing positive statements support our reasoning. That makes our work more agreeable and even more consistent. In everything we read we must follow St. Paul's suggestion to the Thessalonians: "Test everything, keep what is

good and leave the rest." (1 Th 5:21)

7. Metaphysics is the Divine Science, because it applies to a field that leads us towards God, i.e. it is the same science of God, also it is the same knowledge of God, so it is a sharing on the knowledge of God with mere human understanding (i.e. without revelation).

8. Metaphysics is the study of the principles... It was said in class that metaphysics introduces us to the "Beginning" of

things. In other words it introduces us to the same event of creation, which is not an historical moment, not even a process, due to the fact that creation is now and now we investigate on the manifestation of the being - even if the notion of creation does not exist in Aristotle's vocabulary his study brings us inside of the mystery of the emergence of things into existence: the being. Addressing the being, leads us to its ultimate causes.

9. Additional information on Aristotle

a) The Basic Works of Aristotle are: *Organon*, *Physica* (Physics), *De Caelo* (On the Heavens), *De Generatione et Corruptione* (On Generation & Corruption), *De Anima* (On the Soul), *Parva Naturalia* {The Short Physical Treatises), *Historia Animalium* (The History of Animals), *De Partibus Animalium* (On the Parts of Animals), *De Generatione Animalium* (Ob the Generation of Animals), *Metaphysica* (Metaphysics), *Ethica Nicomachea* (Nicomachean Ethics), *Politica* (Politics), *Rhetorica* (Rhetoric), *De Poetica* (Poetics)…

b) Logic is mainly addressed in the *Organon* (Categories, On Interpretation, Prior & Posterior Analytics, Topics, On Sophistical Refutations). Some arguments of logic and metaphysics overlap.

GENERAL PRESENTATION ON METAPHYSICS BOOKS

Short Survey

- Book I (A): Science is knowledge of causes.
- Book II (α): Philosophy is knowledge of truth.
- Book III (B): Investigating over any doubt.
- Book IV (Γ): Metaphysics is science of being qua being.
- Book V (Δ): Substance and accidents.

- Book VI (E): Natural theology.
- Book VII (Z): Investigating deeper upon the substance.
- Book VIII (H): Substance is a composition of matter and form (formal cause).
- Book IX (Θ): Reflection upon the notion of movement (motion and change).
- Book X (I): Unity and distinction in being.
- Book XI (K): Some basic axioms of logic.
- Book XII (Λ): Distinction between matter and form and first being.
- Book XIII (M): Critic of the theory of ideas.
- Book XIV (N): Relationship between numbers, principles and goodness.

Contents of Book A, §§ 1-6

1 "All people by nature desire to know" — or: every human is a philosopher, a metaphysician (§1.) So it is the proper of any human to look for truth. As a conclusion it must be said that Metaphysics is precisely the most properly human science. Metaphysics is wisdom par excellence.

2. In all humans knowledge comes from experience (see Aristotle's Theory of Knowledge).

3. All beings also are characterized by a desire to be, or it is better to say a desire to know (cf. Nietzsche's Will of Power). Aristotle suggests elaborating a hierarchy of beings according to their desire to know. It can be done from minerals, vegetal, animals, humans, angels – Such a classification is properly a classification of all creatures. So God himself has to be excluded from the classification because He is the Creator.

4. Metaphysics needs logic to be expressed and is composed of Ontology, Peratology, Causality, and Theodicy

5. Logic is all organized from the Principle of Identity (See below)

6. As Ontology, Metaphysics investigates on the first principles or first causes of the Being.

7. Peratology investigates on the limited being, as diversity, multiplicity and change.

8. As Causality, Metaphysics investigates on nature and characteristics of change (see below). Here starts Philosophy of Nature.

9. As Theodicy, Metaphysics, or else the Divine Science, applies to a matter that lead us towards God, i.e. it is the same science investigating of God, also it really is the same knowledge of God himself, so Metaphysics is a sharing of the God's knowledge.

10. Metaphysics is the Science of Wisdom, and has mainly six characteristics:
    a. Metaphysics is the most universal science.
    b. Metaphysics is superior to any other knowledge.
    c. Metaphysics can be shared and transmitted by teaching.
    d. Metaphysics is good in itself (honest good).
    e. Metaphysics organizes the inferior sciences
    f. Metaphysics is the most accurate and precise science.

11. In order to make possible a metaphysical investigation, something has to exist (See Aristotle's categories).

Truth is necessary to think

Truth is identity between Mental and Real Being. Identity has to be investigated to prove its validity.

Identity: A same thing or statement has to be always the same under the same perspective. It is the condition *sine qua non* of any discourse, any rational investigation, or any speech. This principle of necessity of the principle of identity is so strong that the ones who tried to deny it, denied themselves (if you say that truth is untruth, your discourse itself is untrue, so truth is true).

Principle of Identity: Discursively: any being has to be what it is and nothing else. Or, formally: always "A is A", and $(A \equiv A)$, or $(A \equiv \forall A)$

Principle of Non Contradiction: Discursively: any being is different with everything is not identical and never can be confused with it, or to say that formally: A never can be identical with what is not A, i.e. $(A \neq \neg A)$

Principle of the Excluded Middle: Any being has to be identical with itself and different with everything else, there no other possibility, or to say that formally: A can be only identical to itself and different to everything is not A, any other eventuality is excluded, i.e. $(A \wedge \neg A = 0)$

Syllogism: If A belongs to B, and B belongs to C, then B belongs to C — that corresponds to the formal formula $(A \subset B) \wedge (B \subset C) \rightarrow (A \subset C)$. The basic syllogism is also said: if A is B, and B is C, then A is C

Note: The basic syllogism is also said in a less accurate way: if A is B, and B is C, then A is C.

Sophism: It is said to many propositions that pretend to be logical as a syllogism and they are not. The most famous of sophisms is the **enthymeme**, in which the middle term B, is not the same in the two first enunciations, it can be formally.

Contents of Book Γ, §§ 1-7

1. Metaphysics is the "science which investigates the being qua being and what belongs essentially to it" (§1.)

2. "Being can be used in many senses"(§2.). So the being is in the same time one and many (See Section E.). Being has to be understood analogically.

3. **"Being is used in many senses"**

BEING
Something that exists.

Real Being is a being whose existence does not depend of my knowledge. A being belonging to the world. Any real being is essential or accidental and exist either in act or in potency

Essential being: Aristotle identifies here all beings that are substances, both in strait and extensive meaning.

Accidental being: Everything belongs to a being that exists as an accident.

Actual Being: Or **being in act**: Any being in its actual existence. Each being in act is in potency of any possible change.

Potential Being: Something that can develop or become actual. Any possibility an actual being has to change.

Mental Being or **Concept** is a being existing only in my mind and not in the reality surrounding me. There are generally some universal concepts (e.g. nothingness, essence, value). They also are called **"rational being."** It is proper to a Mental Being to distinguish between Essence and Existence, which never can exist separately in a Real Being.

Essence: Whatness or Nature of a thing. That which is comprehensible of a thing. The forms which are knowable in a being (substance and accidents). What it is. Essence is the significance of an existence. Essence is investigated as a potentiality.

Existence: The state of being. The fact that a being is present. An existence is always of an essence. Existence is the Act of superintelligibility of a being, for everything is knowable from its own existence.

Intentional Being or **Manifestation of Truth in the Mind**: It refers to a real being when it is present to my mind in the process of knowledge. It is no longer material and not yet mental. However it is consistent. Aristotle calls it intentional. It is in this Intentional meeting between Mental and Real Being that is found the structure, or configuration of a being, i.e. the distinction Matter and Form.

Matter: What is supposed to change. Its source of indetermination, and of opacity. Matter only exists with a Form.

Form: What is intelligible in a being. Source of its intelligibility. Form only exists through a Matter.

F. Some emerging statements

a. "All people by nature desire to know" - Bk A §980a 21.

b. "Experience provides more wisdom than mere study" (Bk A §981a 15).

c. "Those who have wisdom are able to teach" (Bk A §981b 8).

d. "Mathematic knowledge improved in Egypt among people who were not busy" - Bk A §981b 25

e. "Every wisdom starts with wonder" - Bk A §982a 13

f. "True wonder is due to the fact that things do exist" - Bk A §983a 13.

g. "The study of truth is both easy and difficult" - Bk α §993a 30

h. "The being can be said in many ways" - Bk Γ §1003α 35

i. "There is nothing in our mind that was not prior in our senses"

j. Metaphysics is the science of first principles or first causes.

k. Metaphysics is universal knowledge in the highest degree.

l. Metaphysics is wisdom by excellence.

m. Metaphysics books provide basic issues on: Logic, Ontology, Peratology, Causality, and Theodicy.

BEING QUA BEING ONTOLOGY BEING AS SUCH

PRELIMINARY

This is the first note of two, which go together. The following one, on Ontology II, or **Peratology** (see below) is addressed separately, later. These two notes on Ontology and Peratology remain provisional: they will be improved during our reading reflection. Suggestions and comments are welcome. Everyone will interact with the reading.

"*Repetita juvant*" (repetitions help) said the Romans. Several ontological issues have been already addressed in class. Some are gathered here first to support our understanding on the being, and second to improve our reading first of Jacques Maritain in *Introduction to Philosophy* (Part. Two, Ch. V, VI - pp.126-164 or 135-175), then of Aristotle's *Metaphysics*, and Aquinas' *De Ente et Essentia*. The topics to deal with belong to Ontology I. A short intro to the text of Aristotle is also provided.

A. General Introduction

A1. Metaphysics

First Philosophy is the nickname of metaphysics. It is the branch of philosophy that examines the fundamental issues on the nature of reality. It can be divided on **Ontology** (being as such: nature of being, substance and accident), **Peratology** (actual or precarious being: form & matter, causality & changes),

Critique (basic relationship between mind and matter, between the subject, who knows, and the object, which is known; Critique does include **Gnoseology,** or theory of knowledge, and **Epistemology**, which addresses the Meaning, nature and purpose of Science) — and finally **Natural Theology** (ultimate causes and existence of God — It is important to notice that Natural Theology **is not** Theology in its strict sense. Natural theology appropriately belongs to philosophy as its natural way of investigating on God. Such a study opens the way to Theology, which is the specific study of revelation — a good philosophy makes possible any appropriate Theology). **Theodicy**, or theory on God, belongs to natural theology.

The **heart of metaphysics** is included in a section addressing the "being qua being", known generically under the title of ontology. More specifically ontology is divided into ontology I & II. First Ontology addresses the being as such and its many expressions of Essence and Existence, Substance and Accidents. Second Ontology deals with change, or the way the being does change... otherwise Act and Potency and all their implications. That second section is also known as "Peratology", from the Greek < *peras-peratos* >= limit.

In the *Introduction to Philosophy*, Maritain provides the general picture of the whole section on the being with similar assertions → "Conclusion XI - Being as such is intelligible. Everything is intelligible in exact proportion to its being." Then, he added that when "that being, though in itself more intelligible, will be less intelligible to us," for there are limitations of intelligence in our mind. There are beings that surpass human intelligence.

In *General Introduction to Philosophy*, §49, Maritain asserts "What objects do emerge in the mind when we refer to the being?" In addition to the fact that the being is the first object of intelligence it emerges differently, according to the perspective of our inquiry, in other words "this unique fundamental question get a triple answer according to our inquiry perspective of intelligibility, existence, or action" And Maritain to conclude that (1) under the perspective of intelligibility the being is **essence**, (2) under the perspective of existence the being is **substance** (with its proper **accidents**) and (3) under the perspective of action the being is in act and potency.

Let us precise immediately that the first three definitions of the being, essence, substance & accident refer to ontology, which deals with the being as such, while the other two, act and potency, refer to peratology (Ontology II), which refer to the real being in its actual changes… Both, ontology and peratology address real being in its entity, but the first, ontology, deals with the being in its actual existence, while the second, peratology, deals with the being in its precariousness…

A2. Historical Perspectives

After the time of investigation of the Natural Philosophers (Thales, Anaximander, Anaximenes, and followers) and the new founders (Pythagoras, Parmenides, Heraclitus and their disciples) many contradictory statements produced some confusion which induced scholars of the day to believe that there was no possibility to find the truth… therefore, knowledge appeared like a tool at the service of politics and a wave of thinkers believed that intelligence was to be used to prove whatever we like to and the only material to work with is language itself.

The Sophists made language their own expertise. It was a period of uncertainty and skepticism in philosophy. Fortunately one of the Sophists, Socrates, showed up and moved against the relativism and nihilism of the same Sophists. His teaching and especially his example showed that beyond opinions there is truth. So, truth is beyond words. Additionally, truth is near to us. There is no need of a long journey to find her: truth is inside of each one of us. We just need to let her emerge from inside.

The evidence of afterlife provided by Socrates, suggested to Plato the hypothesis of "Recollection Theory," stating that we belong to a world which stands beyond this physical world. Our soul was born there and belongs to it. The knowledge we have is mere recollection of the issues we were familiar with in the perfect world of ideas. Later, Augustine will review the theory of Plato under the perspective of **Illumination Argument**, which follows the natural process of growing in knowledge under our familiarity with Jesus, the **Word**, who is the one we share wisdom with while growing in knowledge.

Aristotle made a diverse elaboration of Plato's teaching. He got the double advantage of showing up after those two extraordinary thinkers and to got his training with his father who was the physician of the court of Macedonian King, Philippe: a physician is not someone who may invent symptoms, but have to accept them, to study them and to understand where they come from and how they may go away. Aristotle started his inquiry with the statement that there are more facts in the worlds than in my mind.

With Aristotle, knowledge becomes first of all the understanding of facts. To do so, Aristotle put himself at the school of the previous thinkers, and made an accurate survey on all his predecessors. His study is very helpful to know them, too. A similar survey is still valid today to appreciate and criticize the partial point of view of every philosophical system… for this is what Aristotle made evident: reality is richer than the mind, when we reduce reality to what we may understand we commit a mistake, a great mistake, which prevents us from knowing the facts.

Aristotle was thirsty for the wisdom of his elders. He also was an amazing observer. He made a panorama of the many ways the being shows up! He evidenced the confusion which trapped both Parmenides and Heraclitus and put one another in total opposition even if they were experts of the same... the being and the logos. Observing the same facts, Parmenides and Heraclitus were in full contradiction to one another, while they made the same mistake... both were dealing with the being but were unable to distinguish the being in my mind (rational being, which, as a being, will never change) and the being in the facts (real being, which continuously changes) Making such a confusion between real & mental being, Parmenides and Heraclitus had to make a choice: Parmenides selected the mental being and denied change, while Heraclitus selected real being and denied permanency... For Parmenides identity, or being, was immutability, for the Heraclitus identity, logos, was change...

A3. Observing the Being

Aristotle was wise enough to refuse to take position between the many theories of his predecessors. He dealt with them with the respect a doctor owes to a patient. Every position was an additional invitation to seek a better understanding of things. He did not make even an eclectic choice as Cicero did in his days, when he was accepting everything and looking for what he liked without any proper discernment between eventually contrasting theories. Aristotle observed everything, considered all possible points of view, then, seeking the truth, made opportune discernment. Aquinas followed his track and emphasized it.

Along with the investigation of his predecessors Aristotle shows discernment and expresses more than once humor: 'There was never such a stupid idea which had not a philosopher to support it!" Observing the facts, Aristotle made the important assertion that **"the being can be said in many ways."** {Mph Book "G"). In other words, "the being is one and many." Such a contradictory statement, shows the concern of Aristotle to accept the observation coming from facts, then, reading the wisdom of his predecessors, his concern was to see how they may fit with each other, without making a priori any discrimination. Such humble address of the facts and of the wisdom of his elders induced him to exert his typical method of investigation, which took name "**Critical Realism**."

His specific method of investigation, **Critical Realism** follows a precise endeavor: it starts accepting a fact as is, then reflecting on it with all possible means, gathering all available information on it and moving to the most reasonable conclusion. A similar method made him an expert on facts and induced him to start new disciplines of study on all the fields of knowledge which require observation like medicine, biology, anatomy, zoology, botany, ethology… Aristotle first mastered those fields of knowledge…. which later became independent sciences.

Addressing everything without previous bias made him capable to deal with opposed thinkers and see what they are believable for and what should be dropped about them. His method of inquiry, Critical Realism, was used 15 centuries later very successfully by Aquinas, and even long after Aquinas' followers are still using the same method today. Among them we may quote Etienne Gilson, Jean Guitton, Garrigou-Lagrange, Antonin Sertillange, Henri Card. de Lubac, Jean Card. Daniélou, Jacques Maritain, Jean Daujat, Oliver Lacombe, Gustave Thibon, to name a few.

Among the investigations that Aristotle worked with, there is the field which goes inside of physics and beyond it (metaphysics), which is properly the expertise of the ***BEING*** as such. His first observation makes a distinction between every item in the facts, the real being, and the items showing up in the mind, the mental being. There is a connection and differences between the two. Here is where logic starts, as the study of how the mind works and addresses the facts, in other words: "how does the mind address the being." At the start metaphysics and logic overlap.

A4. BEING

How can we properly speak about the being, when there is no possibility to talk about it without using the verb "to be"? How defining the "being" without using the verb "to be"? Actually we always have to say "the being is…", which is somehow redundant. It is nonetheless possible. A "**being**" is "whatever does exist". A "being" is "everything which is". It can exist outside of our knowledge (real being) or just in our thoughts (mental being), or even in our imagination and movies (virtual being). As far as it exists somehow and somewhere, it is properly a "being."

A Common Misunderstanding of the Being — The main confusion about the being is to put together mental being (that which exists only in our mind and not in fact) and real being (that which exists in reality, independently of the fact that I know it or not). The distinction was made by Aristotle, to resolve the huge confusion made by Heraclites (whom, such confusion induced to deny consistency of things and to state that everything is change — such a permanent change was called *logos* = Logos) and by Parmenides (whom such a confusion induced to deny any change and to affirm that everything is permanency and the same: If the being is, it is what it is, therefore no change is possible, and any eventual change is mere illusion). Aristotle showed that things are both in the mind and in event or reality, but in a different fashion.

Today such a confusion continues to induce philosophers to deny after Hegel (and rationalists) the consistency of reality, or after Marx and Foucault the consistency of individuals and values, or after Kant (Idealism) and Derrida (Structuralism) to disregard the existence of things, or after Hume (and Empiricists) to state the incapacity of people to know facts and to interpret reality. Such variety of interpretations will not discourage the neo-philosopher that every student is, but oppositely encourage him or her to investigate more closely the events to find out what they are.

The solution suggested by Aristotle and, after him, by Aquinas, is that **every Being is real in its existence.** A being cannot be considered as a mere concept, which would indicate a mental being. Every real being exists right now and it is what it is, with a consistency which includes changes. Under the pole of being (ontological pole) every being is something (whatness or essence), contemporaneously, under the pole of facts (existential pole) every being is supposed to change, so it is pregnant of its future changes (it holds the capability of the changes it is supposed to get further...). Such a capacity is called its potential of change. So the being is said to be **in act** or what it is now, and to be in potency of every eventual changes. Such a capacity to think a being contemporaneously as in act and **in potency** (involving real and mental being) is typical of Aristotle. It will be studied in peratology section.

With such a reflection, Aristotle included the whole capacity of understanding things (their essence) inside of their real actuality (their existence) — He was able to put together theory and praxis, rationalism (idealism) and existentialism. He gave the proper suggestion to address together opposed theories, and to show that every theory usually indicates just a part of reality, as a family picture indicates only a side, a perspective, and a moment of people celebration. Philosophy, according to Aristotle, must restore the knowledge of the whole configuration of reality.

Real being refers to every being whose existence does not depend on my knowledge. It refers to every being belonging to the world. When we adopt the idealism position that only what we know may exist, it would mean that nobody would exist in a class before we knew each other, which is an absurdity. Every real being is in act (every real being is in act of what it is and it is in potency of any possible change). Then, when we talk about

Being in act or **Actual Being** — we refer to any being in its actual existence.

Mental Being is a being existing properly only in my mind and not in reality. It offers to the mind a general configuration that helps to refer to the reality that surrounds me. There are some universal concepts, which exist only in my mind, where I need to produce them in order to think appropriately about the whole of reality, e.g. nothingness, essence, value, etc. People sometimes have difficulty to understand that "Tree" is a mental being. Actually it is. For "tree" is a concept which refers to every being which is a tree, like a pine tree, an apple tree, an oak tree, and so on. Tree as such does not exist, but that cherry tree in my yard does exist. Mental being also may be called **"rational being."** It is the same for all abstract concepts, and even general concepts of things: I use to say door, window, house, and tree: as concepts they are rational beings. When I say tree I do not indicate a real being, but only a possible one. In reality we have not a tree, but an oak tree, a pine tree, an apple tree, a Christmas tree, and those trees in my back yard. As such "tree" does not exist; it only exists as a concept in my mind.

Mental being or rational being must not be confused with **Virtual being**, which is the kind of being which refers to the production of our imagination, either acting in our mind or in some human productions, especially in movies, internet, videogames, etc.

Also, mental being or rational being must not be confused with **Intentional being**, which is the kind of being which refers to a real being when it is present to my mind in the process of knowledge. Consciousness always addresses knowledge as an action of "becoming another", The process through which our consciousness knows is intentional, and what our own consciousness knows is the intentional being, It refers to an event, a fact. It is no more material and not yet mental. However it is consistent. Aristotle calls it intentional. Additionally we must recall that Aristotle classifies the Real Being in ten categories, the Substance and 9 Accidents. as shown below.

A5. Real Being

Among the investigations that Aristotle worked with, there is the field which goes inside of physics and beyond it (metaphysics), which is properly the expertise of the **BEING** as such. His first observation makes a distinction between every kind of items in the facts, the real being, and the items showing up in the mind, the mental being. There is a connection and differences between the two. Here is where logic starts, as the study of how the mind works and addresses the facts, in other words: "how does the mind address the being." Logic and metaphysics go together.

Observing the facts, Aristotle made the important assertion that "**the being can be said in many ways.**" In other words, "the being is one and many." Such a contradictive statement shows the concern of Aristotle to accept the observation coming from facts. Dealing with real being we distinguish the many expressions of what real being is.

As previously said, Aristotle states in *Metaphysics* that the being shows up in different manners… Here is the start of the categories, which are the many ways the being is said. These categories are mainly addressed in *Metaphysics* and more deeply investigated in the studies of *Prior Analytics* and *Post Analytics*, under the way they lead our mind to work (logic).

A6. Living Creation

Another short note must be added before we start ontology as such. Investigating the beginning of the being is actually considering the event of creation. Creation is not only like making a statue, a painting or a machine. Yes, a painting shows the beauty which amazed the painter, a statue shows the emotion of the art is, a machine, or a car goes… Voltaire said that "God made us in his resemblance and likeness, but people did the same with him" — We tend to reduce the entity of God to our own quality of life, far below what God is. Reading F.W. Nietzsche we understand that every being is a living one. He invites us to look at every being as emerging existence, because nothing is dead matter, everything is receiving life and providing relationship with every being around…

To help us consider God in his real perspective, we must understand how we are fully immerged inside of the action, the thought, the love of God. According to Saint Catherine of Siena: "God's love is sweeter than the first kiss that Our Lady gave to his Son Jesus"… God's love is more intense and radiant than everything we dare to imagine… Being created is not at all a sole action of God. Each creature shows where it comes from. All creatures express right away what they are. Again creatures are not mere objects; they are living witness of God's love… Because God loves us, thinks of us, we do exist. It is a living fact.

Being created means answering a call. Especially being part of Trinitarian life. Being brought into creation makes us connected with the whole of existing beings, it requires our attention, our love, our commitment.

B. Ontology
B.1 Essence & Existence

The two concepts of Essence and Existence go together. Essence is always the significance of an existence. Essence goes with existence in a being, it comes alone as mental being in our mind, and i.e. "essence" as such belongs to a substance, an accident, or another being (which it defines). It is however understood an essence as a mental being. E.g. "tree" is the essence of every existing tree. As such a "tree" does not exist. We only have those oak trees, maple trees, Christmas trees that I know in my yard – there is no tree which is only a tree. Every existing tree is a kind of tree. Such existing kind is real being, what I recognize it is, is its essence.

Essence – Nature of a thing. That which is understood of a thing. The recognizable form in a being (substance or accident). What it is: the whatness. Whatever I am able to recognize about the entity of something is its essence. There is curious connection of essence, which as such is a mental being and nonetheless may exist only in reference to the real beings that it defines. Essence goes with existence in a being, it comes alone as mental being in our mind, i.e. "essence" as such belongs to a real being, which it defines, for it is said "the essence of…". Nonetheless, as an essence it is a mental being.

Existence – The state of being. The fact that a being is present. An existence is always of an essence. Essence and existence go together in a being. Existence is said by Aquinas as the act of super-intelligibility of a being. In Heidegger vocabulary, "existence is the revelation of the being", such "revelation" is known as an "essence". As such "existence" is a fact, as a concept "existence" is a mental being. This is not a joke. It is the background of every metaphysical reflection.

In *General Introduction to Philosophy*, Maritain provides a few statements about the essence at the conclusion of a few reflections of section #50.

Conclusion XII - The essence of a thing is what that thing is necessarily and primarily as the first principle of its intelligibility.

Conclusion XIII - Our intellect is capable of knowing the essence of things.

Conclusion XIV - The essences of things are universal in the mind, and considered in themselves neither universal nor individual.

I leave the development of the reflection to the reading of Maritain.

B.2 The Categories

Sometimes the Aristotelian Categories are addressed separately. I dare to include them here, which is the appropriate context to see them.

As Aristotle stressed in Book G, "The being can be said in many ways". In other words there are many manners for a being to be. Aristotle elaborated an exhaustive list of these many expressions of being. They are the **Categories**. They indicate all possible ways of being in existence… Aristotle's Categories refer to two main figures: Substance & Accident. There are ten Aristotle's categories (1 Substance and its 9 accidents), through which the whole Aristotle's metaphysics develops. Metaphysics deals with real being, so the Aristotle's categories are a classification of the real being.

Again, we must stress that Aristotle use the categories that characterize every REAL BEING not a virtual or a generic one (i.e. a mental being) A virtual or a generic being shows a diverse configuration. Actually, when we are dealing with a generic item, we deal with an essence, not a substance, for example "cats", "trees", "flowers" are essences until we refer to a specific one. To say it even more evidently, I like to recall that "tree", "house", "building", "window" are mental being, i.e. "essences" unless we refer to a specific one. Dealing with real being, all substances and their characteristics are effectively existing, actual, too. They all go together. When dealing with a substance and reading its categories they all fit with a specific <somewhere>, <sometime. They actually correspond to the specific <where> and <when> which configure its actual picture.

The Substance is a Being that exists in itself, here and now. Everything existing independently as a real being is a substance.

When dealing with material things, a substance is the interaction of Matter & Form: ex. this computer, this chair, my friend, myself, the moon, the earth, the oak tree in my yard…

Every existing being (real being) has an essence which provides its identity. Essence as such is not a real being: window can be every window in my house, only existing window are real beings. The same can be said about tree: a tree as such does not exist. As a real being we only have a maple tree or an oak tree… and, more precisely the one I know and can see, here, in front of me, or that I clearly remember in my yard, and so on. Usually we refer to a substance though its essence. These habits to use essences to refer to reality make us thing that science (which works only by abstractions) is more real than philosophy, while the opposite is true.

The analysis of Aristotle shows that the substance is known by induction through its accidents: when I see a "chair" I do not see actually the "chair" but its accidents: the legs, the back, the seat, the way they are combined together (position), its color, consistency, practicability (quality), its size and weigh (quantity), where it is (location), when (time), what it is used for (passion), etc. In other words, substances are those things which exist independently and separately in this world. All things are substance. They reveal themselves through their accidents.

As a conclusion a substance is a tangible entity that we easily refer to. It is something that actually exists as a whole, independently.

The Accident is that which exists not within itself but in another which is a substance, like its color, size, quality, position, etc. An "accident" is not "accidental" but every regular (continuous or occasional) and actual characteristic of a substance. Every "potential" belongs to the accident quality, like able to…, powerful, apt to… An accident is every actual constituent of a substance: it is its shape, its name, its coloring, any of it characteristics. Aristotle classifies them in quality, quantity, relation, action, passion, position, *habitus*, time and space (see "Categories"). It refers to phenomenon in modern and contemporary philosophy.

In *Posterior Analytics*, Aristotle shows how some accidents are intrinsic or essential of a substance (like bones and skin for a human), while some others are extrinsic or contingent (like the size of the bones or the color of the skin). Others contingent characteristics are indicate about the accidents. What is important here is to notice the main distinction between substance and accident. A real being belong to one of these categories. It can be an item (a substance) or a figure (accident). If it is an object (a substance) all ten categories apply.

No substance can exist without its accidents. When we see an object, we see the characteristics (accidents) of it. For example we never see a car but its color, shape, fashion, engine, model, year of production, size, wheels, sits, doors, and from its characterics and its shape we recognize it is a car, and what car it is. All these "beings" which are attributes (accidents) of the car (substance) characterize it to the point that we may recognize what it is and call it a "car," a "lemon," or a "limo," my car, my daughter's car, my neighbor's car, and so on.

Emmanuel Kant called phenomenon what is known about the being, i.e. all that which characterizes a being in itself.... The transposition Substance-Accident to Noumenon-Phenomenon enlightens one another from the diverse perspectives.

To be more explicit we must say that **Emmanuel Kant** took the whole teaching of Aristotle, trying to provide a new configuration of the categories. He kept however, the main distinction made by Aristotle between Substance and Accident, insisting on their incompatibility. He gave the name of **"noumenon"** to the being in itself, or the substance, and **"phenomenon"** to the revelation of a being to me, i.e. the accident (or accidents = phenomena) of that substance. Because the substance manifests itself through its accidents there I not direct knowledge of the noumenon, but the relationship between accidents (revelation of the substance) and substance disappear between phenomena and noumena to the point that "nothing can be said about the noumenon," therefore nothing can be said about the being as such, and, according to Kant, there is no knowledge of the being as such: the study of metaphysics has become impossible!

Let us proceed now more systematically with our investigation on Aristotelian categories.

Don't worry if you have the feeling that some topics are said a second time.

A. Being

1. "Being can be said in many senses" (Metaphysics, Bk: G §2.). So the being is in the same time one and many (Bk: E). Being has to be understood analogically (See Note on Reality and Language). Metaphysics is the "science which investigates the being qua being and what belongs essentially to it" (G §1.). The being can be at first identified as => something

2. Real being   A being whose existence does not depend of my knowledge. A being belonging to the world.

  a. Actual being   Any being which is now in existence. Every real being is in act of existence.

  b. Potential being   Something that can develop or become actual. Any possibility of a being to change.

  c. Every being in act is in potency of any possible change

3. Mental being or Concept is a being existing only in my mind and not in the reality surrounding me. There are generally some universal concepts (e.g. nothingness, essence, value). They also are called "**rational being.**" It is proper to a Mental Being to distinguish between Essence and Existence, which never can exist separately in a Real Being.

4. Virtual being or Images in the mind are often confused with Mental Being, it is not a concept (mental being) but a sensorial presence in the mind elaborated as an extension of

images, sometimes referred to "creative imagination." Imagination is never creative, it always a combination of existing images put together in a way that does not exist in the facts: like adding wings of an eagle to the body of a lion to "create", or better to imagine the new figure of a dragon. Virtual being is not an action of intelligence but a sensorial one.

5. Intentional being or Manifestation of Truth in the Mind refers to a real being when it is present to my mind in the process of knowledge. It is no more material and not yet mental. However it is consistent. Aristotle calls it intentional. It is in this Intentional meeting between Mental and Real Being that it is found the structure, or configuration of a being, i.e. the distinction Matter and Form.

B. Substance

6. That which exists in itself

a. Something having existence as a whole.

b. A subject of its own existence

c. Not directly detectable

d. Which expresses itself through its characteristics (accidents)

e. It must exist somewhere, sometime. It is not virtual, nor generic. It is real.

7. It also refers to Noumenon

a. Any being in itself (not knowable as such)

C. Accident

8. That which exists not within itself but in another (which is a substance).

a. A characteristic of a substance.

b. One of the Categories # 2-10 of Aristotle

c. Directly detectable

d. Which is evident here and now - it is never generic.

9. It refers to phenomenon in modern and contemporary philosophy.

a. Only phenomenon can be known.

b. The revelation of the being - Heidegger
c. It has a precarious entity

D. The Categories of Aristotle – Short presentation

Note: After the Substance, Aristotle classifies Accidents in quality, quantity, relation, action, passion, position, habitus, time and space.

1. **Substance** is the First Category. Any being as a whole. Every being existing in itself, showing itself through its accidents. Any being an accident refers to. Any being having attribute.

2. **Quality** 2nd Category. 1st Accident. First evident characteristic of the substance, it can be the color, the species among many. Any differentia of a Substance. Every sort of the substance belongs to. It is what does make the substance effective or defective. It is the easier to identify.

3. **Quantity** 3rd Category. 2nd Accident. Anything can be counted or numerated in a Substance. Every substance is one, but everything is measurable (size, weight, age) belongs to the category quantity.

4. **Relation** 4th Category. 3rd Accident. Any connection of the substance with another one, for example, my book note (the one related to me) is above the table, next to the dictionary, and so on

5. **Action** 5th Category. 4th Accident. Anything is produced or caused by a Substance.

6. **Affection or Passion** 6th Category. 5th Accident. Anything is endured or received by a Substance.

7. **Having or Habit** 7th Cat. 6th Acc. Any constituent part of a Substance that could be itself a substance as well.

8. **Position or Disposition** 8th Category. 7th Accident. Any combination of habits.

9. **Place** (location) 9th Category. 8th Accident. Any actual reference of a substance to a place.

10. **Date** (time) 10th Category. 9th Accident. Any actu-

al reference of a substance to a time.

E. Additional insights on the Categories

I. **Substance:** Again, substance is every being which exist by itself, or in itself (it is known by its accidents) Note that in his book of Metaphysics, Aristotle sees the substance both as an individuals and as a species. So substance is every human being, but also every consistent connection of human beings like family, nation, state, and so on. This brings an interesting issue for a Christian reading of St. Paul, who considered every one like another Christ, but also every community as another Christ. Sometimes we use to call, after St. Paul, the whole Christendom (the Church) the mystical body of Christ, which according to Aristotle would be a substance as well.

There is an improvement between the substance in Aristotle first, then in Aquinas. For Aristotle the whole world is eternal, so every substance does exist "from" itself, while Aquinas give back to the substance its proper consistency of a "creature" that does exist "in itself".

Please, note that the Substance cannot exist without its accidents. It is not independent of its accidents. It is what exists as the entity which expresses those accidents.

II. **Accident:** An Accident is every being existing in another which is substance. It characterizes a substance. It expresses the substance whose it belongs to.

A Few examples (A), (B), (C)

I. Substance:

Ex. (A): Our school

Ex. (B). The moon

Ex. (C): My personal unabridged *Webster's Third New International English Dictionary*

Note: a substance is a being. it has to be precise. It is not an idea. It is a real thing, therefore individual, particular, and contingent (which may include the whole mankind as a specific entity inside of the whole universe). If you say "a tree", "a cat", "a dog", any of these is a substance. They only are essences or concepts, they are not real. To be real an item must be taken some time, some where… A substance is not even your hat if you address it "generally" as it can be home and in your office. No, to be a substance it has to be considered the way it is also sometime, somewhere: like now, while you're reading these lines.

II. Accident quality: Any attribute of a substance that can be appreciated or depreciated

(A) It is a serious and authentic Center of Higher Education in the USA.

(B): The earth satellite, brilliant and attractive (physically, speculatively, psychologically).

(C): The most complete I know as a desk dictionary in one volume.

Note: it has to characterize the substance as a kind of --- (species, brand, distinctive tool or device), for its aspect (color, consistency, material of which it is made), or for what it is good or bad.

III. Accident quantity: Any attribute of a substance that can be counted; age, dimension, weight,

(A): It counts several buildings, students from different nations, faculty, staff members, acres of campus, years of existence, 1 president, a few vice-presidents, 1 academic dean, 1 chaplain, etc.

(B): Its size, mass and weight may be calculated.

(C): Its size is 13 x 9¼ x 4 sq.inches and holds 2790 pages.

Note: it characterizes the substance with a **number**, which indicates its size, age, duration, or value. When you say that a rose will thrive for a short period of time, such a period of time belongs to the category quantity

IV. Accident Relation: Any attribute saying its membership, property, nearness, vicinity, priority, causality, etc. Relation indicates every relationship which would define the substance.

(A): It is a catholic (universal) institution, it's an American institution, for every student in this class and for myself it is "our" university.

(B): It is earth satellite – For someone it is "his/her favorite planet"

(C): It is my best English dictionary; I usually keep it on my desk, or in one of my bags.

V. Accident Action: Any attribute that shows the action committed by the substance

(A): It provides education and formation to the youth

(B): It influences cultures (you must plan your seeds after the last quarter).

(C): It provides invaluable information on American and British language. Also it's very heavy, if you drop it on your feet, it hurts.

VI Accident Passion: any attribute which expresses an action that a substance undergoes

(A): It survived many difficulties and even storms in the past.

(B): Receives light from the sun, was visited by Americans.

(C): It is consulted every day, moved from a place to another in my home office.

VII. Accident Habit: All **integral parts** or components of that substance. Some of these components could be even a substance itself if taken separately.

(A): It includes a beautiful Chapel, buildings, library, bookstore, smart classrooms, students, faculty members, sport fields, library, athletic room, gymnasium, archives, long distance learning program, liberal arts programs, nurse programs, several projects of development, academic policies, faculty policies, student policies, board of trustees, dormitories, etc.

(B): Combination of mountains, picks, craters and valleys.

(C): It is made by means of cardboard and strong paper, and contains four sections: Pronunciation symbols, Editorial staff, Explanatory introduction, vocabulary.

VIII. Accident Position: Internally physical "relations" between the integral parts of the substance

(A): It is in good standing – also position means "university map"

(B): It stands upside down in consideration of the place the Americans landed (mooned) there.

(C): It stands on the shelf

IX. Accident Location (or spatiality): Where the substance is

(A): Its specific location in North-Eastern US.

(B): Inside of the milk way, every time at a precise location between the sun and earth: today it's ….

(C): *In the handy shelf which is at the left of my desk (when I came back from Texas, I could not find it for a while, it was nonetheless somewhere in one of my boxes)*

X. Accident Temporality: When a substance is… All the many cases of the substance relative to time

(A): It's running Fall Session of year 2009

(B): At this time of the year we are in some precise time of moon month. In 1969 Americans visited it and walked on it

(C): Any time since September 5, 1998, when I purchased it.

Hope these 3 examples have been helpful to show Aristotle's divisions.

You may apply these categories to every other example you like: *Yourself, your pet, your home, some personal friend, some relative, your workplace, any specific item, etc.*

No other category than the ones above is applicable to a real being.

Every real being belongs to one of the 10 categories.

If you may find a substance that has not these 10 categories, it could be that you refer to a mental being, or to a virtual being, but you do refer not to a real being. In other words, if one of these 10 categories cannot be applied to an item, such item does not exist as a real being. If you may find an object (substance) that has not one or more of these accidents it is not a real object.

Such a classification will be the pattern of many other similar series in philosophy history. It may be useful to learn properly all Aristotelian categories.

Most works on Aristotle provide only a definition for four or five of them. I considered useful to provide them all in order to have a complete picture of the topic.

B.3 Every Category of Accidents is a specific field of abstraction & knowledge

In other words, the categories are the characteristics of a field of knowledge and science. They are a typical approach of the whole. To say it shortly, let me refer to each category more precisely.

1. *Quality* Art, sculpture, painting, drawing, music, dance,
2. *Quantity* mathematics, arithmetic, algebra, geometry,
3. *Relation* physics,
4. *Action* ethics,
5. *Affection or Passion* Medicine
6. *Having or Habit* anatomy, zoology, botany, chemistry,
7. *Position or Disposition* ethology,
8. *Place* (*location*) geometry
9. *Date* (*time*) astronomy, astrology,
10. *Substance* metaphysics

B.4 Real Being is One

The categories are the characteristics of the being. They are not created by the mind. They really characterize the being. They exist in the facts and intelligence recognizes them. They are the ways the being truly emerges into existence and intelligence reads them.

There is a **mystery** of the being which is contemporaneously one and many. Such a diversity of the being is exerted by every being. If some accident is missing all accidents refer to something which is not real being. It is impossible that a substance exists and does not express its nine accidents. Somehow the categories refer to the many aspects of the macrocosm that are reflected in every microcosm that a being is. It is not obvious to see in the categories the many aspects through which a being refer to the whole of the macrocosm. The question was not fully studied yet and making a tight connection between the two is not always clear.

Nonetheless some examples can be done to show how a human being blossoms through its relationship with the whole. These examples are provisional and need improvement.

Quality shows the dimension of life, it is the first expression of the substance, its vitality…

Quantity allows the exertion of science, knowledge, contemplation.

Relation expresses the dimension of service into the society, the family. People are appreciated according to the people they are related to.

Action & Passion exert the aspect of work and of love of friendship

Habitus may express the field of the Common Good

Situation (position) was seen as the typical behaviors of the body.

Space & Time are the actual condition of people in the universe.

B.5 Kant's Categories

As an attentive reader of Aristotle, Immanuel Kant made a transposition between what is the being in itself (noumenon)

and the being for us, as a revelation (phenomenon). Unfortunately the being in Kant does not refer to the real being. So, Aristotelian categories do help to understand noumenon and phenomenon in Kant. Let us make a short survey on Kant's process.

Kant want to address the rationalism of **Descartes** together with the atomism of **Leibniz** (monads), the empiricism of **Hume** ("who woke him up from a dogmatic slumber"), the scientism of **Newton**, the skepticism of **Voltaire**, the subjectivist idealism of **Berkeley** and the romanticism of **Rousseau**.

Kant emphasizes the Aristotelian distinction between substance and accident, and exaggerates the opposition between unknowable **noumena** (reality) to knowable **phenomena** (appearance).

The substance of things, noumenon, or thing-in-itself is unknowable. The attempt to go beyond the phenomenal world, to apply concepts outside the limits of their empirical application inevitably leads to paradoxes and fallacies.

To say it shortly: people cannot know any substance, but only their characteristics.

For Kant, knowledge comes from a combination of experience and concepts. Without senses we cannot be aware of any object, and without understanding we cannot form any conception of it. Sensibility and understanding interact.

E. Kant used the traditional distinction between **analytical** propositions (starting from the same contents of a discourse) and **synthetical** ones (starting from perception or sensory experience in a process of elaborating concepts) and identifies them under the two categories of *a priori* and *a posteriori*. *A priori* concept is understood independently of reference to sensory experience. *A posteriori* refers to a knowledge that depends on evidence, or warrant, from sensory experience.

According to Kant all ideas proceed from mind categories. Notions of Time and Space are given as *a priori* pure intuitions. They are absolute, independent of, and preceding sense impressions. They constitute the starting point of mind categories. such *a priori* knowledge is innate. Everything is gathered under the notions of time and space and structured in our mind through the categories of thought, which are quantity (unity, reality, totality), quality (reality, negation, limitation), relation (substance, causality, interaction) and modality (possibility, existence, necessity).

Willingly, Kant elabores a "**Copernican revolution**." Objective reality (phenomenal world) can be known only according to the "*a priori*" of the mind, which imposes upon phenomena the forms of its own intuitions (innate ideas of time and space). Mind has the function to elaborate, organize and connect sensual data according a process which he called synthetic judgments *a priori*. This is the only perspective in which synthetic *a priori* statements are possible.

Human judgment serves to mediate between the sensible and intelligible worlds, especially in aesthetic, ethics, politics, and theology. It is mostly a subjective experience, not a universal one. Nonetheless, because of rationality of people, every human experience involves the whole mankind: what is true for one must be true for all.

At the conclusion of the *Critique of Practical Reason*, Kant wrote, "Two things fill the mind with ever new and increasing admiration and awe, the more often and steadily reflection is occupied with them: the starry heaven above me and the moral law within me. Neither of them need I seek and merely suspect as if shrouded in obscurity or rapture beyond my own horizon; I see them before me and connect them immediately with my existence."

As an outcome of above, **categorical imperative** is a universal principle, binding on all humans. It is a pure rational command, an iron law, which founds ethics as a science (compare with self-evidence of pure ideas in Descartes). This absolute moral law is not dependent on ulterior considerations. Its main formulations are: (1) "So act that you could will the maxim of your action to be a universal law;" (2) "Act in order to deal with mankind in yourself and other people always as an end and never as a means;" (3) "So act that your will could be source of a universal law".

In roughly words the morals of Kant is a pure obligation, which is independent of any hope, success, blossoming, result, or even precise perspective. It could be synthesized saying, "Hoping is not necessary to undertake something nor either succeeding to persevere" or "We do not know where we are going to, however we surely are going there, and we have to." Nevertheless morals of will are not entirely useless, for we also can say: "It would be possible to do something good, therefore I must do it," or that other interesting perspective: "I have to do it, therefore I can."

With Kant morals becomes a choice between wrong/right, bad/good, evil/good, i.e. a Manichaeism., which is a poor and improper approach of ethics.

B.6 Judgment of Existence

Aquinas' Philosophy is philosophy of existence. The Judgment of existence, also known as Intuition of the being is the fundamental act of intelligence which recognizes immediately every being as existing and, second of all, as an essence: What it is. A similar exertion is typical of every human being and it is the starting point of metaphysics. the awareness that everything around me does exists proceeds contemporaneously with the awareness that I do exist..This was the starting point of Descartes Philosophy: "I think, therefore I am"

It is the natural need of intelligence to understand the being and to recognize it

At the bottom line of every metaphysical investigation, there is the intellectual intuition of the mysterious fact that emerges with the most common word of our language, the word "to be"… which cannot be explained with another word than itself: "A being is…" Such original awareness makes thinkers philosophers.

B.7 On Substance and God

In Ontology I & II (Peratology), we speak about real being, change, existence, essence, and substance. We make a fast survey on all real beings of creation, from minerals and plants, through animals and humans, up to angels. It was evident that we cannot insert God in the list of creatures because he is the one which everything proceeds from. For God is not a being, on the contrary he is the one who says "I Am". We can only address God as the source of all beings. Every being belongs to him but God does not belong to any being.

Then we consider that every being that does exist in itself is a substance, while the beings that do exist in a substance are accidents. Someone recalled that God is said to be a Substance. It would be improper to say so. It is true that referring to God we speak about transubstantiation, when in the mystery of the Eucharist the bread keeps all characteristics of its accidents but become truly the substance of Christ.

Later the wording of the Creed was brought up, and particularly the section where it is said that "the Son proceeds from the Father and is consubstantial with him. Actually, it is difficult to address properly the mystery of the Trinity asserting at the same time the distinct existence of the three people (Father, Son, Holy Spirit) who are the same only one God. The wording of theology uses the term of "Divine Substance" to express the distinction of the persons in the same entity of God (when the Creed was translated into French, theologians like Garrigou Lagrange suggested, instead of "consubstantial with the Father", to say "of the same nature of the Father and one with it". Dropping the second section of the suggestion the French version failed to be consistent with the original creed, at this point the English version is surely better.

Talking about God as such, it would be improper to say that He is a being (even the words "Supreme Being" can be misunderstood) or a substance. However, talking about the Trinity, we have to express the fact that the Three Persons are One and de facto there is no better expression than "Divine Substance", which is that "Substance which nature is to exist". Such a definition changes completely the nature of what a substance is but save the understanding that the three are intrinsically one.

I hope that this short note will help those who eventually will leave the classroom with some doubts.

Concerning ecumenism the details of some projects which experts are working on in the Church are provided in class as far as they are connected with metaphysics. The given examples were intended only to show that we must be open to the steps that the Lord desires to lead us through. We know that Jesus asked his Father "That all be one", i.e. that we are one day going to be the same family under the care of the Father. We do not know how this will be done. Nonetheless it will happen and we must be ready for it.

Know yourself.
Socrates

Gnothi Seuton
Know Thyself

Ontology II
Change and Causes

Peratology –
The Precarious Being
Good News

As Ontology explains, a being is not a mere object. It is a living creature. According to F.W. Nietzsche, every being wants to be more and is going to be more, just by the simple fact that is going to continue to exist i.e. to emerge out of nothing for more time. According to Augustine "Time" is a creature too. Living in time is an act of being inside of creation. In other words, dealing with "peratology" means to address the mystery of creation. According to the words of J. Maritain, it is a field where "there is more to contemplate than to understand". It is nonetheless a wonderful teaching.

While investigating on the many ways to express the being, Aristotle (who knew nothing about creation, but was an excellent observer of it) sees change, together with the identity of every being. Every being shows capacity, inclination, and ability to change…. Creation does not stop when it is done… Actually, creation never stops to be, and every being, does include change…

Additionally Creation does belong to God, who is eternal, and not just immortal… God is now; He is "I AM", As Aquinas said "The nature of God is to exist." God is permanent source of being... of the whole of creation... Here is why, in the continuous process of creation, every being wants to be, and wants to be more than what it actually is...

Our Inquiry proceeds as a support while reading Aristotle, Aquinas, and Maritain. Our previous study addressed the field of the Being as such, otherwise called "Ontology". It continues now with Ontology Part Two, or Second Ontology, also known as Peratology. To be more specific, let me say that "Peratology" deals with the finite being, the "creature". It is the study of being, emerging out of nothingness inside of creation (this is not theology but pure metaphysics), which follows ontology, as the study of being *qua* being.

This note intends to show some elements of philosophy of nature, which highlight the characteristics and modalities of the finished being, that is to say some major perspectives on diversity and change. The term "PERATOLOGY" is uncommon on this side of the sea. It can barely be found in an English dictionary. Again, it refers to the specific field of metaphysics dealing with what is known as Ontology, Part II, which relates to change, multiplicity and their causation. Again, be careful, it is not just a new perspective; it is the fact that addressing creatures, we must consider what they are called to be. Creation is now. Creation is not something that did happen time ago, millennia ago. Yes creation does happen now. The comprehension of this present note will be improved during class discussion.

Etymologically, "Peratology" comes from the Greek <περασ/τοσ> (peratos) = limits, and λογοσ (*logos*) = discourse, study of. The term <περασ/τοσ> (*peratos*) is often put in opposition with απειρον (*apeiron*) which refers to what has no limitation and characterizes the absolute. Peratology deals with the being which is not mere essence, i.e. universal essence, but gets the limitations of the facts. The particular being has borders in space and time, it is precarious. A finished being is involved in beginning, limitation and change. Peratology asks the question to know what does it pertain to something that exists.

We are going to investigate the notions of existence and essence as they appear in finite and particular beings. A finished and particular being is recognizable (1) **by the fact of its existence** (the fact to be, or his acting to be) and (2) **by its nature or its essence** (what it is, what the thing is, i.e. its whatness). We immediately see that every being shares the act of being. Being in act is common to all that is: each being is a being in Act. In other words, the Act of Being belongs to everything that exists. It is not just mere evidence.

Aristotle was aware of the fact that a substance is directly connected with God the "uncaused cause". Here is why he call substances as small gods and defined them as "Being by themselves"... He knew that a substance shows the present action of emerging out of nothing, emerging now... Every moment is a second chance to be. Peratology, investigates in the manner things emerge out of nothing. It is an inquiry inside of the process of creation.

By contrast, the beings differ from one another through what they are: because of their essences or their natures. The finite being shares the being by its existence, according to the terms of its essence, or of its nature. Nature, or essence, marks the difference between beings, allows establishing discontinuity, diversity among things that exist. Ontology indicates that essence can be accidental (when it relates to the modalities and characteristics of the substance that accidents are) or substantial when it refers to a substance. Thus accidental diversity marks the change of a same substance (the terms of diversity of a same substance), while substantial diversity marks the diversity of beings in their entity.

In other words, the essence delimits in each being its being, which is what does refer to its existence. The essence defines the being in act, or again: the essence marks the borders of the being in Act. Essence is the definition of the being: every existence shows up according to an essence. Essence distinguishes beings, determines the act of being. By its essence I get the originality of each being, but it is by its existence that it is. In ontology we stress the existence, the presence of the being. Peratology looks after diversity and change of beings, the so-called "existent", or rather the "existing" ones, which include the ontological question of change and diversity in the world.

We will consider the precarious being under the mode **(A)** of **change**, **(B)** of **multiplicity**, **(C)** of **movement**, and **(D)** of beings part of the whole picture of creation, i.e. **nomenclature**.

(A) Change

1. Emergence of the question of Change
The fact of change

Change is a fact of current experience. At first sight, change contradicts the being: the fact of change contradicts the principle of identity: "In fact change states that the present being is no longer what it was. It is now another being. Therefore change destroys the identity of being with itself. We may formulate the principle of identity by saying that "any thing is what it is." Change however introduces an alteration: with change a ceases to be what it is to become what it was not, therefore it loses its identity with itself: if something is what it is and is not what it is not, it seems that it must remain what it is and should never be what it is not, therefore change is impossible. Nonetheless change exists. Therefore the question becomes another: what does produce change? Something cannot change according to what it is, because it is already that, and nonetheless it cannot change according to what it is not, because what it is not, consist merely in nothing. It is obvious that from nothing, nothing can happen. The point of view of logic between being and non-being, makes an incompatible reciprocity, and makes the change appear impossible.

It is on the review of this difficulty that metaphysics took birth in Greece, in the Fifth century B.C. The two opposed and extreme positions of PARMENIDES and HERACLITUS are dovetailed, in history of philosophy, by successive systems, which will be necessarily either Parmenidian or Heraclitean.

PARMENIDES asserts the intellectual evidence and the obvious certainty of the principle of identity, to the point to declare in its fragment III: "Think and be, it is the same". And change is for him apparent and illusory, it is an error of our senses: behind this apparent change, reality is perfectly immutable and without change. And there is no other reality that the Being in its perfect and immutable identity, which eternally stands without any ability to change. He said so in fragment VI: "It is required to say and think that the being is: in effect, it is being, so whatever would be against it is not: here is what I urge you to keep in mind".

Today we are able to point out a distinction that appears only later in philosophy. Parmenides identifies real with reason, and secondly he identifies what is relative to absolute being: you cannot be both saved and lost - you are supposed to go either to heaven, or be damned - there is not half measure in what is absolute. Parmenides confuses reason with reality to the benefit of reason and absolute with relative to the benefit of the absolute.

HERACLITUS stresses experimental certainty of change. His discourse denies the principle of identity and the consistency of the being. Being itself is not worth: since nothing stands and continues nothingness is affirmed. There is only change. Change is the only consistent reality. Change is a continuous process, which affirms perpetual contradiction since each moment contradicts the previous moment. Perpetual evolving stands by itself as cause of everything: it causes what is not to exist and what is to disappear. It moves as the incessant contradiction of the stream of perpetual change: "We cannot bath twice in the same river" said Heraclitus, meaning that the stream himself is a continuous moving, which makes impossible diving twice in the same water… Heraclitus gave the name of "logos" to changing facts and "logos" is also the discourse which accesses to the truth of change, i.e. which is able to state what reality is, i.e. that it is change.

Heraclitus did the same confusion as Parmenides but then put the opposite choice. He ignored the distinction, which will appear later with Aristotle between real being and rational being. Heraclitus confused reason and reality to the benefit of reality and confused absolute and relative to the benefit of relative.

Actually there is no other option than to admit contemporaneously the intellectual certainty of the principle of identity and the experimental certainty of change. Furthermore, we also must consider the fact that without identity no change can be said. In order to affirm that my cousin Solange changed it is necessary first to be able to state that the person I refer to is still Solange. Only considering that she is the same person I'll be able to affirm some change about her. Thus there is no possible concept of change without the corollary principle of identity. Similarly, I can identify identity only in a context of change. Identity and change refer to one another: Some changes must occur in the person of Solange in order to assert the identity of Solange despite the changes. Therefore: there is no concept of identity without the concept of change, and there is no concept of change without the concept of identity: change and identity are involved and require one another reciprocally. The reality of the one is based on the reality of the other, the presence of one allows the affirmation of the other: identity and change are corollaries one of the other.

Both of them, Parmenides and Heraclitus, utter a contradictory speech: Parmenides denies the reality of the experience; Heraclitus denies the objectivity of thought and of existence. Both deliver a teaching which is as such inconsistent and impossible to accept. Their disciple accept their teaching because it is intuitively understandable, but in fact irrational.

Aristotle delivered on Heraclitus the ironic sentence: "Either he does not say everything that he knows, or he does not know what he says". In other words: the first perspective he would be a liar in the second ignorant or stupid. But that sentence fits also for Parmenides who denied real being to admit only the consistency of rational being, while Heraclitus affirmed arbitrarily the unique "stability" of pure change, disregarding any entity.

ARISTOTLE (Mph 1005, b 25) states: "it is not possible to assert, with some followers of Heraclitus, that something is and is not, at the same time and under the same perspective " and he added again with a bit of humor the severe judgment: "If we do not thing what we say we assert a lie, when we think so and we show ignorance ". Because, affirmed Aristotle: "it is obviously impossible, for the same spirit, to believe at the same time that the same thing is, and is not". After stating the necessary coexistence of change and identity, it remains to consider how this evident coexistence can be carried out. On the tracks of Aristotle, Thomas Aquinas developed an adequate discourse on the question, stressing the concepts of ACT and POTENCY.

2. Act and Potency
The conditions of change

Ontology taught us that *everything that exists is a being*. And we considered as every being is identified in the mind both as an existent and as an essence. Every being is not undetermined. In order to be identified it had to be specific, it must be recognized as an object or a thing. It is said that in every object or thing we have some undetermined being which has become actual, which has been actualized, otherwise said, which is present to us, which offers actually essence and existence in one fact, which can be distinguish in the mind, but remain the same in facts. Everything we know — through its essence — currently exists. We will say that it is a being in act.

If we were able to only consider the being in act any change would be effectively impossible, because there is nothing at this time that could explain that what was not may now exist and what was no longer exists. The being, as departure point of change, cannot constitute also the term of change.: In fact the being a such cannot operate according to what it is not yet (for nothing cannot actuate anything), and cannot operate either according to what it is, for what it is accomplishes in fullness the entireness of its existence and essence… So what it is cannot produce change for it is already so and so…

Aristotle evidenced an issue that is typical of his brilliant mind. He affirmed that everything is in act of what it is, but his nature, or essence, includes more than what it merely is, that is to say, that the being in act does also include all its possible changes. It is nevertheless not already in act of everything it can be. It is only in act of all the possible changes it may actuate. And change will actuate what it is not yet while nevertheless it is capable to be it. This is not a mental joke, but a fact. Every being in act is in potency of the many changes it may actuate... It is precisely by the change that it will become what it can be and it is not yet. Every change operates according to what a being is in process to be... What it can be (and is not yet) is included in the departure point (of the being Act) and also becomes the term of the change.

In his *Letter to a Friend* (Cf. Marie-Dominique Philippe, *Lettre à un ami*, Editions Téqui, Paris 1978, 11x18, 310 p, or Editions Universitaires, Paris 1990, 16x24, 200 p), father Marie-Dominique Philippe, op. , remarked: that "at the level of first philosophy, it must be noted that what is in act, for example this man, could exist not, since it is in the process of being, i.e. in his process of existing, in his whole evolving progress, which includes eventual corruption...While the substance of the man is indeed indivisible principle in the order his essence, his own existence (his "how he does exist') involves matter, which makes him corruptible. Thus he might exist not. Matter introduces there some fragility. So we may understand that what exists in act implies the possibility to exist and that this possibility to exist is necessarily ordered towards the act" (Ibid. Ed. Téqui, p.183).

A seed does not become a plant because it is seed, not even because it is not a plant, but because as a seed it can become a plant - it is in its nature of seed to becoming a plant. In the seed there is what is needed to become a plant. And not every kind of seed becomes every kind of plant: the essence of a seed includes a specific sum of potentialities. In a general way it must be said that every being includes in itself a number of precise potentials. That number may seem countless to our human capability of counting, it is nonetheless determined.

The notion of essence and of nature is all but a static concept. So a notion is the seat of an immense dynamism, which belongs to the same dynamism of the being. **Every being in act includes the potentialities defined by its proper essence.** Thus, outside of nothingness there is not only the being in act but also the being in potency. Aristotle called "potential" a relative non-being, which differs from mere nothing, which is pure non-being. In fact the potential being cannot be reduced to nothing under the pretext that it is not already in act. Denying the being in potency, denies the essence of the being, too, and its nature, which is the foundation of its potential. Denying the existence of potential being put limitations to the same being in act. Without its potentialities a being in act is not fully considered, for every being in act is rich of what it is in act and of everything it can become.

What the seed is in potency is not simply the non-being because a gland (seed of oak) has not the same potentialities as a hazelnut (seed of a hazel tree). The gland is an oak in potency, by opposition to an existing oak, i.e. an oak in act. Walnuts are potential *juglandaceus* trees, not yet existing tree of walnuts, i.e. in act. The Act refers to what does exist in fact, potency refers to what, which may be or should be.

When Michelangelo decided to sculpt the *Pieta*, he personally went to Carrara and he selected there and purchased expressly to that purpose a large block of marble that he chose because he was able to see in that large stone the appropriate material to his project. He was able to verify that the large rock could become the statue of "Marie bearing Jesus, dead from the Cross" that he had planned to perform. As soon as he began to work on it, in his apartment of the street called today Sistine Chapel street… as soon as he began sculpting the marble block, which was already for his eyes the figure of Marie and Jesus, he started to release from the stone his statue, which was there in potency. His virtual statue slowly began to become effectively the famous statue we are familiar with. The marble block, which was a statue in potency, became under his scalpel the existing statue, the statue in act.

To say it shortly, **change is the passage from being in potency to being in act.** Every change comes from that which can be and it is carried out according to the modalities of what can be. Change operates from that which can be to that which is currently. It is the passage of potency to act. In other words, change moves from possibility of being to actual existing.

Michelangelo sketch

It must be noted that **change is a particular case of multiplicity.** Additionally, the successive multiplicity of moments that differ from one another constitutes time. A changing world is a world existing in time. We said that change consists in the fact that what it was not it is now and vice versa. However, if change was merely the fact that what it was it is not and what it was not it is now, change would only be contradiction. Change would exert some impossibility, due to the fact that the principle of identity shows that it is impossible that what it is it is not. Oppositely, it is quite possible that what it was (formerly) it is not (now), or that which was not (past) does exist (present), but also that what which was still stands...

The passage from past to present is actuated according to changes in beings. Similar changes provide the notion of time.

When I say that what it is today it was (or it was not) yesterday, the same usage of the two distinctive tenses of the verb to be indicates the exertion of a succession in time. This process shows that the being that we know and are familiar with is successive. We deal with a being that exist inside of time. Through change, such a being shows succession and distinction of moments, which differ from one another. Similar differences stress multiplicity. All being considered the question of change, which has been analyzed and evidenced, appears to be tightly connected with the overall problem of multiplicity which we have to address.

B. Multiplicity

3. Emergence of the Question of Multiplicity

Multiplicity raises an aspect of the problem of change with regard to principle of identity: at first sight, multiplicity denies the being: if the being is what it is, there is nothing other than what it is and we do not see how it could be two different things, or how it could get inside the lesser principle of division or of differentiation. It therefore appears that it should be perfectly one: any difference within the being seems to contradict and destroy its identity.

In this connection we meet, as for change, two extreme philosophical positions, essential and contradictory: that of Parmenides which affirms the intellectual truism and certainty of the principle of identity and that of Heraclitus which affirms the immediate evidence of experience which provides without possible dispute the fact of multiplicity. Once again, Aristotle was the first who reconciled the two positions using anew the distinction between being in act and being in potency. Later, Thomas Aquinas resumed his speech.

If there was not the existence of any other kind of being that being in act multiplicity would be equally impossible that change. There would exist only the being perfectly one, undivided, and eternally immutable (which is the definition of the pure Act), such as it was conceived by Parmenides. However, daily experience, precisely, present us multiple beings: the world of bodies is manifestly formed of a countless multitude of individual beings, which consist of indisputable unit and which are separate one another: men, animals, plants and any kind of material bodies...

It is fundamental now to note that the beings that we know by experience are multiple and various only because they are limited. Each one is not limited in the same way that another. Saying limit, we affirm diversity, which leads to multiplicity. Therefore, if the beings we are given in experience are limited, it is because each one is in act of what that it could be. But it must be said in an even more starkly manner: we must affirm that everything which is in act is only and solely what it could be.

In addition, every being is in act of limited potentialities, i.e. it actuates only one or only some of the very many possibilities that its nature constitutes. Change is the updating of a limited number of potential. This limited actuation leaves the door open to infinity of subsequent changes. Such changes however, despite the presence of infinite possibilities, are carried out under specific arrangements: random cannot be invoked. Random has no capacity for intervention. Furthermore, any contingency or fortuitousness contradicts the potential. Although if it is only such or such potential that change updates, it does not exclude the existence (in all its latent force) of other present potential. As for the "entitative" existence of such or such being, the change by which it accesses to its current configuration is not due to a process of pure chance... but it proceeds according to the nature which constitutes its whatness.

When someone undertakes to examine a specifically particular change, i.e. such a precise situation, one can see how a modification is determined by its whatness: "The oak tree is only oak and not cherry tree because the gland could only become that oak and could not become a cherry tree while a cherry-stone can become nothing but that cherry tree and cannot become an oak tree.

When they are closed our eyes are still possibility to see. We are not blind, just because our eyes are closed. Our eye are capable to wee, are in potency to see. When the eyes are open they are in act of nothing but to see. They are not capable to hear because their constitution includes the possibility to see and not the one to hear that belongs to ears. So every being in act, which comes to existence in the course of its evolution, is limited by the power which it carries out the opportunities but which it realizes only the possibilities" (Jean Daujat, *Is There a Truth?*, op. cit. p.68).

In our daily experience we encounter only the being in act, which is limited and multiplied in various beings, which are limited in different ways by the possibilities of being which they are derived. Those actuated being, however, are rich of all the eventualities, the potentialities, the potential, the power that they have according to their own nature, or whatness.

In the extent that multiplicity characterizes the world where we live and seems included deeply in the intimacy of its whatness, it is legitimate to find its origin in a First Being, that religious traditions call God. This calls to lay the foundation of a possible diversity (read: "Trinity") of the absolute... of a real opening of the absolute in itself and out of itself (for what can it be conceivable an "outside" of the absolute). To say it shortly, the multiplicity of the world call for a multiplicity of the absolute!

This multiplicity of beings that we meet around us is presented to us in two major forms: there is the **multiplicity of species** (we will call it "discontinuity") and refers to the diversity of beings and the **multiplicity of single beings** inside of same species (we will call it "individuality") and refer to a diversity of he same. Contemporary philosophy has often difficulty to properly understand the issue because most of the time the being such philosophy refers to is not at all a real being.

4. Limits of Multiplicity -
Otherwise said:
Multiplicity of Species

The word "**species**" shall designate a set of beings of the same nature: all men are the same species because they are all of the same human nature. But there are several animal species. In the same way chemistry classifies bodies in different classes of chemical species: e.g. oxygen is of a different nature, and therefore another species of nitrogen. Hydrogen is as well of another nature of carbon; it belongs therefore, to another species. We are in presence of a multiplicity of species.

Chemical is even more specific and brings further distinctions that make us certain to affirming the discontinuity between chemical species… There is no intermediary possible between two of them. Water is composed of a specified quantity of molecules of oxygen and hydrogen, if I do interfere in the composition (by electrolysis for example), I will no longer have molecules of water. Salt as well belongs to another kind than sugar, which can be physically similar, and the fact that they are similar, by the presentation in grain and the same white color, invites a cook to even better care in order to clearly distinguish them, rather than confuse them, because salt and sugar have in cuisine very different properties. The two are separate beings.

In fact, before the discovery of the existence of molecules and the management of their decomposition into atoms, scientists distinguished each species of physical body according to a **coherent set of physical and chemical properties.** And there is no doubt about the multiplicity of species, because an accurate analysis will never confuse one to another: when it may happen, as for example with sugar and salt, which are similar in their color and in their refined presentation, one realizes very quickly that this is not the same thing, that the species of sugar and the species of salt have not at all the same properties. It is not even necessary to try them in a cup of coffee… I got once in Gascony that definition of sugar: "Sugar is white matter which provides bad taste to coffee when you forgot to put it inside of your cup." Salt would produce be the opposite.

Concerning living beings, we define a species as a **coherent set of anatomical and physiological characters.** This consistency is the sign of a determined nature. This does not preclude the assumption that the living beings can (in the theory of evolution) be from each other. They are well already proceeding from one another in the process of reproduction of a same species. The other question, the one concerning an eventual process from a species to another, remains for the moment in abeyance. This is not the actual question for now. What is at a stake here, it is the effective discontinuity and the current discontinuousness between species. It is considered for each species a coherent set of anatomical and physiological characters, which include then different behaviors in living, eating, relating to other individuals of the same and of other species. Visiting the city zoo would be sufficient to make us recognize the diversity between different animal species. Those who feed animals in their house and keep pets know quite well the difference between a canary, a goldfish, a pussycat and a Chihuahua! Similar diversity among these species is accentuated by the incompatibility of conditions of life (air, water, earth) and of nutrition existing between them.

This discontinuity is so evident that, when one wants to force nature and produce mutations (such as grafting in plants, or hybrid individuals in animals, such as a she or he mule), these single beings so artificially newly engendered are sterile: they do not reproduce; they do not start a new natural species. This fact confirms discontinuity among species.

5. The Borders of Individuality
Otherwise said:
Multiplicity of beings pertaining to the same Species

Usual experience shows a multitude of individuals existing inside of each species. These individuals belong to the same nature, and notwithstanding they also are different to one another. I see it around me for example; as I walk in the woods beyond my back yard I can admire a multitude of squirrels, or in North Park, where there is a multitude of ducks. On the Roman Aventin Mount, I used to admiring a multitude of roses and rosebushes and, on the edge of the sea, near to Fiumicino Airport, I was pleased to walk under a multitude of pine trees. All of these configure multitudes of individuals of same species.

Etymologically, **individual means what we cannot divide without destroying it.** Thus, for example, South-East of Rome, in the hills of Latium, near the shrine of the Virgin of the Divine Love, everybody can meet flocks of sheep, that is to say groupings of animals which are sheep. We can divide these herds into smaller groups of animals and again, until we arrive at a single sheep. But when we arrived at a single sheep, we cannot split it again without destroying it.

The concept of individuality is more difficult to identify among inanimate beings: I can divide a stone in a number of fragments, make pebbles, gravel, or even sand, it is still of the stone, even if it is no longer, strictly speaking, a "piece of stone". I can reduce the wholesale sand, usable for mortar, in smaller powder of sand which will serve to make cement. Fragmenting the individual units of gravel, I change their nature and disclose new units which are individuals of course, or even units of sand.

In cuisine, I can crash cooking salt in order to get fine powder of salt for emergency need. I've made smaller single units of salt. It is still salt, divided in smaller individuals. If I take a quantity of water, this division will be even more subtle: I will need a container for seize it. The water would appear to fragment for infinity of smaller entities, but this is not the case: modern chemistry tells us that there is an indivisible unity of water, the so-called water molecule, composed of a specific number of atoms of oxygen and hydrogen that I cannot divide without destroying it. And I shall no longer have water. There is a limit beyond which I can no longer divide the quantity of water. When this happens I reached the individual level of a species.

Each individual is identifiable by the precise limits beyond which I would amend its being. There are therefore individuals, which constitute the diversity of each species. **A species is formed of a determined number of individuals.** And even if I cannot always count that number, it is a determined division in specific units of individuals.

In the diversity of beings of the same species I see that the multiplicity of beings is achieved by the multiplicity of individuals. Between them discontinuity exists. Discontinuity means a break in continuity. There is the existence of separate entities which cannot be further divided. Coming here, I had to walk in the campus streets, where I passed over several waves of cars, or more precisely of vehicles. The example confirms that I may find pieces of traffic that I can divide into vehicles, but when I get the unit of traffic with the kind of beings which are vehicles I cannot divide more my investigation on the traffic. Vehicles are individuals. A traffic flow can be divided into a number of vehicles, but I cannot divide it below the unit of a vehicle. Each vehicle as such, i.e. as a vehicle, is indivisible - even in the case of a composition of two vehicles that are a truck with its trailer, it must be stressed that for moving the trailer does not go without the truck, both therefore compose a single autonomous vehicle, indivisible as such. Yes, each vehicle is indivisible and is distinguished from any other vehicle... It is indeed beings of the same kind. Of course we can classify subsequently these vehicles by category (truck-trailer, truck, pick-up, van, car, motorcycle, scooters, bicycles), by brand (Ford, GMC, Chrysler, Ferrari,

Alfa Romeo, Fiat, Peugeot, Citroën, Volvo, Mercedes) and by model to the interior of a same mark (Toyota Matrix, Toyota Echo, Toyota Tercel 1995, Toyota Tercel 1992, etc.), by cylinder capacity, either on a general way (900, 1300, 1500, 2000, 2500 cm3), either to the interior of a same model (Clio-1.2, Clio-1.4, Clio-1.8, Clio-2.), but this classification according to the different types of vehicles does not detract us from the fact that each car, or each vehicle, constitutes as such an indivisible entity.

Same comment can be done for plants that surround Porziuncola Chapel. When I was used to teach at Regina Mundi, Rome, I was used to walk along the side of Tevere River, from Napoleon II Museum until the Pontifical Institute along two rows of trees, of maple species, located on both sides of the avenue that runs along the Tiber, which each tree - each <platanus> - constitutes an individual, i.e. a basic entity indivisible of plane-tree...

C. Matter and Form

Before addressing any reflection concerning MATTER & FORM we must be aware of the fact that what we usually call "matter" is not actually matter and what we call "form" is not a form. The ignorance of the real nature of "matter" and "form" is the cause of the misunderstanding of many philosophers on the issue. Such misunderstanding does characterize every philosophy based on a system and not on the observation of facts. Among the philosophers who made similar a similar misconception on the two issues we must quote René Descartes and all his followers, including Immanuel Kant and Georg Hegel.

6. Emergence of the Question of Matter and Form

Every individual has a particular configuration and a certain consistency. It is often referred by the synonymous term of body. The body is often defined by its scope. It is then defined as a uniform scope, as a portion of space. But this definition does not fit with the constitution of a body. One can still define it as a portion of matter. The concept of portion gives the idea of division and of individuation. The concept of matter gives the idea of the material used in that portion.

The principle of individuality consists in the matter by means of which bodies are made: two individuals of the same kind are organized the same way and are distinguished only by the portion of material which constitutes each of them. But this differentiation makes each one a unique entity. There is no doubt that they belong to the same species and kind as many other individuals and each one however, is unique in its proper existence. Matter, therefore, has a determinant share in the process that brings each individual into existence. Each individual is identical to other individuals of the same form. At times it can be confused with one or another of them. It is another one, however, by the portion of material which configures it and makes it completely separate, unique singularity in the world. Two pieces of the same stone are not consisting of the same portion of stone. They differentiate one another relentlessly through the different quantity of matter which constitutes each one. Such diverse quantity of matter introduces them into existence as two unique entities that are though identical in their intelligible nature.

Thus the specificity of a body will be the structure according to which is organized the matter by means of what it is made. When we say that two pieces are made with the same stone, we indicate that we recognize in each of them the same characteristics of the stone, the same form, even if they are two diverse pieces of its matter. We call actually FORM the configuration of the body. More specifically, the shape will be the principle of specificity, i.e. what does give the body its configuration, which allows recognizing the nature of its species. Specificity principle means, the principle of determination, and therefore the principle of intelligibility of the body.

When we speak of matter, we refer to everything commonly perceptible by senses, that is to say everything which is essentially to the constitution of mineral solid, but also all substances which made plants and animals. But when one speaks of substance, one usually intend to refer to some matter which already has a form, like plaster, cement, stone, marble, wood. All these fields identified as plastic, silk, iron, steel, copper, bronze, etc., flesh are substances which have already a form! And it is thanks to that form that we recognize in their proper subjects the characteristics of plastic, silk, etc... We have a common definition of matter. It is said to be the substance of what the body are made of.

All the same, when I speak of the form, I cannot conceive it but as what that is inside a body, i.e. in a material. Therefore, in the whole of reality around me, there is no form which does not have a material, or a matter that has not already its form. Notwithstanding, speaking in the strict sense, matter is an undetermined element (because without form still) which comes in the composition of beings (i.e. receiving his determination of the form). Matter has been precisely defined as **"what may change form"** Matter is what is likely going to change. **Matter is all that is able to be transformed.**

The composition of bodies in form and matter allows a first assertion: as such **matter is unintelligible** since it is defined to be "without form". Being intelligibility only comes from its form.

We stated that **MATTER** is **principle of individuation** of body, since it is by the matter which are made of that two diverse bodies of the same nature or the same species, may exist, while having the same form: for example two chickens, two geese, two ducks, etc. So considering that matter is principle of individuation we may affirm therefore that **matter is faculty of change** of bodies (since matter is what distinguish diverse things, and bring into existence what they are, here and now). Oppositely **FORM is principle of intelligibility**, or principle of identity of the bodies. Being so, we understand that **form is principle of stability** of bodies (It is because of its form that we recognize the whatness of a body, despite its hardware changes in space and time). It should be noted here that form and matter are always present together in every real being and consider how the two interact one another

It must be stressed how the concept of matter is alive and revolutionary. After Aristotle, Aquinas considers matter to be quite the contrary of a static entity. Matter is that which gives to reality a particular manner to be evolving. Matter is what is supposed to change... and be individualized and allows every existent to distinguish itself from another. Matter is also linked to quantity, to the gravity of the being. **Matter is mere opacity**... and at the same time **Matter is capacity to change.**

Any static entity belongs in fact more from abstraction than from matter: a static entity can certainly be composed of matter, but the permanency which defines it comes from the form — through which it is recognizable — and not from its matter which is likely to change. On the track of Aristotle, according to the doctrine of Saint Thomas Aquinas, matter is defined by its **availability to diversity and to change** — which will be actuated under the action of such or such form. He defines matter as a "passive power".

There is a subtle game of perspectives which contemporaneously involves matter and form, in a continuous interaction that engages them at every level of the beings. According to the perspective of the observer it will dominate the availability of matter to change, or the action of the form which updates such change.

In order to make language more adapt to the topic we are dealing with, I like to stress the **matter in general**, **original matter**, or **natural matter**, or else the **nature of matter** are employed in the discourse as synonymous. The same can be said about <form in general>, <original form>, or <natural form>, or even

<the nature of form> which are all expression to refer to the undetermined nature of form in its mere pure entity.

As to matter in general — whatever it is already organized or not — we must state that **matter is substance in potency while form is actuated substance**. Here the formula of Aquinas is illuminating:

> In effect, matter as such is in potency to form. It must therefore be considered that matter itself is in potency to the forms of all the things which it is the common matter. On the other hand, matter becomes actuated by a form only because of its relationship to this form. Matter remains therefore in potency of all other forms (*Summa* I Q.66, art 2 - Ed. Cerf p.611b).

Therefore MATTER is properly what makes change possible, even if ultimately the change is actuated according to the form which intervenes. But it would be ambiguous and even misleading, to assert - without further clarification - that the change comes from the form... The nature "form" promises identification, precision, intelligibility, consistency, identity with oneself, and needs the natural "matter" through which organize it. In other words, **natural "matter" is a co-principle of natural "form"**. One does not exist without the other. Matter is to the form its possibility of activation.

It is therefore the union of natural matter with natural form that actuates existence and change. And the configuration of change comes from natural form: in this sense, any change is change of form. When one says change of form, one says that matter left a form and assumed another. There was change in the field of matter by substitution of form. This puts us in presence of a clear and very subtle game, which evokes the prosperous modifiability of matter and the large number of forms suitable for transforming it. Certainly the potential for adaptation of matter is a mystery. Matter, which is one, adapts to countless quantity of forms...

7. Intrinsic Worthiness of Matter

The clear presentation of Aquinas touches the **mystery of matter**. A similar entity goes far beyond what we could at first feel free to consider. Let us raise a little more the veil which hides such mystery, trying to disclose some aspects. Some would like to refer to the problematic and famous words, attributed to Pierre Teilhard de Chardin and quoted by Card. de Lubac: "God is matter". God can certainly not be identified with plaster, stone, wood, iron, or leather... A similar identification would lead us to idolatry. The affirmation does merely mean that "God is all in all", i.e. that for those who are able to see, literally speaking, nothing is extraneous to God, because everything is part of creation, therefore everything belongs to God's breathing, or if you wish, everything belongs to God's quarters, or even God's neighborhood. A similar assertion "God is matter" could appear to be pantheism when we do not stress the evident difference between God himself and his creation by which he expresses himself and through which we continuously meet him: To give an example, a similar mistake would be done when we confuse somebody with his behaviors, or some of his deeds. There is a relationship which stands between the two and nonetheless together with the familiarity some difference also exists between someone and his deeds. Similarly, affirming the distinction between creator and creature we understand that "God is matter" affirms the presence of God in the dynamism that Matter is.

There is another perspective to consider in those words, affirming the presence of God in matter... Reading the *Carnets* of Teilhard, his notebooks, we witness his particular devotion to the Sacred Heart of Jesus, in which God became flesh and remain flesh for us for all the time we need him. That heart beats for us with all his love. A heart of flesh and matter... It is difficult to identify all the meaning which includes a similar expression which reveals a particular intimacy with Jesus... to the point that even the vocabulary is insufficient to express the mercy of

God hidden in matter... Here the apophatic vision has not yet been fully expressed in cataphatic sharing... Similar expression, however, offers the opportunity to better consider all that matter includes and hides in Aquinas language. Only a deep spiritual intimacy with God, enlightened by faith experience, may enter a similar mystery. So a natural original matter, excluding any form, expresses a natural power that is difficult to understand in a scientific language, which touches a mystical vision, which Aquinas was used to.

The word "God" can be adopted here in the same sense that Aristotle was used to. Aristotle was accustomed to refer to the Prime Being, which, according to Aquinas, religious traditions call "God". A philosopher is allowed to do so, i.e. to borrow from religious tradition a word which deals with an entity that philosophy recognizes even if it is barely able to properly refer to. Therefore, if matter is ability to change, a statement like "God is matter" takes here an illuminating sense. Ultimately speaking, matter needs to find in God — and not out of God — the origin of its own nature, which is capacity for change, also said principle of change. It is exactly what Aquinas affirms attributing to God every capacity since "the power of God is infinite" (*Summa* I, 105: 8). And also attributing to God every initiative, invoking Isaiah: "All our works, you made in us, Lord" (Isaiah 26:12 quoted by Aquinas, *Summa* I, Q.105, art. 4).

If, for a wrong behavior, we would establish outside of God the capacity and the principle of change, this would be denying God: it would be tantamount to establishing outside of the Prime Being a reality which would be foreign (and therefore which would report to another being). On the contrary, when we affirm God as source and principle of change, we set up a fact that finds its proper source in a multiplicity of the absolute, which establishes in his immutability the source of his diversity. Similar context enlightens the words "God is matter," which express in cataphatic language the intuition that science found in matter traces of Trinity. The discourse leads us here to the source of all being, toward the Prime Being, that religious traditions call God. We have now posted one of the major issues of theodicy. And we must proceed further...

Recent scientific discoveries confirm Aristotelian perspectives on original matter. Perfect example would be the existence of entities identified under the **theory of quanta**: unit of quantity of matter so discreet and small that it is not measurable in its accidents of space and time. It is however identifiable by the tiny trace of energy left by its emerging presence. It is a discrete value of matter related to a small manifestation of energy. The quantum theory is the set of theories and methods of calculation elaborated from the hypothesis of quanta of PLANCK energy, which was first applied by **Albert Einstein** in the nature of light, and by **Bohr** and **Sommerfeld** to the physics of atom and, closer to us, in-depth investigation by **Louis de Broglie**. We also must refer to the theory of relativity, in which a substance is defined by its potential energy and not only by the deployed energy as for the theory of quanta. Here is the famous formula of Albert Einstein: "$M = C^2/E$ (or $E = mc^2$), which defines a quantity of matter by its potential energy and not merely by its manifested energy... The fact that at the onset of existence, science assimilates matter to energy, as a principle of action, encourages us to confront it with the very notion of matter in Aristotle, which was so wonderfully synthesized under the prospect that evokes strangely the sentence of Angelic Doctor: "Considered in itself matter exists only in power" (*Summa* I, Q.66, Cerf, p.66a).

Then he said: matter is essentially indeterminacy. However, the form, which organizes the subject, never reaches to deplete the surrounding uncertainty of matter, i.e. its countless possibilities of adaptation, of actuation. This explains the persistence of change and of movement in the universe (Cf. M.-D. Philippe, *Cours de métaphysique*, op.cit. p.7).

Bohr, Einstein, Sommerfeld

Broglie

8. Second Causes

While we have to continue our metaphysical investigation, we cannot miss to refer occasionally here, on what Aristotle and Aquinas call **Second Causes**, which are nothing but the fact that the Prime Mover (which religious communities call God] is acting in the world through the pure spirits, according to both Aristotle and Aquinas, with the difference that "pure spirits" refer in Aquinas to God's messengers, or else the ones we commonly know under the generic name of Angels.

In order to properly understand the whole discourse, we must draw a distinction between (1) what is called **prime matter** which is pure indeterminacy, which is nothing but the nil that God discloses to himself, i.e. that he raises before himself and (to say it with human words) without which he could not express himself outside of oneself (in such a case, matter is **radical indeterminacy**) and (2) what will be appointed as **Second Matter**, which is the opaque uncertainty which forms corporeal beings (that is to say, a **primordial matter** barely informed, a first stage of matter and form, which constitutes the primary stage of material beings. It should be noted about opaque matter that "the material things which are lower than our intelligence, are in our intelligence of a simpler way than they are as such"(-*Summa* I, Q.50, art. 2, Cerf, p. 513b).

Professor Giuseppe Zanghì, an emerging figure of Sophia University, Loppiano, Florence, Italy, also known under the nickname of Peppuccio, suggests to see Mary as the symbol of this nil which allows the creative act manifest: Mary is the type of nil (fullness of transparency and renunciation) in which the Verb can express himself, almost like (but forgive the comparison) a blackboard, very clean and black, promotes and stress the writing of the chalk. This exemplary concept of the role of Mary is very close to the position of Fr. Marie-Dominique Philippe, who made Mary the exemplar type of philosopher: as the person who is so transparent to the truth, to let it speak. On the track of Mary, every true philosopher should be the blackboard which allows the reading (the truth) to be produced by the white chalk of wisdom. In other words, the task of a philosopher consists more in a passive way or even in a sort of denying oneself in order to manifest what is supposed to be expressed, and tell the truth... The "negative" is understood here as a nil relative, a true and positive action of availability, which allows the positive to effectively intervene and be, in his revealing act of emergence into existence. As well as in spiritual life, transparency (the acting non-being, or non-being as such) opens the doors to the spirit, to wisdom, and makes us sage, and discloses us to ourselves, although equally we can understand how, analogically, the emergence of corporeal beings (or the existence of beings inside of matter) reflects this same process which is present in the whole universe at every level of being.

To clarify the difference between pure and opaque matter, it is useful to recall that after Aristotle, St Thomas states that only prime matter (the one without any form) enters in the composition of pure spirits, that religious traditions call Angels — "It is not the same matter which intervenes in the formation of celestial bodies and in the composition of earthly elements, except to an analogous process, provided that all things make sense in the unique concept of potency" (*Summa* I, Q.66, art. 3).

All the previous reflection was to show the nobility of matter. As an outcome, all Christians will understand how important can be the care of bodies in their lives and the care of the whole society.

G. Zanghì stresses that ignoring Marie would penalize matter (*Lecture of 27 June 1991*, Mariapolis Ctr, Grottaferrata). Mary is the flower of the whole matter. She is the one who is left without contamination directly by the Spirit of God. She embodies the largest indeterminacy, to accept the best of every possible form, the One who is the Verb. Mary is not even mere matter. Matter is at the image of Mary. If we want to know what matter is, we must consider the figure of Mary.

Actually matter is nothing other than that principle which is at the origin of the constitution of so-called material beings... In the strict sense matter is not something other than that principle. So well rehabilitated as we did, matter appears transfigured, and we can now understands why there was in history or even in current time currents of great exaltation of matter in human thought...

Matter has also a privileged place in the full picture of creation... it is (if we may say so) its first step, it shows in the first place. The eastern tradition gives an illustration, breathtaking in its clarity, on the nobility of matter: as well as Man is the icon of the Verb and Angel is the icon of the Holy Spirit, Matter is the icon of the Father. "Oh, Matter how much beautiful you are! Notwithstanding you only is the onset of the universe, raw material, the poorest part of it. I understand now what a mystery called Jesus to become flesh, to come nearer to you..." The whole discourse on matter is now transfigured. And it is easy now to understand the excitement that men, philosophers, scientists, or poets got in front of the tangible world. "The substance has so much power, it must contain a spirit. The soul of the gods is attached to its images ..." (Gustave Flaubert, *The Temptation of Saint-Antony*, chap. 5.).

Schongauer's Temptation of St. Anthony

9. Intrinsic Worthiness of Form

At each level we can read in the same bodies a proper distinction of reality. The distinction is established by the nature of form in the nature of matter. For example, observe what it means in ethics the moral value of an act. After you have identified the material quality of an act in its execution, we need to reflect on the interior act of decision, which exceeds the outside act of implementation.

Another example more precise and may be simpler: observe a carpenter in the act of manufacturing a table. It manufactures the table from some material that is wood. We may distinguish at least three levels of evaluation, related to three different levels of form, in addition to the paramount level (i.e. the raw material, which is pure power, pure indeterminacy, without form). Many factors interfere in the process: quality of the table, rationalization and economy of material, purpose which the table is for, and eventually how the carpenter will handle it. More specifically I like to state:

(A) According to the draft table to undertake, the craftsman chooses the wood the most appropriate. It chooses the wood according to its quality: nature of the tree originating in the wood, position in the trunk, presence or absence of knots, quality decorative scratches, etc. That is the first degree of assessment of the quality of the material, according to the natural form of wood.

(B) Then, in the second degree of quality, according to the more or less great capacity of the artisan and cabinet maker to work woods, there will be a different quality of execution in his work: the table will be more or less proportionate, solid, useful, beautiful, etc. Here matter is the wood itself appreciated in the form that it is given under the craftsman's hand to actuate the draft. The table has become a piece of art, comparable to the statue of a sculptor, the paint from a painter, the partition created and executed by a musician... We are at the presence of a human act which commits intelligence, in its dimension of creativity: the work reflects the professional, artistic and even vocational qualities of the craftsman.

(C) There is however a third degree, that belongs to the moral and spiritual dimension, beyond the pure creativity of intelligence. The matter will be here the work of art itself, the table which has been achieved, and its form consists in the quality of love that the craftsman has put in its implementation. For the same table, we may have different qualities of the same act: Saint Joseph the Worker in his work was used to include a quality of love that many carpenters ignore. Sometimes that upper level of from is determinant in what the table will promote in society...

Human actions have beyond immediate their intrinsic value a spiritual value that the result of the actions does not allow to assess directly. While human actions are immediately evaluated according to the criteria of social consensus, they have a spiritual point of view which offers a higher quality of assessment, since they commit our eternal life: "When I spoke all languages of the earth and the sky, if I do not have charity, (...) if I lack love, I am useless" (1 Co 13:1-3)

Irrespective of matter, it is the form which has the character of intelligibility, spirituality... The form is indeed... what "forms" the body, that is to say which gives the body its own configuration (its form). Form offers what is identifiable in the body, what is apprehensible by our intelligence. It is why we will say that the form is what is intelligible in bodies. And since it "forms" the body, **form is principle of intelligibility of bodies**...

As well the assessment of the value of a being is to be sought on the side of the form... and a moral action, because it belongs to a higher form, will express an order of value higher than mere psychological, logical, physical, or material action. Ethical motivations show priority on the motivations coming from psychological, physical, etc. interests.

It is important however to notice that there may exist physical or psychological actions which may contradict one another but remain indifferent from the point of view of the moral assessment or spiritual evaluation: There are different plans of action that may not be necessarily implicate.

Actually, the diverse levels of activity do not necessary interfere for the evaluation of a being. Consider, for example, the conversion of St. Paul on the road to Damascus, such as it is counted in the Acts of the Apostles. A phenomenological description of events is given (dropping from the horse, voice heard, blindness) which cannot jeopardize the eventual psychological interpretations. Similarly, the psychological interpretation that was made in fact by Frederick Nietzsche in the Twilight of idols, and in the Antichrist, show his will of Power (guilty complex typical of every Pharisee before the law, which leads him to the bright idea, to luminous, which it provokes him to fall from the horse ! - Then the liberator aspect of becoming disciples of the "way" to be free from the Pharisee psychological oppression in spite of the difficult process of adaptation and understanding - which produce a psycho-somatic blindness and allow interim accommodation with recovery of view). So a psychological view may be true and nonetheless does not deny the higher spiritual interpretation, which appears so clearly in the Acts of the Apostles.

Jesuit great scholar F. Prat confirms the psychological analysis of Nietzsche: at the time, a Pharisee used to live a psychological drama, which was almost unbearable face to the condemnation of every single act, as it was then interpreted. Nonetheless, even if a similar psychological perspective remains consistent, it does not at all exclude yet the spiritual fact which allows Paul, on the road to Damascus, to recognize the one who he loves so exclusively and on behalf of whom he launched his combat the followers of the "Little Way". Here is the reason why Paul recognizes on the road to Damascus the One he loves so much in the voice he heard: yes, Paul recognizes in the One he suddenly meets the same One he was combating and that One is the same that then talked to him. Such a consideration includes the comments made by Nietzsche on the psychological level and psychosomatic aspects. The highest level of survey explains the least.

The psychological analysis cannot take account, in its entirety, of the event. The spiritual dimension escapes the psychological investigation, which does not know it and therefore cannot deny it, otherwise by incompetence. The least cannot account the more. Actually, the spiritual event exceeds its psychological outcomes. What is said however by Nietzsche on the psychological level remains acceptable to that level: F. Prat - who does not know Nietzsche reference - makes the same analysis as Nietzsche on psychological level, but then he completes it, as a scholar, on the spiritual level.

He must avoid to confusing the orders of value. Conversely, a morally good action will not be necessarily artistic, and the largest art may not necessarily be expressed, if the artist (due to particular spatial or temporal conditions) is deprived of a suitable material. There is some independence in the order of values... All of these considerations, however, do emphasize the importance, autonomy and specific value of the form.

I like to quote here the words of Maurice de Guérin (1810-1839): "Form is the happiness of matter, the eternal hug of its atoms drunk of love. In their union, matter enjoys and get holiness" (The green book). There are also these surprising words of Charles Baudelaire: "Any form created, even by man, is immortal. Because the form is independent of the matter, and there are not the molecules which constitute the form" (Essays et Notes: Mon coeur mis à nu, LXXX).

In other words, what does make the holiness of our daily actions does not lie in our human perfection... but in the love we are putting in our deed... That is why the slightest of our actions may assume an immeasurable value, regardless of what we do, of the substance of our actions. All the same, every deed handled by Mary in the lesser of her housekeeping in Nazareth retains a value greater than that of the most grandiose saint... because it is animated with a greatest love of God, and a greater intimacy with God...

In Short: the form is worth better than the nature of our acts: a lack of love is more damaging than a scalpel error. Some paragraphs behind, we illustrated matter as the icon of the father in the Trinity, but we know that there is no form without matter... that the Father is father only through his relation to the Son... Thus the pure form - which is Spirit - finds its excellence in the Verb, the Word of God... Metaphysics opens naturally its reflection into theology, which it needs to supplement its proper investigation.

It is now important to examine how differentiation operates. In other words, it is time to consider what the causes, which produce diversity and change, are.

D. How do Bodies Change
Otherwise said:
Accidental Changes and Natural Changes

The intelligibility of organized matter (physical objects) registers a double originality. Existent show a difference coming from both (1) what the bodies are made of and (2) the form they assume. However, that which creates such or such specific change, that which gives determined contour to a substance, it is the form: **all change proposed by matter is actually caused by the form:** "In body movements, we call mover the one who produce the form, which is principle of movement" (Summa I, Q.105, art.3, Cerf, p.857b).

We are entering then in a dilemma seemingly intractable: in a first context, it is stated ,on the one hand, that matter is defined as what may change and, secondly, that form is what determines such or such matter to become, or to exist... then in a second deepening, following Aristotle, Aquinas claims imperatively that **matter is principle of continuity in the being, while form is principle of change**. There is some contradiction to be solved.

10. Accidental Changes of Bodies

The facts emerge with great simplicity. The answer lies in the facts more than in the complexity of the words. To answering properly the question, it is sufficient to look realistically at material world.

Let us take a being at a precise level of its existence, freely chosen. When, for example, I seize a plaster bag and that I mix plaster white powder with water, I can use it to spread it along the wall, it is still plaster, but it is changed in its aspect by means of the water substance I added: I have no more plaster dust, I have layers of plaster on the wall. The applied material has changed aspect and shape, but it has not changed its nature, i.e. its substantial form remained the same: I still have plaster. It was through the addition of some other organized matter, water actually, that I could produce some change in the configuration of the soft white powder; notwithstanding, through its substantial form, I still recognize the continuity of its identity in its spatial and temporal originality, which is plaster. However when I consider the organized matter that is plaster, I notice that the structure of plaster as such remains the same, but something was changed in its aspect: I have not white powder of plaster in a bag any more I've got plaster layers applied on the wall. Its chemical structure and properties was not changed, but, yes, its physical configuration has become another, its external shape is a new one. The plaster has changed in its aspect: one of its accidental forms was changed.

Let us start by saying that on one side matter is mere availability to change, on the other side it is form which is the principle of such or such particular change. It is so particular form which achieves so specific change. Thus, an accidental form is identified, which caused the change. As a first outcome, we distinguish then the substantial form that ensures continuity of the substance and the accidental forms which actuate the changes of the substance according to the potential included in the nature of the body and belong to the substance, i.e. what the prime matter united to the substantial form established in the body, in that precise body which was just here examined. This body, as such defined, becomes (because of its matter) principle of continuity, compared to the accidental forms which are the principles of change of the body. We have then cleared up a first contradiction which would remain insoluble if we wanted the face the question without considering the difference between prime matter which is not yet organized and the organized matter of a tangible being. Also, we must refer to the specifically known structure of a given body, which is determined: we must respect the structure of matter. Every analysis invested on a body examines it at a specific level of its being. We scrupulously must respect this rigor of analysis: a philosophical reflection does not require less, but more rigor than a scientific approach.

In a word, we observed that **form defines the identification** of a body in its being (i.e. in its identity and in its changes) while matter constitutes its ability to change, and its continuity along changes.

11. Natural Changes of Bodies

Every level of facts witnesses that the concept of matter and the one of form must therefore be adapted (it will be said proportionate) to reality according to the distinctive characteristics into it is considered. When I observe the plaster as plaster, I consider some matter which has taken already the structure, the form, the organization of plaster. But in the case of some work carried out with plaster, the subject to consider is no longer plaster as such, but eventually the wall, the bulkhead, the wall decoration, or the ceiling in the constitution of which plaster is involved. Plaster constitutes the means by which the wall, the ceiling is composed. In the case of a statue, I shall take it as the subject, which plaster, marble, or bronze may be the matter that takes the form of the statue: in this case again **matter is what may change and form is what operated the change**. Again, Aquinas defined the form as **principle of change.**

Please, notice here that when we say principle, or power of, it is nothing but what it is said. Do not try to imagine something different in order to understand better what matter and form are. One is mere indetermination the other one is principle, act of being… There are nothing more than what it is said. Then, they actuate each other in the objects we are familiar with… We cannot use imagination to represent what matter or form is. We must use intelligence, and intelligence works with definitions. It is nothing more but also nothing less, than that. The precise identity of both is becoming clearer along our investigation today…

An exemplary case of change in the nature of bodies can be found in the daily experience of a chemist. For example when the chemist exposes a greasy substance to the action of a base product (e.g. a vegetable oil with potassium or alkali), the action of the one with the other produces a soap, the quantity of material used remains the same, it is the form which has changed. It is understood then that the matter employed in such course of action (the matter of alkali and of the one of grease) continues to exist while the forms of the two are changed in one new product. The matter which is involved shows continuity of being. The forms of such quantity of matter changed. The same quantity of matter remains under a new form. Aristotle and Aquinas give a special attention to matter under the accident of quantity. The same does happen when combining quantity of base with some quantity of acid, we get salt… Under the category of **the accident called quantity**, matter is principle of individualization (produces individuality), but also **matter is principle of continuity**.

The power of matter to change form is realized in an eminent manner in every change which involves the nature of a body. This transformation can be checked in the natural cycle of carbon, in the natural process of photosynthesis, in that of animal nutrition process. This change concern us typically in the process of generation (childbirth) and death: in the latter case, matter loses body's form, to provisionally assume a corpse form... and we know that we can refer to a corpse only for a body which has just died, later we appoint it as mortal remains, even by what it remains, whatever it is bones or relics. Most often the body decays to reorganize in symbiosis with the surrounding soil. Then matter remains the same, it is the form which changes.

Significant is the cycle of carbon, i.e. the passage of carbon in different stages according to successive combinations inside of living beings, the soil and air. The process evokes the assertion of Jean-Baptiste de Monet, Chevalier de Lamarck, who stated that nature produces "only individuals which succeed one another and which are similar to those which produced them" (*Philosophie zoologique*, chap.1), according to which that was fixed in the famous formula: "nothing is created, nothing is lost, everything is transformed", which refers to the old Latin proverb: "*Natura non facit saltus*", that Louis Pasteur expressed with his own words: "after death, life

de Monet

Pasteur

reappears under another form, and with new properties" (*Lettre adressée au ministre de l'Instruction publique, avril 1862*).

We will express all this, saying that **matter is principle of continuity**. But a similar continuity comes in fact from the elementary form owned by the prime matter. Take the example of water: "H^2O" is a molecule of water, where "H^2" and "O" are three molecules which include two separate molecules of hydrogen and one of oxygen, which can be separated by the intervention of catalysis. It is clear that the principle of continuity is due to the basic structure present already in the body of water through the hydrogen and oxygen molecules that makes it up. Because of the prime matter which organizes it, water keeps in its nature the capacity of change, which will operate according to the model and under the impetus of the new form that eventual possible change will adopt.

The concepts of matter and form are concepts to be use in a proportionate manner with the object we are observing: the stone, the wall or the statue. When I consider several reproductions of Michelangelo's *Pieta* in some touristic store of the Roman neighborhood near the Vatican, these *Pieta* reproductions are differentiated by the (quantity of) matter which they are made of.

In corporeal beings, I recognize their identity by the form, because only form is identifiable. Matter is known to me exclusively by its form. And I recognize the **material continuity and discontinuity of a body by its form**, even if the individuality of a body is only due to matter, under the accident of quantity. And it is the persistence of a same form within the change that makes the continuity of "matter". This also applies to raw, informed, or paramount matter. Strictly speaking, the absence of form introduces a continuity of the form of matter, which is then pure power. What is said about the organized form must be said about the original informal matter: **matter is the principle of continuity**.

Bodies multiply and diversify in existence by their own material consistency, not by the form, which is precisely what updates bodies among the beings. Behold, if we consider the common matter of bodies, i.e. the matter which all bodies are made of, it is well by the form that they are identified. To be precise we should even say that it is by their forms that they are differentiated under the light of intelligence, and that it is by their matter that they are differentiated under the light of existence. Synthetically, we should say that form provides originality to matter, precisely because **matter is real capacity to change**.

E. Movement

12. Principle of *"Raison d'être"*
Otherwise said:
Principle of Causation — Causality

Corporeal bodies emerge into existence inside and because of the change in which they are produced. To say it otherwise, they move from a status of potential being to the status of actuated being, from a being in power to a being in act. Every change is a passage from being in power towards being in act. Each body accesses into existence in a material (indeterminate), according to the modalities that it is given by the form.

The assertion of the principle of identity (and of non-contradiction which is its corollary) enabled us to see that it is the nature of the essence of being to be what it is. We also must agree with another principle which characterizes the existence of beings, it is the so-called **principle of *reason d'être*** which formula can be expressed in the following assertion: EVERY BEING WHICH IS NOT BY ITSELF IS BY ANOTHER. Otherwise said, if you wish, whatever does not exist by itself does exist from another.

We cannot deny a similar principle. Whoever would like to try to deny it would fall into contradiction: but if this is not by another, then it is by itself! Similar principle determines all the understanding of change and the diversity of beings. This induces us to introduce the notion of cause.

13. The Four Causes

For Aristotle the world is composed of individuals (substances) occurring in fixed natural kinds (species). Every individual develops and grows according to its proper nature, which direct identity, growth, purpose, usefulness, and every possible change. Although science studies general kinds, according to Aristotle, these kinds find their existence in particular individuals. Knowledge grows by discerning, inside of experience, what is intelligible. Everything which exists stands out of necessity. Every fact, entity, or particular is known addressing several questions: what, when, why, where, how, etc., which are as many questions as many are the sources of existence of every being.

While his predecessors affirmed that only one sort of cause can be really explanatory; Aristotle proposed four: two intrinsic sources, the formal cause (which is the shape, species, kind, or type), the material cause (the matter out of which a thing is made), and two extrinsic: the efficient cause (the source of motion, generation, or change), and the final cause (the goal, or full development, of an individual, or the intended function of a construction or invention, and in every case the last ste4p of a change). Taking for example the Michelangelo's Pietà, we recognize its material cause in the marble which it is made up, its formal cause is the shape of the statue, the efficient cause is Michelangelo himself, with all his expertise and tools, who shaped, and its final cause is the realized project, enriched by a reading of Dante. In different contexts, the causes are the same four and they apply analogically.

In each context, Aristotle insists that something is understood better when its causes can be stated in more specific terms. For example, it is more informative to know that a sculptor made the statue than to know that an artist made it; and even more informative to know that Michelangelo chiseled it rather than simply that a sculptor did so. Aristotle thought his causal pattern was the ideal key for organizing knowledge.

Other relevant issue is the interaction of causes, their reciprocity: each cause being first in its own perspective. Then while formal cause indicate us the identity of a being, its material cause produces its capacity of change. By its form a being is in act. Its potency of change is proportionate to the indetermination of the matter it is made of. So every change happens by emendation of form, towards it the being is in potency. Every substances, then, is recognizable by its accidents, or characterizations. A Soul is the form of a living Body (different types of soul will be found in different type of creatures: plants, animal, human, pure spirit). The Body is the material expression of the soul, while the Mind is the speculative expression of both (Trinitarian model). Morality is fruit of a free decision according possibly the best knowledge in order to make the best decision we can towards happiness.

Besides, people have no Innate ideas. At birth human mind is "*Tabula rasa*," a blank slate, totally empty but not totally inactive, for the mind of people naturally wants to know. that desire to know makes the whole difference with animal which are born with instinct while people are born without any knowledge but with a great capacity to learn and babies learn from their immediate neighborhood, family, friends, society. This explain how, when a baby is grown with animals it gets animal behabiors, among people it grows with human behaviors..Later on the consequence of it is that "nothing exists in consciousness that has not first been experienced by the senses"

In metaphysics we call "cause" everything that contributes to constitute something in its being, i.e. everything that something would depend on in its proper being. Causality is in the nature of things. What is in power cannot by effect of oneself become effectively produced and be actuated: it takes an intervention which produces the transition to the act. A cause is necessary. If the effect exists, therefore the cause exists, too.

The notion of cause answers the questions which are raised up about an object. There are four ways to give a full account of an object, as we have seen that four factors are involved about it: matter and form, then being in power and in act.

Aristotle said that **there are four ways to respond "why" about an object**.

On the tracks of Aristotle, Aquinas identifies first the ones called **intrinsic causes**, which constitute the object as such and are known as material and formal causes. Then he distinguishes those called **extrinsic causes**, which interfere on the object and produce change in it, and are known as efficient and final causes.

We will follow his tracks,

(1) **MATERIAL CAUSE** is what by means of a thing is made: it is "this quantity which may exist" and does exist under such or such form. Material cause explains why this object is possible in its own entity. In the case of a cherry, material cause is the quantity of organized matter which constitutes it.

(2) **FORMAL CAUSE** is the definition or the model of a thing. It is the determination which organizes the quantity of substance which is and identifies a thing. Formal cause says what such object is; it tells me that it is this or that. In the case of a cherry, it is the form which organizes the matter which the cherry consists of (color, taste, cellular structure, etc.). Its form allows me to recognize that it is a cherry. The form "causes" me to identify a cherry for what it is. I recognize the formal cause inside of what the nature of a thing is, in what is intelligible in it.

(3) **EFFICIENT CAUSE** responds to the question "where is this from?" Efficient cause indicates the why of the evolving of a thing: it responds with the external causes which have caused the activation (Act of being) of something in the organization

of matter under a precise form. It reflects the external elements which have produced the object. Efficient cause finds its source outside of the object and its point of arrival inside the object itself. It explains the change that has led to the formation of the object here and now. This cause is often the most obvious of the four ones:. Usually, when the term "cause" is used alone, it refers to efficient cause. Dealing again with a cherry, we may recognize that efficient cause is the whole of elements (air, water, sap of the tree which has fed the pulp, care of the gardener, etc.) which intervened and brought out as a result the constitution of the cherry.

When, for example, I move a chair, I rise on the object that is the chair according to the accident called action. I produced an action which the displacement of the chair is the result. In this case, it is I which am the efficient cause of the displacement of the chair.

(4) **FINAL CAUSE** responds to the question "in view of what' some change does happen. Final cause says why, or better in view of what, a thing exists. Final cause finds its origin is in the thing itself and its point of arrival outside of the thing, in its end, in what completes the object or thing as its perfect development. In the case of a tree producing a cherry, we may consider final cause as the end of the process which produces the cherry, i.e. the cherry as such. Then considering a cherry we may observe that it includes the kernel (seed) of cherry, which the pulp inside of the cherry is the humus paramount in view of reproducing another cherry tree. Final cause expresses the last step towards the essential power of thing leads to become.

In the case of the displacement of a chair, it is a transitive action. Every transitive action is an outside change. Similar action is defined as a change from an initial situation towards a final one... In the case here examined, the end indicates simply the situation toward which the action tends and is intend to go forth and stop. An action tends necessarily toward a change which is its end - otherwise there would be no change. In this example, final cause is the culmination of the action.

Let us add **more examples**. If we take the example of a statue: material cause is the matter which it is made (bronze or marble), formal cause is the figure it represents (a Pieta, a Crucifix, Our Lady), efficient cause is the sculptor (Michelangelo), or the producer (reproduction company), final cause is the purpose embodied by the sculptor (beauty, contract compliance, concern to expressing a religious experience, production of a gift to thank a benefactor, etc.). In case of a producer, final cause could be the purpose to make available religious figures to a large amount of people and raise devotion, etc.

As for the notions of form and substance, power and act, the concepts of four causes must be recognize for each object, considering the issue proportionately to the thing. Concerning the sciences which make use of mathematics as their operative language and which usually claim today to be the only ones that specifically deserve the name of science in true sense, there is a curious phenomenon to observe..: Because of the abstraction that is made on the subject investigated, science is not addressing a real being, but only a being of reason. Every mental being, by the mere fact that it only exists in our mind has only a possible intelligible consistency, which refers to the formal aspect of things. Therefore, a scientific object does possess neither matter nor purpose. As a result it can only be considered in its immediate external aspects, that is to say, in its efficient cause. This is why, positive sciences are predisposed to only seize the efficient cause of things. But every scientist, who reflects on reality, must relearn to reason on real facts, which should include the four causes. However, this is not an exercise to which a scientist is accustomed.

14. Reciprocality of Causes

After recognizing that there are four kinds of cause, we

must realize that each one is in its proper order the cause of the other three. There is a particular reciprocity between material and formal cause in the constitution of the object as such and a privileged reciprocity between efficient and final cause in the evolution of the thing, in its change.

But the four causes always intervene in reciprocal concomitance, in interaction to one another: We will never stress enough how each cause is first before the other three in its proper order. In other words, each cause is in its order is cause of the other three. It is appropriate to say that the other three depend on each of them. That is what is expressed when we speak about the interdependence of causes, but this term is less expressive and even appropriate that the term of reciprocity. I would like to talk about the **interdependence of effects** and the **interaction of causes**.

A little brutal is to affirm that since all cause as such is naturally prior to its effect, as a result each cause is, in its proper order, previous to the other three. Each cause intervenes in priority in its order of own causation. Taking again the example of a cherry example which becomes a cherry tree: **material cause** is the quantity of material which incorporate the cherry and the quantity of elements involved in its transformation towards the tree; **formal cause** is its identity of cherry, which is neither an oak, nor a plant of another genus or species; **efficient cause** consists in the external interventions causing the decay of the kernel and its successive maturation; then final cause is the final step that is to say what it is reproducing according to its nature, or its essence, i.e. the new being that a cherry seed has the potential to become, otherwise said: a new cherry tree.

However, without the external intervention of the efficient cause (by the burial of the cherry in an appropriate field), the final cause could not act, or actuate, i.e. achieve itself as a cherry tree. Vice Versa, the adequate conditions (efficient cause) need the final cause to realize its own process: it must be a core of cherry, i.e. a seed that has the potential to be repeated. It would be unnecessary for example to bury, in the same conditions, a piece of wood which would not have the ability to reproduce, which would not cause to process towards its final step. Without the final cause, the other causes remain without effect. As an outcome, in order to be effective, every change needs the interaction of four causes.

The interaction of causes helps to understand that **what is cause in its proper order is in another order the effect of another cause**: under different aspects the same object is both cause and effect of another object. For example, a walk is cause of health as its efficient cause and vice versa health is the cause of a walk as its purpose, its outcome, or its conclusion. Similarly the body because it is matter of the soul (its form) makes possible by its good conformation (health) the existence of my bodily substance, it is its cause, and yet it is the soul, as a form of the body, which animates it, i.e. which organizes it, which causes it. Under material point of view it is ok to affirm that the body is the first; from the formal point of view the soul is the first, as the organizing principle, it gives life to my body. From the point of view of the extrinsic causes, I am the fruit (second) of everything that constitutes the outside (efficient cause) as creature and, in final analysis, I am created by God (first efficient cause), and I exist yet positively in a free act (first) according to my own nature which consists to know and love God (ultimate final cause).

Additional reflection on the concept of reciprocity of causes will help to illustrate the importance of this concept to understanding the typical behavior and freedom of a human person. A theological debate forced the Magisterium to combat both Pelagianism (doctrine which puts divine grace depending on the merit acquired by human action) and Predestination (Lutheran doctrine stating that God's grace operates and saves us regardless of our behavior in respect of God). We easily understand that the correct position requires the concept of reciprocity of causes: is priority belonging to divine grace or to human merit? The solution requires the reciprocality of causes! Each one in its proper order, divine grace and action of man, is the first. It is in this coincidence of the primacy of divine grace on one hand and on the other hand the full freedom of people that we can properly consider the whole loving relationship between man and God.

The principle of reciprocality of causes allows a subsequent reflection about the concept of creation: the intervention of God, who creates, cannot be done at the level of one of these four causes which are all interacting to one another. Creation, therefore, belongs to an order which exceeds the dimensions of time and space, where these four causes interact. As a result the question of creation cannot be addressed at the level of extrinsic causes, efficient and final, which would be the case when raising the classic interrogation, which ask if the egg existed before the hen. The intractability of this questioning emphasizes the principle of reciprocity of causes.

When someone wants to place the establishment of creation under the guardianship of one or the other of the four causes, one would reduce creation to the production of a creature and would make the whole world deriving from one of its parts: which is unacceptable. The more cannot arise from the less. As an outcome, we must consider creation as creation of the world in its entirety and as maintenance of the world in its current vitality. If creation is not dependent on time, it is therefore time which is dependent on the creator act: since always creation is now, it is now that creation establishes the world (in its entirety) in its very being. The four causes, being nothing but the definition of the relationship of changes in the universe, they fall within the created world. The four causes are also created with the world, which they are integral part, which they belong to. Their intimately reciprocal relationship argues in favor of the efficient present actuality of the creator act. It always operates here and now beyond time and space. Here is introduced the notion of transcendence which characterizes the Prime Being.

F. Nomenclature of Beings

15. The Scale of Existent Beings

It may appear impossible to attempting to elaborate a complete inventory of existing natural beings, i.e. of those beings, which are not manufactured by human expertise, trying to sort them according to the quality of their kind, or species. Yes, it is almost an impossible endeavor.

I'll try to introduce here a systematic draft, which normally would require to opening a new conversation that would take name of SOMATOLOGY, namely the analytical study of bodies. We will not do it in details, and it is not necessary to do so. It will suffice to allude to this nomenclature in order to increase the understanding of peratology.

Referring therefore to a similar inventory will illustrate one of the aspects (there are other) of the specific reality of peratology, namely the great variety of bodies which constitutes the world in its entirety and **which vary by their matter as individuals and by their form as species**. From the point of view of their form, beings are classified according to an order of increasing complexity, ranging from raw material, such as stone and other elementary minerals, where matter is dominant and form appears in its lower complexity, moving up to spiritual beings, which are pure forms.

This being said, it is necessary to operate the classification of beings according to their kind, or species, i.e. according to their form. However, the kinds or species are regrouped in turn into five major categories, called "kingdoms" or "worlds".

(1) In **MINERAL KINGDOM** all beings that define themselves through a molecular structure own, without autonomous

movement, i.e. of forms which do not provide themselves any change, but which need an external efficient cause to move or to change. These beings are also defined as bodies, which substances fall within inorganic matter, as opposed to the reign kingdom that is immediately above it and that is said "organic world", because it is "organized" by life.

The science which deals with the structure (the form) of bodies belonging to mineral world is chemistry. Inside of the reign of inert bodies, which is the mineral world in broad sense, bodies will be classified according the growing complexity of their molecules. Molecules, however, are already body compounds. In effect, molecules are composite of atoms. The complexity of atoms goes hand in hand with their weight. Bodies which identify with a single atom are the so-called simple bodies. Since atoms enter in the formation of all existing bodies, which they are the composing elements, they are rightly called elements.

It is only since the XIX century that chemists have been investigating on the simple bodies that atoms are, and they eventually found in 1839, with German scientist Johann Wolfgang Döbereiner, that there was a direct relationship between atomic weight and the chemical properties of each element. The important discovery rendered possible the classification of atoms.

Similar classification shall bear the name of Periodic Classification of Elements, which was given by the Russian scientist that addressed and developed first a similar panorama, and precisely the chemist Dmitri Ivanovitch Mendeleyev. He started elaborating this scale in 1869, when he found some correspondence in the atomic structure of elements having identical properties. These similarities or connections enabled him to rank the elements by "periods", and then to complete the table along the following years, imagining even missing bodies, guessed and elaborated as intermediate structures having a definite atomic weight, which were placed between bodies that were already known.

It is not necessary to give here detail contents of the table, let's say only that, in natural conditions of temperature and atmospheric pressure, the table identifies among the chemical elements, sorted from the lightest (the most simple) to the heaviest ones (the most complex)... The table identifies all physical kind: gas (hydrogen and oxygen, in particular), liquid (brome and other halogens), and solid (iron, copper, gold, lead). It is among solid bodies, that we identify the minerals, in the narrow sense of the term, which gave their name to the "mineral world". We will not go further into the details of this classification, because it would lead us then to develop an even more elaborate classification of complex bodies (i.e. compositions atoms) that molecules are. For the purpose of this investigation (addressing only inorganic molecules) we must only say that molecules are sorted into a series moving from micro-molecules up to macromolecules... The inventory would be too broad to report here. To know more, it will be sufficient to refer to a good chemistry manual.

The ancient classification of the four elements, which characterized the time of Aristotle (water, air, earth and fire), has undergone profound transformations. It is now the knowledge of atom and of molecule which allows a precise identification of the bodies which compose elementary gases, metals, crystals, rocks, minerals (that is to say all material containing substances in pure state or in form of mixture, including one or several specific chemicals, in such ratios as they can be industrially isolated), and other bodies like boulder, pebble, gravel, sand, silt, slime, mud, clay... The three main commonly admitted categories of gas, liquid and solid are not usable here, for an investigation of mineral world, due to the fact that a same molecule may appear under these three gaseous, liquid and solid forms according to certain physical conditions, such as temperature, altitude, atmospheric pressure, etc. There are therefore physical conditions (at the limit of possible in certain cases, but really verifiable) where each of those bodies simple or complex exists under the state of steam, of liquid and of solid, i.e. mineral. The easiest example could be referring to water (made up of one oxygen atom and two atoms of hydrogen), which can adopt the three diverse configurations of gas, liquid and solid.

(2) **VEGETAL & PLANT KINGDOM** brings together the beings which show a certain degree of structural autonomy, i.e. an internal organization which produces specific changes inside of the same being from birth until death, and performs common functions. These are beings which are endowed of the faculty of transmit such autonomy replicating themselves. In his *De Anima* (*Treatise on the soul*), Aristotle says that "among natural bodies, some know life and some know it not. Life means feeding themselves, growing, and autonomously declining" (*De Anima*, II:1). Aristotle also asserts that life is what distinguishes animated bodies from inanimate ones. Here, too, classification shall be done from the "form", i.e. from the structural complexity of being a vegetable, a plant. In other words, classification proceeds according to the organic complexity of the being, from the seasonal blade of grass (phanerogams), up to the giant redwood (sequoia, which longevity can reach 6,000 years old) passing through daisies, roses, cherries, etc.

There is an irreducible gap from mineral world to vegetable world. This can be expressed using the words of Chevalier de Lamarck: "We may assert that between raw material and living bodies stands an immense **hiatus**, which allows neither to settle in the same row these two kinds of bodies nor to undertake to linking them through any sort of nuance" (Jean-Baptiste de Monet, Chevalier de Lamarck (1744-1829), *Philosophie zoologique*, chap.4). He added later, "all attempts to connect the two kingdoms miserably failed".

Up to 1995, botany, which is the science of plants, had identified more than 450.000 species of vegetables (including 250,000 which have flowers, among which 500 are carnivorous). Each year more than 5,000 new species are reported. At the bottom of the scale we find cellular cryptogams (blue-green fungi, *Cyanophyceae*, bacteria) some of which barely differentiate from mineral world, then come vascular cryptogamic (ferns, horsetails, *lycopsids*), afterwards are quoted the phanerogams (flowering plants), among which there are woody plants that trees are.

Some vegetal beings are at the lower limit with the mineral world. There are even cases that naturalists are not able to classify. It happens with some corals, because they are not able to identify their nature, uncertain if they are mineral or living bodies. It is clear however that if these bodies know life they are plants, if they do not possess it they are minerals. It happens all the same that happens at the upper limit of the vegetal world with protists.

(3) **ANIMAL WORLD** differentiates vegetal kingdom by the presence of sensitivity: it gather bodies which are alive, as plants are, but gifted of sensitive acquaintance. There are cases when a man cannot distinguish if such living unicellular organism belongs to the kingdom of plants or the one of animals. It happens with *protists*, that were recently quoted, notwithstanding, the philosopher has no doubt. Even if a technical response, from botanists and biologist experts, is difficult to provide, the philosophical answer is simple: if there is not sensitivity that body is a *protophyta* (vegetable), whether there is sensitivity, it is a protozoa (animal).

The science of "Systematics" pushed further the classification of the living beings belonging to animal kingdom. Starting from the basic unit which is genus, it elaborates the construc-

tion of successive units that are species, order and class. These four categories (genus, species, order and class) have been set in 1758 by the Swedish naturalist Carolus von Linnaeus (+ Upsala, 1778) who had the habit to indicate the first two degrees by a binary nomenclature binary: the name meant the type, or genus, and the word indicated the species.

To be specific we will say that he used for animals the same method that he employed with plants. He organized the framework for identification of beings, using one Latin (or Latinized) word to represent the genus and the second to distinguish the species, the first name (genus) being a noun and the second (species) a qualifier (adjective). Also, the author who first described a particular species is usually indicated after the double name.

Classes are grouped into their BRANCHES, starting the classification of animals from the bottom. So we have (1) first the radiated (who have no internal structure and reproduce mostly by duplication, like freshwater polyps, coelenterates, medusa, coelacanths, intestinal worms,, echinoderms, amoebas, heterotrophic, protozoan, sporozoan, etc.), (2) the articulated (classes of insects, arachnids, crustaceans, annelids), (3) the mollusks (classes of acephal, artiozoar, cirrhopod, bracchiopod, gastropods, pteropod, cephalopods), (4) vertebrates (classes of fish, reptiles, birds, mammals).

(4) HUMAN BEING - Above animal is located rational animal, also said political animal, that man is. The world of man is characterized by the being, which includes all animal characteristics plus intelligence. Intelligence explicates the originality of this new world of beings, which includes humans and clearly shows the epistemological fracture (to resume the term of Gaston Bachelard) existing between the animal kingdom and the human world.

Gaston Bachelard

It is not necessary to add much since the whole section on gnoseology deals with this topic. Intelligence includes in human world a spiritual dimension, which provides immortality and which is also studied in some section of metaphysics.

Concerning the eventuality of classifying people depending on the quality of their form (the soul), a careful examination of human soul shows that, precisely, **there is nothing to classify: all men are equal among themselves**. It is also said that they are brothers.

It was precisely the undue endeavors of making some classification among men in categories of "races", or "species" (and, more recently, in social "classes") which produced abuses such as racism, and all forms of social oppression, provoking social conflicts (class struggle).

Nonetheless, as for every other class of beings, each human individual is unique. Every individual is unequaled in its proper existence… Prof. Giuseppe Zanghì liked to stress, the remarkable, the incomparable single excellence of each human individual. He also used to say: "God's thought on me is not identical to God's thought on you!" (Conversation ofu 27 June 1991)

Ancient times knew the class of slaves, clients, and free men... Many diverse classifications existed in history between people, dividing them according to their origin, wealth, political power, etc. French Revolution of 1789 put the footprint in our cultural baggage as the last great battle waged against these divisions of human society in three categories: nobility, clergy, and the people (third-state) which included peasants, craftsmen and tradesmen (bourgeois).

The whole of mankind is constituted by a same species. Any attempt of classification within the world of human people which would forget that this world is composed of only one race, the human race, would jeopardize the same characteristics of human nature. There is only one single nature of people, which is expressed in cultures and ethnic groups, which are improperly called "races", but in a restrictive meaning. The events characterizing different peoples are integral part of the whole same human history. Geographical locations do not count: the history of men is the history of the earth.

(5) **PURE SPIRITS** - Above mankind, nothing, absolutely nothing, allows us to exclude the existence of beings which share intelligence, but do not share sensorial acquaintance, as it happens in humans. It is the field of beings which does not share material existence. Even if our culture recognizes their presence through the context of experience of faith, inside of sects, in Masonic rites, intermediation of mediums, witchcraft, spiritualism, etc. their existence is often disputed. Nothing, however, authorizes a philosopher to exclude pure spirits from human reflection and experience. The data collected about pure spirits fall under the blow of human experience which is investigated in philosophy. Given that "nothing that is human must be ignored" (Seneca), every specific element collected within my personal experience must be considered by philosophy, even when this experience is carried out in a particular social, cultural, or spiritual context.

Our days make difficult and delicate sometimes to speak of pure spirits. It seems easier to speak on material and tangible items... Few people dare to speak on that part of reality which is not merely physical, social, business, or political... Some however, dare to do so, because of the care of offering a full panorama of human fields of knowledge. In such perspective angels must be included.

As a preliminary word I like to stress that oppositely to what happens among people, whom we communicate with through our senses, every communication with Angels goes directly through intelligence. Thinking of an Angel, our Guardian Angel for example or any another one, opens him in our immediate presence, or if you wish, instantly, brings us in communication, in "conversation" with him, if we want to. In such a case, while dealing with angels in class, they all are present to our discourse, if willingly we accept them. As an outcome, they are among us, even when we cannot hear, see, smell, or touch them sensibly. If we only agree with, a conversation on Angels is a time of prayer. In case it is not, it could be that the discussion is not properly talking about angels. The same is in force while we are reading the note.

We will confine our discourse here for what it needs in reference to the existent scale. We only are interested for the moment about their "presence" among the beings. As regards to their nature, their role, their nearness to us, their interaction in human endeavors, it is a topic that belongs to an appropriate study. Additionally, the study of pure spirits in their function of God messengers - Angels - pertains to the domain of revelation and should be address inside of theology. As a philosopher, one must however, verify the possibility of their existence and examine what it is possible to know about them in the field of metaphysics.

Along the elaboration of the scale of beings, everyone is scored according to its form. As well as we asked a chemist to classify mineral beings, a botanist to classify vegetable ones, and a zoologist to identify animals, and a philosopher to address people, we now need the theologian to tell us how to score pure spirits, also known as angels. The theologians of our days are often curiously "silent" about them! Reference can be done with Augustine and Aquinas, who are two great masters who address the presence of angels on earth and also speak as philosophers.

As such, the study of pure spirits belongs to philosophical tradition. On the tracks of Socrates and Plato, Aristotle introduced the presence of pure spirits as organizers and managers of the world. Dealing with sidereal world, or sidereal space, Aristotle identifies pure spirits as the movers of stars and planets (we now would say galaxies), as secondary causes. You may find these references in Aristotle: *Meteor*, 3, 340b, 6; *Physic*, VIII 259b, 28 and particularly 259a, 12, where Aristotle affirms that the movers of celestial spheres are nothing but their souls (their forms). Aquinas develops Aristotelian reflection providing Angels with an important function in the management of universe and the correct endeavor of mankind (*Summa*, QQ.106-114), granting them a business which fits with the nature of second causes.

Whatever we may say we mostly have to stress that to this degree of beings, they are pure forms. While among people there is only a single species, in which persons differentiate through the quantity of matter they are made of, at the level of angels there is no matter... No matter does enter into the constitution of those who are known as "celestial bodies". In other words a principle of paramount differentiation gives shape, capacity, intelligence, task, behavior, limitations to each one, when emerging into existence. In the field of pure spirits, however, such differentiation is not provided with some quantity of organized matter that would be "mixed" with form... There is no organized matter involved unless as mere principle of differentiation, which is technically prime matter... i.e. mere capacity of change. Matter as such is absent as an additional presence in the form that could make ulterior differences in species. As far as there are angels, and not just only a single angel, and due to the fact that they are pure forms, they are, therefore, distinguished only by their same form. Each angel is a specific form. Each angel himself is a species.

Due to the fact that each member of the world of pure spirits is unique in his existence, each member of the kind is in his existence a full species and there is not another one of the same species... We usually may call them "angels" even if it would be more appropriate to call them "Angels", with a capital "A", because of their uniqueness. We are dealing in such a heavenly neighborhood of so highly celestial issues that the whole word should be written in capital letters... We are limiting the capital letter to first one of the word, in order to stress the unique nature of Angels.

The many testimonies in the bible (Cf. Genèse XXXII, Exode VII et XXIII, Rois III, Tobie XII, Job XXXIII, Daniel IX et X, Malachie III, Luc XVI, etc.) and writings of saints (The list here would be far too long. I suggest that everyone refers to his favorite saint, or the one who is the protector of the chuch, chapel, or university he/she is used to visit), those written references induce to believe that their number is incalculable. It is not countless, however, but surely too high for people to count. Notwithstanding, authors are not unanimous on this point. At times, someone would like to reduce their number because of the fact that it is difficult to imagine too many angelic natures. Notwithstanding, more common is to find writings which advocate a very large number of them: many authors consider Angels innumerable. Though it is, any indicative number about them was ever provided. Yet a certain popular piety, which is consolidated by eastern and western iconography and by the major religious traditions (Jewish, Christian and Muslim) claims that their number exceeds by far the number of human beings.

We like to stress that when the Catholic Church reformed liturgical calendar, in 1969, the celebration of Guardian Angels remained and was fixed on 2 October, just a few days after the celebration of the three Archangels, fixed on 29 September. Concerning Muslim tradition it will be sufficient to recall that Muhammad claimed that the whole Koran was revealed to him by Archangel Gabriel, and that the Koran confirms the action of Angels in human life as referred in the Bible. Many publications help to see how angels are present in our lives (Gilles Pageot, *Les anges existent-ils encore?* Diakonia Service, Audiocassette n° 85).

Since the time of Middle Ages, Haylemon, Origene, Pseudo-Denys, Augustine, Aquinas, James de Voragine, Honoré d'Autun, Popes John III and Paul I, the Councils of Bragan and Latran IV, and specialists range the pure spirits into three groups of Choirs, called "Hierarchies", and precisely Epiphany, Hyperphany and Hypophany. Each Hierarchy is in turn subdivided into three main categories of Angels, called "Choirs". We have thus nine Choirs of Angels as the Book of Revelation refers to (Rev. 12:13). There is some flexibility in the distribution of the Choirs within the Hierarchies.

One of the most authorized inventories is the one elaborated by Augustine. We will follow it as our best reference on the topic. As a result we like to disclose the following panorama: Seraphim, Cherubim, Thrones (in Epiphany), Dominations, Powers, Virtues (in Hyperphany), then Principalities, Archangels, Angels (in Hypophany). These are therefore the nine Choirs of Angels. The number of Angels within each choir was never indicated. The first Choir is entirely absorbed in the contemplation, adoration and worship of God, the second is turned to the management of powers of the world, the third is directly engaged into human business (on land kingdoms for Principalities, major events or great vocations for Archangels, on each person of mankind in particular for Angels). It is at this last level that each one of us enjoys, among the world of pure spirits, the precise action of a specific Guardian Angel. It is all the same for each legal or moral person, family, organization, small community, which has its own Guardian Angel. Nations, however, have their protectors out of Archangels.

Of course, these pieces of information are sensitive. They refer to topics which are delicate to handle. It was however essential to providing the presence of pure spirits on earth and emphasizing that a treatise of philosophy that would address real being, i.e. all creatures, and would miss to refer to pure spirits would remain an unbalanced and incomplete study of the facts.

G. Important Note

16. God is not a mere Being

Otherwise said: God does not belong to the Nomenclature of Beings

With the world of pure spirits the nomenclature of creatures is complete. There are not other beings in the whole world.

It would be a serious mistake to try to add the "Prime Being" in the list… whenever we like to put it on the top or on the bottom, both positions are equally inaccurate. When you make the inventory of furniture before moving are you supposed to count your children to? Identically, you do not count the workers of the moving company either… even if they are also in the house among the furniture. No you don't. People are not furniture. It would be a similar mistake adding the "Supreme Being" in the list of universe beings…

We cannot insert God inside of the scale of beings, because the scale itself comes from him. Inserting God in this scale would be removing his prerogative of foundation of everything: "I AM". And it would not even sufficient to assert his unique difference, for every being in the list shows some unique difference, too. Including the name of God in the list would induce the reader to imagine God as a being among the others, although more perfect as any other being. God is not only more perfect than anyone else: he does not belong to such a list. God cannot even be an object of thought, unless we name him as different to whatever we may think about him. God is incomparable. God is not only above all beings, he is also present to all beings in a more thoroughly manner than every being can be present to itself. Inserting God in the scale of beings would ultimately be a way to give reason to Voltaire, when he says that "God made man in his image and likeness and man rendered him the same courtesy"!

Before proceeding further we must behave and be sure that we are not talking about God as another being, as something existing in the universe. God is not even a mental being. Actually, if we really were properly thinking of God we should immediately enter in ecstasy. Anyway, before proceeding ahead in our conversation, let's be sure to put our heart and our mind at the presence of God. This is actually something we should do before every activity or every study as Aquinas used to recall. Here is why he used some specific prayer before every human commitment. To be consistent with such endeavor, I am pleased to add, at the end of this note the famous Aquinas prayer before study. You will find it in the original Latin, with my personal English translation.

This note is just an occasion to remember of not confusing God with any being of the world, not even as the Prime Being, unless we understand that he is not a being. So let's call eventually him as Prime Mover, as Aristotle does… And Aquinas is pleased to add: "Prime Mover that religious traditions call God."

Because all being is depending fully on God, who stands behind and beyond us by all sides (outside, lower, upper, before, after, inside, etc.) but above all God manifests himself within every being, which he provides life. Addressing theodicy, as a metaphysical section on the study of God, we consider all what that human reflection is able to say about God. For the moment let us consider that the best approach towards God is probably today the one which was cleaned by the wave of atheism. .while atheism denied God presence among human beings, it actually made also a good job: it accustomed people to understand that we cannot meet God as a simple other being, as someone to talk to the way we talk to other people. Meeting God is actually much more easy that meeting other people. After a wave of atheism we got the best background to meet God faster...

Remember how God taught Jewish people the evidence of his being beyond every being... and how Jewish people refused to pronounce his name for not confusing him with any other creature. As a result, in the Bible, JHVH is not a name, it's an abbreviation, a sign to indicate we are talking about the One, whom we are not allow to name: "You will not pronounce God's name in vain" (Deut. xxx). Even Jesus, does not pronounce his name, but once, when dying on the Cross "Eli, Eli…" in all other occasions he referred to the Father, the Heavenly Father. "Whatever you do in secret, my Father will reward you…" (Mt xx), "Be perfect as your Heavenly Father is perfect" (Mt xx). Many times, Jesus uses a periphrasis to refer to God: "Ask and you will be answered; knock and you will be opened…" Jesus doesn't say "Ask and God will provide…" Even Jesus in person follows Jewish tradition about the one we are not supposed to refer by name, but to indicate in order to understand we speak about the One who is far beyond everyone we know or are familiar with.

It can be interesting to consider a certain parallelism between the Biblical language about God ("Knock and you will be open", where the passive tense replaces "JHVH", who is "Unmentionable") and a certain language common in atheism. When at the beginning of the XX century France was ruled by a government which wanted to behave as secular and atheist, rulers wanted transform the whole society according to an atheistic political project and decide to cancel from school books any trace of God inside of literature. This is how several tales of Jean de La Fontaine were processed: instead of reading "small fish will grow and become big fish, provided that God grants it life", the Ministry of Education ordered to print: "Small fish will grow and become big fish, provided that it is granted life". In a certain way, but without noticing it properly, atheistic governance took into account the notion of the transcendence of God, as it was suggested by Holy Scripture. It was, I believe, transitional stage of maturity of human thought.

God is transcendent. He cannot be assert but beyond every being of the world. The Bible appoints him as the Eternal will provide… Actually **one cannot think properly of God unless entering into his presence**. In other words, to properly speak about God, we must convert or, if you wish, turn our eyes towards him, and looking at him, let speak the One who is unmentionable. Any other attempt to thinking about God would be referred to a being or a concept, and therefore it would be a thought on something which is diverse from God (cf. theodicy).

H. Recap — Provisional Glossary

It is important in our endeavor to distinguish but not to separate any step of ontology in large sense (ontology + peratology) from the whole body of metaphysics, while dealing with the primary evidence of the being and its primary source of existence.

Being is something that exists. The being may have different consistency. Aristotle affirms that "the being can be said in many ways."

In fact we meet first ***Real Being***, which is a being whose existence does not depend of my knowledge. It is a being belonging to the world.

But most of the time people deal with ***Mental Being***, which is a being which exists in the mind but not in reality. Mental being helps to address speculatively all aspects of real being, considering its whatness, or essence. Every real being is in act.

Actual Being, or **being in act**, is every real being in its actual existence. Each being in act is in potency of any possible change. Every being in act includes the potentialities defined by its proper essence.

Potential Being is whatever an actual being can develop to make actual. It refers to every possibility an actual being has to change.

Matter that we know only exists with a form. Every piece of matter we know and recognize is organized matter, i.e. matter brought into existence by form. Every matter that has a specific name has already a form, and it is said "organized matter". Matter is what is supposed to change. Matter is mere opacity, and source of opacity... It is mere indeterminacy and source of indetermination. Matter is essentially indeterminacy. Primordial matter is radical indeterminacy. Matter is what, by means of which a substance (real being) is made. It is source of change, of opacity, and indetermination of a substance. Matter is what may change form. Matter is faculty of changing. Matter is capacity to change. Matter is what is going to change. Matter is all that is able to be transformed. Matter is unintelligible, it is source of opacity. Matter is principle of individuation. The principle of individuality consists in the matter by means of which bodies are made. Matter is source of continuity of a substance during its changes.

Form is what brings matter into organized existence. It is what does provide intelligibility to a being. It is what is intelligible in a substance. It is that which is comprehensible of a thing. It is source of its intelligibility. Form we know only exists through Matter: it gives shape to matter. It shows what a being is in act. While matter is always in potency, Form is in act. In other words, while matter is power, from is act. Form is principle of intelligibility. It is principle of intelligibility of bodies... Form is principle of stability, too. It is principle of identity.

Substance is a being that exists in itself. Every substance is the interaction of Matter & Form, expressed through its own accidents... Matter is what the substance is made of, and what may change in the substance. Form is actuating the substance. Substance exists because of its form. We also may say that substance is subject of organized matter. Natural "matter" is a co-principle of natural "form". They coexist in every substance.

Change is the passage from being in potency to being in act. It is a particular case of multiplicity. All change proposed by matter is actually caused by the form. Matter is principle of continuity in the being, while form is principle of change. Matter is what may change and form is what operated the change. While matter is effective power to change, form is effective principle of change or, if you wish, it is the act of change. We may recognize the material continuity and discontinuity of a body by its form. By their matter substances vary as individuals and by their form they vary as species.

Multiplicity shows the possibility to divide an entity into several beings. Many beings compose a multiplicity. There is multiplicity of species ("discontinuity" of chemical, physical, and eventually biological properties) and multiplicity of single beings (individuals) inside of species

Individuals are the basic unit of multiplicity. Etymologically, individual means what we cannot divide without destroying it. Individuals vary according to the quantity of matter they are made of... They are recognizable by their form.

Species is a coherent set of anatomical and physiological characters. A species is composed of a determined number of individuals.

Principle of Causation — Whatever does not change by itself does change by another, which is called "cause". In every change four causes are involved: material and formal (intrinsic), efficient and final ('extrinsic). What is cause in its proper order is in another order the effect of another cause.

Reciprocality of Causes — All causes work together. No one is absolutely first. Each one is first in its own order. Reciprocality of causes means interdependence of causes, but this term is less expressive and even appropriate than the term of reciprocity. We should talk about interdependence of effects and interaction of causes.

Nomenclature of Beings includes minerals, vegetables, animals, humans, and pure spirits. For mineral, vegetal, and animal orders the form classifies specifically the beings in gender, species, classes, and branches. Among people, there is nothing to classify: all men are equal among themselves. Among Angels, each one is a unique species. There is no other being in the universe out of the above five orders. While dealing with the first three (mineral, vegetal, and animal worlds) people "command nature obeying its laws." At human level, the interaction among people changes individuals and makes society. People are substance both as individuals and as society. People blossom individually and collectively, the two sides are essential in the natural improvement of people. At Pure Spirit level, the more we know, the more we are changed and improved.

Prime Being — Aristotle asserts that the being as such can only proceed from a being which nature is to be, that is to say, from a Prime Being, also called Prime Mover, who -Aquinas stressed- is the one that religious traditions call "God". Metaphysics produces its search in the field of being and investigates further without the help of Revelation or Theology, but also without totally ignoring them, just in order to refer appropriately to everything with a proper vocabulary and suitable identification. The study of Prime Being is the highest search of metaphysics.

Aquinas Prayer before study:

Creator ineffábilis, qui de thesáuris sapiéntae tuae tres Angelórum hierárchias designásti, et eas super caelum empýreum miro órdine collocásti, atque univérsi partes elegantíssime distribuísti: Tu, inquam, qui verus fons lúminis et sapiéntiae díceris ac superéminens princípium, infúndere dignéris super intelléctus mei ténebras tuae rádium claritátis, dúplices, in quibus natus sum, a me rémovens ténebras, peccátum scílicet et ignorántiam. Tu, qui linguas infántium facis disértas, linguam meam erúdias atque in lábiis meis grátiam tuae benedictiónis infúndas. Da mihi intelligéndi acúmen, retinéndi capacitátem, addiscéndi modum et facilitátem, interpretándi subtilitátem, loquéndi grátiam copiósam. Ingréssum instruas, progréssum dírigas, egréssum cómpleas. Tu, qui es verus Deus et Homo, qui vívis et regnas in saécula saeculórum. Amen

Ineffable Creator, who, from the treasures of your wisdom, have appointed three hierarchies of Angels, and have established them in marvelous order above the fiery heavens, and so wisely have marshaled the portions of the universe, you are proclaimed the true fountain of Light and wisdom and the primal origin raised high above all things. Pour forth a ray of your infinite brightness into the darkness of my understanding; remove far from me the twofold darkness into which I was born, namely, sin and ignorance. O Lord, who makes eloquent the tongues of little children, do refine my tongue and pour forth upon my lips the goodness of your blessing. Grant me keenness of understanding, capacity of memory, method and ease of learning, subtlety of interpretation, and abundant eloquence of speech. May you instruct the beginning, direct the progressing, and perform the achieving. You are true God and true Man, who live and reign, world without end. Amen.

GNOSEOLOGY

HOW DO WE COME TO KNOW? WHAT DOES KNOWLEDGE MEAN?

Preliminary

Gnoseology is integral part of metaphysics (as a section of **Critique**, which also includes *Epistemology* and a few sections of *Logic*), together with **ontology, peratology** (also said **ontology 2nd**), and **natural theology** (As already said on St. James Street). Studying the way we know is investigating a process that we already are familiar with. The study is done both in metaphysics and in logic. The discourse deals with the process of demonstration, and finally the meaning of words. In fact it takes time to realize the way we know.

This note on gnoseology can be considered as a general preparation to the coming reading of Maritain on Ontology (I & II), the ones of Aristotle on Metaphysics, and the one of Aquinas on Being and Essence. Each of these pieces of reading suppose the awareness of the **theory of knowledge**. Afterwards, all statements become easier to understand. According to Aristotle *"Every teaching or learning through discourse proceeds from previous knowledge"* (*Second Analytics* 1:1), here is one of the keys of knowledge.

Process of knowledge, **theory of knowledge**, gnoseology are synonymus. they all introduce us into the process through which we come to know. The investigation on that process started with Socrates and was reported by Plato, which **Recollection Theory** was improved by Augustine as **Illumination Argument**. It happened the same with Aristotle and Aquinas: Revisiting Recollection Theory under the light of Critical Realism, Aristotle elaborated the synthesis, which later was better explained by Thomas Aquinas. Commentators said that often Aristotle is more understandable in the writings of Aquinas than in those of the same Aristotle. it must be stressed, however, that Aquinas wanted to make more transparent the Illumination Argument and he did it throught the categories of Aristotle.

To say it again more panoramically, after Plato (fl. 370 BC) a new pattern was provided by Aristotle (fl. 350 BC).. Later, under Plato's influence, Augustine (fl. 400 AD), made a new elaboration. Finally a full perspective is offered by Aquinas (fl. 1270) as a synthesis of the previous ones.

All the views of Plato, Aristotle, and Augustine, were made more evident by Thomas Aquinas. Dealing with human knowledge, Aquinas makes us aware first of the way information is provided to people through senses: observation, perception, and sensations. They compose our first step of sensoriality. Later on, intelligence reads inside of things what they are. It is a first step of awareness, called rational knowledge.

Important Distinction

Do not confuse the natural process of understanding, with the homonymus spiritual gifts of the Holy spirit: they come upon us to complete the natural process not to replace it. They work in the same field of knowledge under two diverse and complementary perspectives.

The gifts of wisdom, understanding, knowledge, These are the **supernatural graces**, which individual Christians need to fulfill their mission in the **Church**.. These gifts are indicated in the letters of St. Paul, at first to the Romans (Chap. 12), then to the Corinthians (1st, Chap. 12), and to the Ephesians (Chap. 4). Also the first letter of Peter (Ch 4), evokes the spiritual gifts. The gifts are seemingly related to both, the "natural" behavior of intelligence and some "miraculous" ability added from above. All spiritual ("intelligence" is "spiritual") gifts are empowered by the Holy Spirit.

The study of **Natural Intelligence** belongs to the field of metaphysics. It includes comprehension (capacity to grasp — which traditionally has its seat in the heart) and reason (capacity to deal with the connected issues — which traditionally sits in the head).

> The article is divided in four sections:
> (1) Historical process
> (2) Gnoseology as such
> (3) The Tree of Wisdom
> (4) Historical Survey
> (5) The Knowledge of God

Socrates

Plato

Augustine

Section One

Socrates, Plato, Augustine

Historical process

A. Socratic Maieutics

Let's go by steps.

"**Maieutics**" is the art of Teaching elaborated by Socrates. It is the Socratic art of awaking people to some inside truth. According to such method, students do not properly learn from a teacher, they only recognize the truth that a teacher points out. They "discover" something they knew but were not aware of. Teacher's suggestions and student sharing improve a common knowledge.

People live in space and time, but through knowledge and love they experience facts that overcome space and time. Through knowledge and love people share eternity. The propaedeutic of truth properly exerts in people the process of illumination theory. It is a natural process for it is natural for people to be born for the truth. "Everyone seeks truth" – Aristotle. To say it with other words, the truth which gave us birth and is still acting in us wants to meet herself in the neighborhoods of our life. When such event happens we know that we are finally backed to our future. We get a small exertion of it when suffering to solve a problem we suddenly enjoy saying, "I got it!" That temporary enlightenment is a small and very short instant of illumination theory.

Augustine stressed the proper outcome of Socrates' conception of teaching. Augustine considers that **teaching** is not properly a process by which knowledge is transferred from one person to another. For knowledge is not the simple result of an external process of explanations and proofs. After Socrates Augustine believes that every teaching is waking up in a student the truth hidden inside…

Augustine develops his reflection on the topic in the dialog he wrote and entitled *The Teacher*. As the dialog between Adeodatus and his father Augustine indicates, words are signs which refer to what they indicate. So using words move other people to look at the same facts… Words do not provide the facts they show them… So be it for teaching and learning. Every teaching is an invitation to experience the facts. It helps to enlarge the knowledge of the facts. When a teacher speaks, it belongs then to the interlocutor to look personally at what the discourse leads to. This was the reason why Plato left most of his dialogs unfinished… they were supposed to put in the minds of listeners seeds of wisdom to grow and develop autonomously.

Teaching and learning is not a mere process of recollection as Plato affirmed, it is similar but deeper. We are made by the truth and made for the truth. We are exerting the distance between what we already are and what we are not yet. In the meanwhile the human task is to strike the distance, to erase the gap between the two. The Gospel of Luke says that Jesus, the son of God, was growing in age, size and wisdom. He said "he was growing." In fact Jesus was living properly in time and space, moving successively and progressively. Living in time and space makes everything a process. No development is immediate, even the faster one. So every action of teaching and learning proceed by steps. The same Illumination theory is a growing process.

Explanations and proofs are the occasionally incitements, the stimuli by which students awake from ignorance to knowledge. Students experience the internal jumping into flash of insight, seeing the truth. The enlightening is caused by external suggestions as teaching or sensorial experience. According to Augustine, however, the enlightening process of teaching is even more than a simple awakening endeavor.

Augustine considers that The "Word" (the "Logos", alias "Jesus," the Son of God) is present in every consistent discourse. Through the discourse God acts in our lives. Jesus' spirit illuminates our mind from inside of every discourse. So he states, "The power that reveals the truth to us is Christ as the Teacher operating within us." Augustine emphasized the maieutic process indicated by Socrates, who claimed to be the one who, like a -midwife for future mothers, helps people to deliver the truth which is prisoner inside of us. Philosophy is an action of delivery the word dwelling in us!

Knowledge is not merely an automatic process, but the fruit of a willingly free decision. So circumstances, neighborhood, education, help us to improve in what we "potentially" are at birth, then, little by little, we grow in knowledge and love. This is why, we have such a great feeling of familiarity, when we learn something true, which nonetheless is new for us, for we are made for truth, and everything is true is "conatural" to us, it fits us. So everything we "known" appear like it was recalled even when it is new.

This note follows Augustine's text, with the enlightenment of comments provided by Aquinas and analysed from Jean Guitton. We must distinguish at first what is knowledge, according to Augustine, and how does it proceed. Hope the students will excuse if my attempt to be explicit is somehow technical. Remember that in this Augustine's issue faith and knowledge go together, and "we need to believe in order to understand." In fact it would be impossible to understand properly something that we barely believe it exists... Similarly Socrates behavior was faith in truth...

B. Plato's Recollection Theory

Later Plato, following the steps of Socrates, elaborated "Recollection Theory". Illumination theory starts is an improvement of Plato's theory. Plato was so impressed by Socratic Maieutics and by the fact that actually Socrates was able to deliver the truth from the mind of his interlocutors that he had to find an explanation for such a delivery. His attempted of explanation was to believe that truth was inside of people from previous experience. He did not realized that what Socrates exerted was a process of improvement. Socrates had the capacity to provoke people to reflect and to help them to improve in their own capacity to think. His admiration of Socrates hid from him the real picture. Plato believed that people lived in a previous world of perfection and discussing with Socrates was awaking them from precarious ignorance.

The soul is able to remember, to recollect, what she new in her previous life. Such perspective of awakening is not good enough to explain the origine of the body and the fact that knowledge is growing all along human life and improving from a generation to another. The awareness of knowledge is not standard: if it was a simple process of waking it would be mistaking sometimes and would not be progressing all along.

For Plato the body does exist from another source than the soul and is only the shell of the soul. Such a rudimental approach is defective. Aristotle will adjust the whole picture as we will see below. Augustine, however, made consistent recollection theory under the light or creation: in God all knowledge was perfect while we are created, but the knowledge of people is not mere remembering.

While Recollection Theory (Plato) is recalling something already known, Illumination Theory is bringing forth some knowledge present in the mind only as a potential. Such a potential wakes up under the provocation of discourse or experience and develops accordingly… It is not already in existence in the mind. Otherwise it would be mere Recollection. Illumination Argument takes its name from the fact that every new understanding is like an enlightening process, almost like every discovery provokes an instant of enjoyment. Additionally, because we are made as the image of God, while we improve in knowledge we improve in what we are, we improve in His image. This image is not totally performed at our birth it needs our participation to blossom. Flowering in what we are, makes us blossom in the WORD. We are members of the Trinity Family by adoption and we are called to become, little by little, another Christ.

C. Augustine's Illumination Argument

Illumination Argument remains the preliminary background to any study of gnoseology. It is preliminary historically and logically. Illumination argument is a second elaboration of Plato's Recollection Argument, and the ground of investigation that influenced greatly Bonaventure and John Duns Scotus. The best understanding of it is elaborated through the systematic gnoseology that Aquinas developed later with Aristotelian categories.

Illumination argument has a tightened connection between study and prayer. Somebody may believe that Logic, knowledge, and Prayer have nothing to do to one another. The opposite is true. It is in his dialog with his son Adeodatus, entitled on *The Teacher*, when dealing with the meaning of words, that Augustine addresses the issue of prayer. Prayer is an issue that shows the borderline of logic and knowledge and helps to better understand how human mind works.

When a scientist finds the result of his search, the truth, his search ends. Science is done, because science deals with objective issues that never change.. When a philosopher finds the truth, his whole inquiry is transfigured in a better endeavor. When a metaphysician meets the truth, what does happen is proportionate with the quality of the truth which is looked after. Sometimes, such event can be the mere end of a long search, like the simple result of an arithmetical addition, but most of the time search is more likely similar to the result of some physical operation when a critical mass is reached and an explosion starts. Meeting the truth is a fact that changes human life and illuminates the mind. Often the words are barely able to show the complexity of interactions and connections that are involved in a so simple and so clear endeavor. Philosophy moves inside of a context made of rich configuration of energetic situations. Some situations need to be experienced in order to be fully understood. The understanding comes, anyway, with the desire to know and the experienced intelligence.

Augustine offers an original investigation on language. The way of speaking reflects the way of reasoning, and through it we share knowledge, we communicate. Augustine's The Teacher, is an inquiry on the nature of speaking. In the first page, Augustine addresses the form of human communication that prayer is. It could be surprising for somebody, today, that at the onset of the dialog between Augustine and his son Adeododatus on the nature and configuration of language they want to spend time reflecting together on prayer. After due reflection it is not at all inappropriate that at the beginning of an article on the nature of language, Augustine wants to indicate one of the best form of communication that prayer is. According to Augustine prayer is the criterion of proper thinking. When human communication gets the intensity of the dialog between people and the above, then there is true communication.

Prayer is everyone's experience. Augustine's teaching performs the delicate task of addressing the paradoxical situation of an individual meeting the Absolute. Augustine is leading his Congregation in days of confusion. Soon, his teaching was extended to the whole Christendom… His formulation is universal, i.e. valid for all, and fitting everyone's belief. Whatever religious tradition we come from, prayer is a common field of improvement for every human being. In The Teacher, Augustine says that "there is no need to speak when we pray… there is no need of spoken words." That means that there are situations when the words are useless, like when two enamored people look silently together a sunrise or spontaneously help one another in home care activity, or when two people look at a same great situation and understand each other without a word... These situations exist. After the tracks of the Eastern Fathers, like Basil, John Chrysostom or John of Damascus, Eastern Christians believe that at the end times people will get their own body in the fullness of its consistency. People will not be trapped in the dichotomy of time and space anymore and will spontaneously be in touch by their willpower. There will be no need of words to communicate. This is already the experience of prayer.

All being considered it is proper to be open to the behavior of prayer during a philosophy course. Philosophy deals with wisdom. Intelligence seeks truth, as willpower seeks the good, as an artist strives for beauty, a politician for justice, and every person for the happiness to be experienced at an upper level. Prayer is communication with the above. It is the privileged instant of betterment in the field of communication and language. I said an "instant" for through prayer we live in eternity, i.e. in a permanent instant, also called "present." Prayer is the place where time meets eternity.

We live today the threshold of the amazing growing process of globalization. Whenever we like it or not we are in it. The teaching of Augustine is the understanding of his historically neighborhood at the threshold of a cultural gap. Surprisingly, his time and our time have a strong resemblance. He witnessed the fall of the Roman Empire, which produced the explosion of chaos in the Dark Ages, which provoked a reaction that, eventually, led to the blossoming performances of the Middle Ages. Today we are involved in the process of the world moving from many countries into a world made with only one unique large village.

Augustine's teaching provided insights which led Christendom in its endeavor of building a new civilization over the chaos of the migrations of people, which crushed down the Roman culture of his days. It is still insightful today to enlarge our vision and enlighten us beyond the partial perspectives of many writings and common ideas of our days. It already helped many to overcome the limitations of readings like the ones of Luther, the Upanishad, or El'Hallaj. These different perspectives do not deny Augustine, but eventually integrate it inside of the intercultural and multi-confessional behaviors of our present culture, This is also the thought of Pope Benedict XVI, who is an expert of Augustine, and likes to quote him in his official speeches and Encyclicals. He stressed several times the issue since the beginning of his pontificate, during his trip in Germany, and especially while visiting the Blue Mosque in Istanbul in company of the Great Mufti, on November 29, 2006, praying together the same God. Members of other religious denominations witnessed a large consensus on spiritual and cultural issues. Praying together goes beyond the best possible human meeting.

As the truth is far above every reasoning, God is far above every prayer – "No eye has seen it; it has no color. No ear has heard it; it has no sound. It has not entered man's heart; man's heart must enter into it." So Augustine wrote to Proba on Prayer. Nonetheless such a relationship with God happens. Those who are believers have at least once in their life experienced the presence of God, which exerts beyond words. Then it happens again. Sometimes, in spite of their provisional character, occasional conversation are helpful to show how most often human communication is far below what people would like to exert and are capable to. F. W. Niestzsche like to stress how human behavior and communications sometimes deceive us for people need more, they have inside the desire of the transcendent in everything they do. This desire awake us towards true knowledge.

D. Illumination Neighborhood

According to Jacques Maritain in *The Degrees of Knowledge*, in the chapter on St. Augustine, the illumination that Aquinas refers to is the same as the one of Augustine, interpreted, or better, understood under Aristotle's terminology. He ascribes this fact as the outcome of the suggestion given by Albertus Magnus to Aquinas, when he invited him "to follow Augustine in theology and Aristotle in philosophy." This means that he had to follow Augustine as the master of his personal convictions and Aristotle as the teacher of the language to use for expressing and understand these issues. In other words, Aquinas follows Augustine and explains his teaching amending Aristotle's doctrine. This is the reason why, Jean Guitton, Copleston, and other experts say that Aristotle is more understandable in the writings of Aquinas than in his own.

In the chapter on St. John of the Cross (*Juan de Yepes* §20-22), Maritain is even more explicit.. Aquinas and Juan de Yepes agree on the fact that "contemplation is experiential knowledge of love and union" and "while such experience is growing, Charity transform us in God so that a knowledge reaches directly." This love, however, is an outcome of faith which unites our intelligence with the abyss of deity: our faith is the source of our mystical experience... and "contemplation itself is experience of darkness." Our soul does not understand clearly and nonetheless proceeds ahead. It is a condition of intense purification. It is therefore a true action, in which because of faith the soul joins God directly and not through intelligence. Maritain indicates how this dark contemplation provides "a secret wisdom," which love transmits to the soul, unknowingly and before the soul may understand what happens to her." This secret sageness is present in the soul and at the same time it purifies and enlightens it in a way that the soul itself is unable to describe (Se also *Sum. Theol.* IIa-IIae Q.180 a.1).

In the human process of growing in the intimacy of God, Maritain's §21 explains that mystical wisdom hides the soul in a huge solitude, where the soul discovers to be far from every creature in an abyss which reveals her its own condition. So, moving up towards God remains a secret track, which the steps are the same paces of our loving knowledge that God infuses in the soul, which Maritain indicates as the living fire (Str.3.3), adding that " loving knowledge is received passively according to the nature of God not according to the nature of the soul (Cf. Aquinas' *Comment on the Sentences*).

As an example, we may refer to the assessment of Jesus on the cross, when his intelligence is tested during his forsaking. People have lost the intelligence of things because the Archangel who was in charge of intelligence near the human beings — Lucifer — failed. This is why today, salvation goes through the three theolagal virtues of faith, hope, and charity, which are managed by Michael, Gabriel and Raphael, who remained faithful to God and are still in charge. On the cross, Jesus passed the test of intelligence. Experiencing the darkness of the mind, he repaird the misdeed of Lucifer and gave us back the integrity of our natural condition up to a stage which is similar to the situation we had before the original sin. We only need to stay constantly inside and over the restoring sore of Eucharistic Jesus.

Illumination theory is not unusual in philosophy history. Every knowledge develops, through ordinary sensorial vision, an enlightening coming from intelligence activity. There is a specific activity of speculative light, which illuminates object of every kind and make them intelligible — even those which are purely rational or spiritual — making them "visible" to our mind. According to Plato such light comes from the shape of the perfect world of ideas, people belong to. According to Augustine, that light is produced in us by God himself. According to Aristotle, and later to Aquinas, such a light is integral part of the nature of the same intelligence. The three different theories on illumination are not incompatible with each others. For Augustine, the perfect world people come from (as in Plato) is the same mind of God, who created us at his image. For Aquinas, it is natural for people to be endowed of intelligence, for God respects in his creation the same process of natural law which reflects his creation. For creation happens now. And the human soul comes from a "natural" action of God. To be more specific, we should say that God creates people at his image, acting inside of the human biological process. This is something that many people have difficulty to understand, today, for they believe that creation was something which happened in the past. Augustine showed how time is also a creature, and it would be a non-sense speaking of something before time started, for creation is now.

According to Augustine, the natural light of reason is a gift from God, who makes us capable to know and therefore to run the whole world, acting above the other beings in the whole of creation. Such a gift enlightens all human knowledge.

Again, words are the presence of the Second Person of the Trinity among people and they are the tools of knowledge. Growing in knowledge is proceeding in a deeper understanding on words and through them (as signs) in a deeper awareness of the whole world.

E. Illumination is a "natural" process of improvement.

The spiritual perspective of Illumination Argument does not denies the natural process of understanding. It is not a supernatural endeavor, but the full perspective of human process of being, the complete panorama of what being human consist of. Knowledge is the main characteristic of the human being: people are language.

According to Augustine, words are signs, which help communicating knowledge. People communicate through language. Nonetheless the contents of our thoughts are not totally determined by the words. The words help to refer to reality & experience. This is why the same expressions (or formulae) have not necessarily the same meanings for all attending on a same conversation. Every expression "speaks" according to the experience they refer to. It is another perspective of Aristotle's words that "every learning through discourse develops from previous knowledge." Each one has a different approach to reality, for each one has a different identity — That relationship to reality makes our own identity. Every discourse supposedly refers to some known reality. Language refers to facts and to the knowledge present in people.

It may happen that a discussion debates about things, the words of which never are pronounced. This shows that the Words as such are not the key of a conversation or a communication, but the reality they refer to is the key. It also happens that a so called conversation is in fact two mere parallel monologues. To have a true conversation includes listening to reciprocally. A mutual understanding is required. Here is why the best interlocutors are the best listeners. In any conversation there is some dissociation between language and thinking: each word speaks in proportion of the familiarity the listeners have on the dealt issue.

Language does not create reality. People do, i.e. an order does not create anything until someone obeys. Only when a discourse influences human facts we have a reciprocal impact between language and facts. Every new perspective on reality becomes a human issue through the adhesion of other people on the same issue. Words help people to produce new concerns, to improve on managing reality. Changes depends more on the capability of people to change. Greatest changes are produced by conversion, not by a change of structure if people are not deeply changed inside. Contemplative life support active life, not the opposite. However there is complementarity between contemplative thinkers and the surrounding community.

Words reveal issues that are already present in the mind. A word cannot introduce new ideas: they all are introduced by facts. A teacher produces in his/her students nothing but issues that had some latent presence in their mind. Looking for truth is a personal process inside of our own mind. No one else can enter in such a personal process of knowing or learning. Teachers suggest only. No teacher can replace the concern of a student for the truth. The Truth, which lies in student's soul, is what a teacher is supposed to make emerge in his/her mind. Aug. gives the example of preaching the Gospel. In his prologue St. John says: "He was not the light but witness of the light." Every improvement towards the truth supposes a previous knowledge. Good teachers stress and start from student's previous knowledge, using examples, analogy, study case, common pattern, etc.

Human souls are properly able to share eternal truth. In our precarious bodily existence, we share imperishable thoughts. Eternal truths or everlasting thoughts cannot be a product of our own precariousness; we cannot generate them. Such kind of imperishable thoughts, ideas, and truth cannot come from a precarious human being and must come from above. No one can get them if the above truth does not reveal itself, does not make her known to people. All along his life Augustine has been seeking the ultimate reason of things. His endeavor became almost a failure when finally he met St. Ambrose in Milan. He went to Milan to fight the doctrine of Ambrose and it was the wisdom of Ambrose who won his mind and his soul.

Jesus is the revelation of the Father. He is the Way, the Truth, and the Life. Any truth is a sharing of God's Truth. Any word belongs to the second person of the Trinity. Every process of improving in knowledge is a way to enter more deeply in Trinity life: we are successively source, minister, relationship of the truth. Human act of knowledge is part of Creation process: it is the human answer to Creation. Any experience of knowledge is part of the betterment described by St. Paul: "Everything belongs to us, we belong to Christ, and Christ belongs to God." It is proper to say that we may only speak through the Second Person of the Trinity. When we speak we belong to the one who is the Word. We speak properly the truth if inside of us it is Jesus, who is the one who speaks. And every time it happens for us to say the truth, like St. Peter in Mt 16.16, we need to be taught from above. Doing so we become another word in the one who is the Word. And through Jesus Christ we enter inside of Trinity life.

This includes a new step of spiritual life, which involves the whole community we belong to and is the body of Christ. We are either expression of the truth (Jesus) or related to her (Mary). Everything that makes us more ONE, fresh, young is related to her. Vice versa the truth makes us integral part of the mysterious game of Love: God is love. God is the only Master inside of the Mind. He is *Pater intelligibilis lucis* (Father of the intelligent light), *Pater illuminationis nostrae* (Father of our own enlightening). "He is nearer to our soul than our own cloths are near to us. "God is nearer than our own body" — Becoming aware of that is correct and amazing enlightening.

God is the one who introduces with our souls all divine ideas, and continues to do so. The process is both somehow natural and somehow divine: we are made for the truth and the truth makes us what we deeply are. We need the truth we are made for. The natural seeking of truth wants to meet with the everlasting truth. Getting the ideas of things, *"formae,"* species, *rationes, regulae*, etc. is both a natural want, and the integral step of the course of creation, in which the continuous action of God requires our participation. The process through which sensible objects awake our souls into God's ideas is named **Illumination Argument**, for it is a mystical relationship with the truth.

This process requires humility and the capacity to continuously die (carrying our cross) to our own opinions in order to move further towards the truth of the facts.

F. The Theory of Illumination in Saint Bonaventure

Bonaventure disregards one of the keys of Augustinian Illumination (intimacy with the Word) to stress more systematically the triune configuration of the macrocosm and microcosm moving towards the end times from inside, outside and upside. According to Etienne Gilson St. Bonaventure retained the basic Platonic configuration of Augustinian Illumination, adding both insights from St. Francis and Aristotelian principles in a more cosmologic perspective.. Bonaventure underlines three sources of illumination: inside of us, outside and above. They all lead us to God. He believe that the "light" which is quoted above is the same that Augustine refers to. He says, "This is the light of Eternal Truth, since our very mind is formed immediately by Truth Itself'". St. Bonaventure stresses how "the outward, inward, and upward light leads to glory, praise, and honor of the Father, Son, and Holy Spirit."

G. Epilogue

At the time of Augustine's death the Vandals are at the door of Hippo, and the Goth are pushing at the borders of the Roman Empire, some of them have even broken into Rome City. In 410 the Visigoth ransomed the Capitol, Center of the Urbs (Rome). Previously, the whole of the Roman society had been developing a period of opulence which favored decadence. In less than a century the whole configuration of the Western Roman world will be destroyed. Nonetheless Augustine wisdom will survive and help culture to survive the struggling days. He was the last great thinkers of the dying empire and it is then the builder and forerunner of the culture to come.

Aristotle

Ambrose

Albertus Magnus

Aquinas

Bonaventure

Section Two

Gnoseology

A. Gnoseology or theory of Knowledge

1. Both indicate the same: it is the study of **the way we know**. In other words: how does it happen that we move from ignorance up to knowledge? How do people become aware of reality around them? First step of investigation on knowledge is to go through the steps of awareness. Gnoseology is the study of the human process of knowing. It includes all aspects. It is the study of a very common human activity, which de facto, we are not so easily aware of.

2. Etymologically "Theory of Knowledge" (from "Theory" (*Qewria*) = pilgrimage, processing, observation) indicates any serious speculation on how knowledge comes up. It is also called Gnoseology (from "Gnosis" (*gnwsis/sews*) = knowledge, and Logos (*logos*) = discourse).

3. Theory of Knowledge investigates on the relationship between subject (the one who knows) and object (what is known). It considers what kind of presence are the things in our mind and the way they emerge in us as sensitivity first and finally as knowledge.

4. The process of knowledge is the typical behavior of people. It is what make people human. A human being is language. There are two steps in such a behavior, first a natural process, which study belongs to metaphysics, then a supernatural process, our constant communication with above, which study belongs to theology. Please do not confuse the natural process of understanding with the spiritual gift of "understanding" which transfigures the whole process and makes people divine being: never address in metaphysics what does belong to theology (beyond "natural theology").

B. Sensorial acquaintance

1. **Sensation or perception is grasped immediately** by each sense, according its proper specificity:
- Touch apprehends consistency, temperature, texture, roughness, and superficiality of things (feeling)
- Smell gets the chemical and physical emanations of bodies (odors)
- Taste distinguishes the chemical or physical composition of aliments (flavor)
- Hearing seizes intensity and frequencies of air vibrations produced by objects in motion (sounds)
- Sight discerns shape, luminosity, and colors of objects (images)

2. **Sensation is a direct contact** with particular facts and objects. Human beings have no way but sense to be connected with the world. This is why Aquinas affirms, "We have no knowledge about what we have no experience." Such sensorial acquaintance involves actions, reactions, emotions, reflexes, instinctive behaviors, passions, etc. This is why methods of learning tend to be interactive to be more effective.

3. **U.S.O.** — Unidentified Sensorial Object — is the first level of any perception. At first we perceive the presence of items, which we do not identify immediately. Then the cooperation of different senses, acting together, gives identification of the item.

4. **All perceptions working together produce "internal sensation"**, which is the coordination in the mind through which people reach the point of identification of things (their image). We get the sensorial awareness of objects or facts through the confluent activity of two or more senses. This coordinated sensation is also known as internal sensation, for it happens inside of the mind.

5. Such acquaintance ends up the process of perception. It is the gathering of images we have in our mind from senses. **Image** is the trace that perceptions leave in our mind — each

sense prints a proper trace of each perception that concurs to the elaboration of the image of an item. Technically speaking we could say that "image" is the first word of sensorial knowledge.

6. Beyond images: **Memory** is the permanent trace in our mind of two or more connected images. **Imagination** works with images. **Creative imagination** does not exist; it is nothing but association of existing images. It could be a creative combination of them.

7. Knowledge through senses is the characteristic of animal knowledge. It is the first stage of human knowledge. Note that Sensorial acquaintance is an **immaterial act** of capture of material and sensorial reality.

8. Senses do not read surrounding informations, they write them into the mind, where intelligence are reading what they are. Senses provide images and nothing more. Intelligence read in images what they are: through abstraction intelligence provides understanding of images. In other words we may say that senses provide the fact, intelligence get their understanding.

C. Where IDEAS come from

1. Similarly to images which come both from things and from senses (they are the impression that things make on our senses), ideas have a double origin: they are the product of images and intelligence (they are the impact that images produce on intelligence – intelligence reads images as well as senses perceive things). In the same way that senses get information under their own expertise: sounds (ears), shape (eyes), color (eyes), taste, touch consistency… intelligence get inside of images the whatness of things. Intelligence is capacity to read inside of things (through their images) what they are.

2. Suddenly a gap is made. Our capacity of understanding leads our mind to read through the images what things are, their whatness, their essence. Intelligence reads inside of facts through their images in our mind. From the images the mind

produces ideas. An idea is the extraction, actually called abstraction, of the universals characteristics hidden inside of things. Every idea ultimately identifies some kind that the thing is Our Knowledge develops from a double source like the two legs of every walk: facts provide images and intelligence reads their universals; through the images the mind understands what things are. Intelligence identifies the teaching of facts. Such teaching is expressed in ideas, through words. To say that with an analogy: an idea emerges out of an image that intelligence made pregnant of it.

3. **Senses are first, they are necessary for intelligence and nonetheless senses are inferior to intelligence**. They offer the starting point of the process of knowledge they are not the cause of it. They are used by intelligence, almost like a brush is used by a painter. A brush is not the cause of a painting, but it is the tool used by the painter to make the painting. The brush is mediation between painter and painting as well as senses makes the connection of humans to surrounding reality. Without senses we cannot communicate as well as without brush (or fingers) the painter cannot paint.

4. As its immaterial expression ideas are concepts. They need a sensorial expression to be used in the mind (with reasoning) and transmitted to other people: the words are the physical expression of ideas, and sentences make more elaborated concepts.

D. Rational Knowledge

5. To say it again with other words… Intelligence addresses sensorial issues in a deeper understanding. Senses are only the medium while intelligence gets the insights, almost like a TV decoder gets the contents of a cable. Without the cable, the TV set would not work, however the TV is more sophisticated than the cable. In our mind, intelligence is almost like a canvas which receives, through the brush, the genial work of a painter.

The canvas could not exist without the brush and nonetheless expresses much more than the brush could do. Every creature expresses itself to our senses, but our intelligence is able to get the traces of the creator in them.

6. Again, **Abstraction** uses senses, depends on senses, starts through senses, and nonetheless it is integral part of a process of knowledge which is **superior to acquaintance by senses**. Such dependence from senses produces a higher level of awareness of things and a better intimacy with things. Intelligence is a deeper contact with the whatness of things even if it is not a direct contact. It brings knowledge to a universal level.

7. Inside ("intus") of images, human intelligence (from "*intus-legere*") reads or selects ("*legere*") what things are, i.e. the being, the whatness of things. This process of "extraction" of essences from existing items is named "abstraction". In the same way that sight get images, hearing gets sounds, smell get odors, taste get flavors, inside of our mind intelligence get the nature of things, their essence. We must be aware of the specificity of intelligence, which characteristic is to get the whatness of things.

8. Rational knowledge is not a direct apprehension of reality; it is an indirect capture of things through their meaning, which is get inside of their images. Such capture is mediated through senses. Knowledge is an indirect contact with things. Abstraction is the process of identification of what is intelligible in things - which we are aware of through senses (images). – Intelligence provokes a higher level of awareness on reality. Fruit of this abstraction is the whatness, essence, concept or else "idea".

9. Like senses produce images (the gathering of images composes sensorial acquaintance), intelligence produces ideas (the gathering of ideas build up knowledge). Images provide description, ideas offer definitions. Through ideas rational knowledge emerges above sensorial acquaintance.

10. Each **Idea** is said by a word. Each idea or concept is

properly a basic "word" of rational discourse. Composition of two or more ideas forms a proposition or **judgment**. Two or more judgments compose reasoning. A gathering of reasoning makes a discourse. Every **discourse** is the formalization of thought. We think through words in a discourse.

E. Intelligence Breathing

1. Initially knowledge comes from experience and education, which teach how to understand experience, and introduce to language a civilization. Experience and education interact accordingly and improve knowledge. After a while such improvement in rational awareness has formed a patrimony of knowledge in our mind. Then people never stop to improve by reflecting on the knowledge they already own, or getting more from experience.

2. So, a concept (or idea) may come from a previous discourse, as the result of a previous reflection, independent of experience (at that time). It is called *a priori* (anterior to experience). — Dealing with a priori contents, a judgment is **analytic**, and the corresponding reasoning is **deductive**.

3. A concept (or idea) may be the result of experience. It is called *a posteriori* (after experience) — trying to "comprehend" the intelligible contents of experience from a posteriori ideas a judgment is **synthetic**. A composition of synthetic judgments forms an **inductive** reasoning.

4. **Intelligence Breathing** is the constant process of moving from facts to concepts and vice versa. (1) **Induction** — When the concept comes from experience it produces a synthetical proposition, and an inductive reasoning and (2) **Deduction** — When the concept comes from general knowledge, it produces an analytic proposition and a deductive reasoning

5. Synthetic and analytic judgments are complementary. They need each other to fully comprehend, like we need two

legs to walk, we need to inhale and exhale to have respiration. A priori and a posteriori idea produce deductive and inductive judgments, and extend in deductive and inductive reasoning. They are the two waves of every process of thinking. These two waves are constantly interacting. They represent the "breathing" of intelligence.

6. In this context we must stress the complementarity between intelligence and reason, or intuition and demonstration… Intelligence as previously said is the capacity to grasp to get to synthesize to have a vision on things. Reason is the capacity to deal with details, causes, characteristics, perspectives that make things what they are. In every process of demonstration inductive and deductive there is also interaction between intelligence and reason.

7. There is not a field of knowledge that uses only one of the two waves. Even science, where deductive reasoning looks predominant involves induction, too. As soon as you see numbers you know it is arithmetic (induction) or you see a figure and you know the roles of geometry do apply (induction again)

8. There is more: every concept coming from previous knowledge provides analytics propositions or arguments, every experience provides synthetic arguments. Synthetic propositions make an inductive reasoning, while analytic propositions provide a deductive reasoning. In every context of knowledge, inductive and deductive reasonings work together.

9. It is said sometimes that science is deductive while art and humanities are inductive. It only shows that in each field there is sometimes a predominant wave, nonetheless intelligence works always with the full exercise of intelligence: we cannot walk with one leg only, we need both. It is the same with reasoning: it always needs to work both ways.

F. Reason & Love make true knowledge

1. Knowledge is awareness of facts; it involves humility, rea-

son, and love. As such the term "knowledge" is ambiguous, for philosophers uses it under different meanings: it may indicate reason, comprehension, and what we know. Grounded knowledge indicates scientific expertise. As a process of awareness it is synonymous of reason and needs love to exist in fullness. Sometimes, knowledge is taken as the mere process of understanding by the only faculty of intelligence; it is then identified with reason.

2. Philosophy is "love of wisdom." Beyond knowledge, wisdom is intimacy with truth. Such an intimacy involves companionship, amicability, conviviality, and confidence. So, philosophy is love of being intimate with the truth. At the start, wisdom requires love and knowledge. To be proper a study of gnoseology must include the whole process of moving towards the truth, which involves all human faculties: "We must go to the truth with all our soul" - Plato.

3. Reason & Love are the two essential faculties of people. They are interdependent, in a reciprocal enrichment – they interact as a virtuous circle (the contrary of vicious circle). Both make a common endeavor: the more we love the more we understand. The more we know, the more insightful our love will be. To say so in a few words: We understand better what we love and we love better the truth we know.

4. As the body needs two legs to walk, a person needs intelligence and willpower to grow up; these two aptitudes transform us from an individual into a person. Love wants Goodness as Intelligence wants Truth. Love seeks value, intelligence seeks facts. They interact to one another.

5. Philosophy is the science which combines the two. That is to say, philosophy is Love of Wisdom (Pythagoras), which means: going to the Truth with all our strength (Plato). In the same perspective, philosophy is also said as "the art of putting intelligence at the service of love" (Marie-Dominique Philippe), or "the art of contemplating the Truth in order to bring the

world back to the Truth" (Maritain), such activity of knowledge is source of action.

6. Love is capacity to address the other, to grow in relationship, sharing up to unconditional love. Love is desire and capability of what makes me better, happier, more realized. Love is the desire to become all the reality surrounding me and to express it. Love is capability of self-denial to become another; it opens the way to know, for it is capability to get out of what we are to become another as different of what we are – without the process of becoming another, no knowledge is possible.

7. There are several degrees of love: Eros, love of friendship (the definition comes from Aristotle), agape, charity: (1) **Eros** is love at its physical level: Eros is pleasure, is enjoying a presence. It is the first step of love. It is a good start, which encourages going ahead. In his first Encyclical, Benedict XVI insists to express the beauty and goodness of Eros; (2) **Love of friendship** is its psychological level. To be expressed in fullness it must be reciprocal. Such a love, however, will be real if each side expresses unconditional love, then, the reciprocity explodes at the upper level of (3) **Agape**, which is love expressed and shared inside of a family, a community, a team, a solid group – It is the level of sociological love: where there is a collective, a common sharing... (4) **Charity** is love at its spiritual level: "*Deus caritas est*" = God is Charity (John, Augustine)

8. Love is not mere kindness not even good feeling. Looking at the different levels in which loves expresses itself helps to understand something more. When we deal with passion, we now understand that passion is only one of its possible expressions. There is more. Love reflects the exact nature and configuration of reality: all things interact with each other in a dynamic process. Looking at facts without love would be like trying to realize or perform some work without breathing, or like talking offering a lecture to a group of American people using a different idiom… It would be ridiculous and even dramatically wrong.

So, claiming to deal with truth without love would be absurd and perilous. This is why to have knowledge of something we must love that thing.

9. **Love and knowledge (as reason) continuously interact one another**: "Knowledge inflates with pride but love builds up" (1 Cor 8:1) — "In love and knowledge reasons are not the same" (Pascal) — "If I have all knowledge... but do not have love, I am nothing" (1 Cor 13:2) — "When love is lacking somewhere, sow love and you will get love" (Juan de Yepes).

G. Knowledge – Additional perspectives

1. **Knowledge** is a grounded conviction — In Plato's Theaetetus, it is a certainty supported by evidence.

2. **Intelligence** is the human aptitude of knowing — Etymologically "intelligence" comes from "*intus-legere*", which means the capacity to read or select (*legere*) inside (*intus*) of facts. Capacity to grasp the understanding of facts. Capacity to get the whatness of things.

3. Intelligence exerts two different faculties which go along: **Reason**, which is the capacity to debate, to ponder, to reflect and **Comprehension**, which is the capacity to embody, contain, to realize, in other words to gather in one concept many different issues. Both comprehension and reason work continuously together towards full understanding.

4. Aquinas' definition requires a particular reflection: "**knowing is becoming the other** (the known object) **as another**, i.e. as different of the subject who knows. He stressed the kind of mystery that knowledge is, for it is the capacity to become another without ceasing to be what we are. It is the capacity to become "intentionally" another, to share in our mind another existence, without ceasing to be what we are. Even more, knowledge improves human being; it is a characteristic of every human being. Through knowledge we improve in what we are and become more and more capable to handle the world

around us.

5. There are different degrees of Knowledge according to the neighborhood of human activity people deal with, from sensorial knowledge, opinion (common sense or superficial beliefs), science, philosophy, theology, up to mystical knowledge. At every level it is still knowledge, but in a very different meaning. Scientific knowledge allows to work on the world around and to develop techniques which adapt according to people needs. This is why F. Bacon said "We command nature obeying its laws," so, knowing its laws make us capable to change the world we live in. This is why "knowledge is power."

6. In **mystical knowledge**, it happens the opposite: we are changed by the one we contemplate. With Nicolas de Flüe we may say: "God take me the way I am and make me the way you want." Mystical knowledge is real knowledge of spiritual entities.

H. Degrees of Abstraction

1. Definition: "abstraction" is extraction of the being out of things (through images). It is the capacity to identify in the mind "what a thing is" i.e. the **whatness**, or the essence of things. It is called **idea** or **concept**. Righly speaking philosophers distinguish four degrees of abstraction. We say it roughly because we may considerer more distinctive differences in the process of abstraction. Nonetheless generally speaking philosophers use to make four essential steps:

2. **First degree** of abstraction is opinion — See Plato and the allegory of the Cave in the Republic. It is the step when we move from mere reaction to the circumstances into the capacity to speak. At first we enter in the field of Common Sense expressing opinions and dealing with them. First degree of opinion is when we enter into the dimension of language. At this steps almost full language is equivocal.

3. **Second degree** is identification of general nature of things (genders, species, natural laws). Natural law identifies

typical relationship between beings – It is actually the proper specificity of thinking to do so. It identifies diverse characteristics of things out of their individual existence. This degree of abstraction is particularly evident in **physics**, when formulas identify connections between entities without considering the specificity of those entities like speed (relation between time and distance independently of the entity that moves, whatever it is a cat, a dog, a horse, a car, or a plane) weight, temperature, resistance, attraction, etc… At this degree of abstraction, we deal with scientific formulae which are proper concepts that cannot be misunderstood. There language is univocal.

4. **Third degree** of abstraction is identification of individualities (numbers, figures,). It provides all scientific language which use **mathematics** (arithmetica, geometry, astronomy) and so on. Language is at the top of univocity.

5. **Forth degree** of abstraction is identification of essence (**metaphysics**, First science, natural theology). There we get concepts or entity which essence is richer than the same language. Here is why, in philosophy, esp. metaphysics, uses analogy to be consistent. We say that its language is analogous.

6. Strictly speaking, beyond the metaphysical degree, there is no more abstraction but it is revelation. Above knowledge is less a typical process of abstraction than a typical capacity to listen from above — See Maritain in the *Degrees of Knowledge* — It requires the humility of intelligence to accept a higher light and understanding.

7. Mystical and spiritual degrees of knowledge start from there. It is another human dimension as deep and spectacular as a new birth as Jesus said to Nicodemus. It is a new birth in the sense of a new kind of life, similar to the spectacular change that happens to a baby from the womb of its mother to outside delivery — Mystical knowledge also refers to the human knowledge of God.

I. The Division of Speculative Science

1. According to Aquinas in the comment to Boethius, which translated into Latin the Greek text of Aristotle, Speculative Science is a generic definition to indicate the whole field of grounded knowledge. It includes all sciences, because all of them need the usage of human reason, together with some additional faculty: observation, imagination, intelligence… They are called speculative sciences because they involve speculation, reasoning, reflection, discourse, demonstration, and so on.

2. The diverse specificities included in speculative science embody physics, mathematics, philosophy, metaphysics, and divine science.

3. Such a panorama of knowledge does not include the study of Revelation. According to Aquinas, Revelation includes the Holy Scriptures (the Bible), the Tradition of the church, , the example and insights of the Saints, and the teaching of the Magisterium. Such a study is properly speaking theology. Because theology works with Revelation it is not included in the Speculative Science. Only, divine science, or natural **theology**, which does not refer to Revelation but to the same sources of metaphysics, is included in the Speculative Science.

4. Aquinas distinguish for each science, according its degree of abstraction, its specificity, the nature of its object, and the method used by the human being to do it. We will follow this process even if Aquinas does it differently, studying first the degree of abstraction, then the specificity of each knowledge and finally their respective method of study. To make easier the reflection to the student we will approach all aspects of each science, one by one.

5. **Physics**, or natural science does not study some "abstraction" as such but the facts and the natural items.

6. The field of physics includes biology, botany, anatomy, zoology, …. and properly speaking physics at such

7. **Mathematics**, There are obviously intermediary studies

which use is extraction of essence out of the being. It is the capacity to identify in the mind "what a thing is" i.e. the **whatness**, or the essence of things. It is called **idea** or **concept**.

J. The Range of human Knowledge

1. It would seem curious for a few that there is a range of knowledge for people, as there is a range of sight (not too near, not too far), a range of watching (not too bright, not too dark), a range of sensibility to the colors (from infra red to ultra violet), a range of sounds that people are able to perceive (most animals have a better audible perception than people) etc. Similarly, there is *de facto* a range of knowledge

2. Like for our senses the capacity to know of our mind moves between two limitations: the opacity of matter, and the hyper-intelligibility of the spirit… There are some material issues that remain out of reach of people, like there are some spiritual issues which remain in the mystery of God.

K. The Purpose of Knowledge

1. Rational acquaintance provides power. "We command nature obeying its laws" — Francis Bacon.

2. Knowledge is a tool in our life, not its ultimate purpose. Knowledge must be at the service of life. In such a perspective, knowledge helps people to blossom especially with love (see "Love and knowledge"). Knowledge may end up in contemplation — which cooperates to the work of creation.

3. Such a power that knowledge is must be put at the service of human blossoming. Such exercise of knowledge is properly what Marie-Dominique Philippe calls philosophy, "Philosophy is the art of putting intelligence at the service of the heart."

Section Three
The Tree of Wisdom
Historical survey

The Tree of Wisdom refers to the human patrimony of wisdom as evidenced by the whole history of philosophy since the beginning of the human endeavor seeking for the truth. All main topics and waves of philosophy along its history are pieces, or branches of the Tree of Wisdom.

(A) ADDITIONAL TOPICS
1. Can a Discourse Lead to the Truth?

According to René Descartes, truth depends on my thought ("*Cogito ergo sum*" — I think therefore I am) and from a proper idea it depends its own existence. So reality depends on a coherent and consistent discourse. If we admit with Descartes that it depends of the discourse to get the Truth, we should ultimately recognize that Truth does not exist by itself and it is only a "subjective" issue, i.e. the issue developed by the speaking subject. Then "truth" will become just an opinion.

On the opposite, from Emmanuel Kant, objective reality (*Noumenon*) cannot be reached by any thought. We only can reach its expression or "phenomenon". Then a discourse is never supposed to reach the truth, it only can get something else. Both philosophers lead to a position which finally refuses to deal with the truth.

In such a perspective Friedrich Nietzsche says: "there is no truth, there are only interpretations," even when they are referring to facts — Then, a discourse will be poor or rich in proportion of the quantity of meaning or interpretation it discloses! In both cases "no truth can be disclosed by any discourse" we only can say what we feel, we experience, we know. From there on the only issue to get some truth is the way opened by Husserl, called phenomenology, which deals with our experience of knowledge, due to the fact that "when we know, we know something." Our mind is intentionally directed to something. Such intentionality is the key of what we can be aware of. So on side contemporaneous philosophy has almost given up its investigation on truth.

On another side, a scientific approach would pretend that Logic is in Charge of Truth. Only what is logical can be true. The question was investigated previously in this Note, dealing with the identity of "Logic.". We concluded saying that Logic is supposed to be an excellent servant of truth, but pretending to submit truth to logic would be a fatal mistake for our civilization.

Logic is propoedeutical to the truth. It is not the castle where truth should be kept prisoner. Between the two opposite pretensions: the one which claims of not knowing the truth (contemporary thinkers) and the one which subordinates truth to the discourse (wrong interpretation of logic & scientific approach of reality which pretends to replace philosophy, like Auguste Comte (1852) or Jacques Monot (1962) the only realistic approach of facts is **critical realism** which invites philosophy to recognize the necessary humility of intelligence addressing reality in order to get some truth, following the words of Shakespeare, "there is more in the world than in my mind."

Monot

Comte

2. Degrees of Knowledge and Degrees of Truth

In Jacques Maritain *The Degrees of Knowledge* we see the different option people have to address reality. It can be by opinion, by proved experience, by theory and experimentation (science), by speculative and spiritual reflection (philosophy), by Revelation, religious traditions, and scriptures (theology), or even by some personal experience of the absolute (mystique). At every level of knowledge it corresponds a different mode of talking (see definition of equivocacy, univocacy, and below of "analogy") and also a different consistency of truth.

Each science has its own language and addresses reality under a typical different perspective. Somehow, every science has its own definition of truth, which requires consistency with the rules of its investigation and with the configuration of its own formulas.

Such different "perspectives of truth" has been classified according to the quality of investigating reality, going from the poorest to the most insightful. Such categorization was improperly said "Degrees of Truth" – It indicates the degrees of investigating on reality

An issue that could appear the rule at a level of investigation may be contradicted at a superior level, like in the example of "life" – It is not the same to talk about life for a plant, for an animal, a human person, a pure spirit (Angel), or God. The word "life" remains the same in spite of very different meanings, which nevertheless are connected. There is a kind of similarity in spite of effective unlikeliness. Such proceeding by degrees inside of a same issue, progressing by intensity of meaning is said "**analogy**."

Life is "analogically" similar for a plant and a human even if it is not identical. Nonetheless the same word defines the activity of both. People use the term "analogous" to indicate many degrees of compatibility between very different meanings (or truths) concerning identical issues existing in different degrees of existence. It is the case for justice, intelligence, being, beauty, good, etc. Such issues may have very different meanings according to the situation they refer to and nevertheless they also remain the same and fit with the term which is used to say them: the good of a tree (ecology) is not identical with the good of a person (individual blossoming), and with the good of the society (economy, family, globalization), and "good" remains appropriate in all cases. They all are supposed to go together accordingly (common good) even if they offer at each level a very different configuration.

Unlike analogous, equivocal is a change of identity while there is some confusion of words.

Also univocal cannot change of density of meaning like analogous but remain the same.

For such a reason many philosophical concepts are addressed by analogy. This is the reason why a scientific discourse cannot replace a philosophical one, to say the less. The same should be said about equivocality even if, philosophy needs common sense and science to be consistent. This is an issue to develop later.

3. Science and Philosophy

Teaching **science** requires, at every generation, recurrent updating, which includes the rejection of many previous obsolete methods and theories. As well as science, philosophy needs to be constantly upgraded. Science updating influences changes in philosophy, too. Philosophy needs current acquaintance on sciences and all fields of knowledge. The roots of philosophy are in all aspects of human culture: "Everything is human concerns me" (Seneca). Philosophy started together with the development of sciences and arts. Without a tight science background there is no authentic philosophy. Vice versa, without philosophy science may lose its own identity. Nonetheless,

Philosophy reaches the truth in a more consistent manner than science. Every science book older than a generation (25 years) or even less, is already obsoletes and, eventually, has only an historical value. Oppositely ancient books of philosophy, even the ones older than two millenniums, are still valid today, and may help us to understand human people, civilization, and the nature of things. In fact we still read with amazement the works of Plato and Aristotle.

In this neighborhood, **it is essential to understand that philosophy is not a subjective discourse**, or an intuitive knowledge of the unknown. Oppositely, it is the full knowledge of reality, beyond science and behind theology. While science uses theories and checks them with the facts by experimentation using mainly the faculty of reason, mostly as an extension of the abstract language of mathematics, and addresses pieces of facts or general perspectives on them, philosophy uses personal observation, available intelligence, and capacity of discernment to address the whole in its entireness. Science uses symbols, addresses problems where objects are not real (when you have to solve a problem about how many fruits will make a sum of pears, peaches and apples, it does not count if these apples are unripe or seasoned, red or golden, for a scientific problem deals with symbolic apples not with real ones... Philosophy is nearer to reality than science for it addresses the facts without rational prejudices (theories) or symbols and address a fact as is. So it is the task of philosophy to direct science toward a better performance and usage at the service of people.

The main waves of modern and contemporaneous philosophy shows that if we try to get in philosophy the same sort of certainty that we obtain in science, we confuse thoughts and reality, we lose our capacity to deal with truth, and cannot make the necessary distinction between life and knowledge – and fall in a complex field of contradictions. Unlike science – in which all discoveries are solutions, which end up a research – every discovery makes philosophy increase the intimacy with truth and enhance its research. Philosophy offers higher certainty than science. We may say that as well as science improves technology, philosophy improves culture. Both are indispensable to correctly address reality, like two legs are necessary for every human being to walk.

To say so otherwise, Philosophy is a method to reach the truth. It has many branches that depend on what questions are asked, or the field of interest. Philosophy can be considered as the intimacy with the truth (General philosophy & metaphysics). This involves the whole person as well as all of their surroundings associated with that person. It is not a specific, but more of a generalized approach that applies to the mass. Philosophy is not dated; it applies today as it did centuries ago. Philosophy looks for ways of explaining the big picture - how does everything fit together.

4. What is real? Is there a Reality?

It seems easy at first to say that reality is what does exist. Reality comes from real. So, reality should be the neighborhood of what is real. According to Plato, Aristotle, Aquinas, and most philosophers, "Reality exists even when I do not know it." Also reality may offer different aspects and even change. Also reality is what stands under appearances. From such a statement we may provide the definition that reality is what things actually are.

Well, it is not actually so easy to say it. Martin Heidegger stresses the gap between facts and language. It relates to that popular question, which each of you in the course are familiar with: "If a tree falls in the woods and nobody hears it, did it really make a sound?" In the same respect if a bird chirps - but you even do not understand the meaning of the word "chirp", is it really happening? Or does a run bubble if nobody hears it? Yes, it occurs. It happens, even when nobody is able to properly refer to it. Things happen, even without a clear understanding of them. Knowledge follows the facts.

Heidegger also stresses that thinks happen but only people know it. At dawn and setting the sun makes gorgeous colors in the sky, the sun does not know it, people know and appreciate. The clouds make incredible shapes in the sky, they even announce through their shape the coming weather; the clouds do not know it, people know. A bird shows beautiful shapes, behaviors, and color… it is not sure what is the level of conscience that animals are aware of about their own behaviors, nonetheless people know such behaviors and study them… Heidegger defined people as the kind of being by which the whole world is aware of itself. It can be said that a human being is the being through which reality becomes knowledge.

In the society there is a tight connection between knowledge and facts. Economy is the field when opinion creates facts. When for some reason people believe that some food will be missing, they all try to purchase it and prices grow up. Similarly there is no reason to know why gas and food prices are going up and down. They move the same. Isn't it? Is there somebody able to monitor and manage price speculation? Even if nobody does it, prices continue to go up and down. Did a car accident happen if nobody witnessed it? Aren't you a thief when nobody sees you? It is not the quality of language which makes the consistency of facts. Language only refers to our awareness of the facts, not on facts as such. This is a first important step about language, knowledge, and facts. There is some flexibility in between.

Some philosophy currents which do not recognize to people the capacity to know the facts, or recognize to them only a partial capacity of it, like idealism, existentialism, materialism (which ignores spiritual facts), phenomenology, structuralism, deconstructionism, etc. These currents state that "facts are what I know!" In such a case there is no possibility at all to provide a definition of what is knowledge, because for them facts do not exist out of the mind. Therefore there is not such a thing that reality. Following them, we must agree with Nietzsche, "There are no facts, there are only interpretations." At this point, what a word signifies indicates my awareness on facts, not the facts as such. Saying so about those philosophy waves, I wanted just to quote here these theories to make more precise what reality is... I leave to further investigation more discernment on those theories. According to such perspective nobody should exist before I know them, which is clearly doubtful. Very roughly, I would only say at the moment that there is the fact that such theories exist, even when I do not know them. Similar statement confirms our previous position that facts must exist before I know them.

Yes, there is flexibility between language and facts. Such flexibility indicates how far we are from the truth (see below about **Truth**). It happens the opposite, when we are speechless before some event. In this context we also should recall that contemplation is the capacity to look at reality even when we are unable to say it.

5. Aristotle's and Aquinas' Method of "Critical Realism"

Let us stress again that Critical Realism is the so called method of inquiry started by Socrates, and then developed by Aristotle, Aquinas, Maritain, Gilson, Guitton, Daujat, Garrigou-Lagrange, Sertillange – to name just a few, based first on facts and second using intelligence. Critical realism accepts the priority of reality on knowledge: while idealism accepts only what I know, Critical Realism agrees with the fact that even if I do not know you, you may exist...

Such a method suggests that every philosophical inquiry must consider the facts, pay attention to possible pieces of information, perceive comments about, and examine related discourses... even those we dislike. Critical Realism is a method which observes everything and then reflects personally on collected data... We must go beyond the trap of the words in order to discover the solution inside of the contemplation of the mystery of reality.

When we are facing some aporetic question or contradictorily statement, we must seek a higher level of experience, which offers a more homogeneous perspective, a more insightful sight on it.

Critical realism is not naïve realism. (See Maritain's *Degrees of Knowledge*) for it rejects the view of naïve realism that the external world is as it is perceived. In the same way, Critical realism does not correspond to any of the following theories, which make an improper use of "realism" like Metaphysical realism, which holds that there exists a mind-independent reality. In scientific realism this reality is the material world; in theological realism this reality is the material world and also, primarily, God; Semantic realism, which holds that science and theology contain propositions, that is statements capable of being true or false in the sense of correspondence to the reality to which they refer. In scientific realism the focus is on propositions about unobservable entities; in theological realism the focus is on propositions about God; Epistemic realism, which holds that it is possible to put forward propositions that are approximately true, that some propositions actually are approximately true, and that belief in their approximate truth can be justified. In scientific realism this applies primarily to theories and theoretical propositions about unobservable entities; in theology it applies to propositions and theories about God.

Section Four
Historical Survey

All along history, doctrines on knowledge were elaborated by philosophers... Here is a short selection which allows having a synthetical survey.

1. **Platonic Realism** (Plato, Malebranche) affirms that universal ideas exist in themselves in an ideal world. Knowledge consists in awaking and remembering (collection argument) the formal world our soul belongs to.

Malebranche

Critique: Platonician Realism reduces consistency of present life to mere appearance and believes in a previous life of the soul. Soul is a prisoner of the body.

2. **Empiricism** (David Hume — 1711-1776) states that everything stand in experience and experimentation. However there is two stages of empiricism, those who believe that above mere experience there is a human capacity to learn and understand (like Locke) and those (like Hume) who claim that out of experience we do not know anything and deny consistency of science.

Hume

Locke

Critique: Empiricism stresses the consistent view that all knowledge comes from senses. Unfortunately it denies later the faculty of intelligence to grasp whatness from senses, to produce ideas from images, and reduce human knowledge to mere imagination. Ultimately, empiricism would consider knowledge as a human disease.

3. **Idealism** (Descartes, Kant, Schelling, Fichte, Hegel, Feuerbach, Marx, and Engels) affirms that universal ideas belong to the mind, which describes reality according to its own categories (especially time and space, which are innate ideas). Categories are the conditions in which our mind knows the surrounding reality.

Descartes *Kant* *Schelling*

Fichte *Feuerbach*

Marx & Engels

Critique: Idealism is contradicted by a few facts 1) children learn by education and do not know spontaneously through innate ideas; 2) If a human being was supposed to know everything according to the categories of time and space he/she could not have any notion of eternity; 3) If the mind was organized by innate ideas there was no room for cultural improvement through generations. Besides all civilizations should be the same.

4. Nominalism (Sophists, Boethius, Roscelin, Abelard, Okham, and most common contemporary waves in phenomenology, existentialism, structuralism, linguistics) upholds that intelligence works giving names to things. So knowledge is nothing but management of names (which are the same as ideas and concepts). Then language gives knowledge; if some language misses a name it is missing the corresponding idea.

Boethius

Abelard

Roscelin

Okham

Critique: Nominalism is insufficient to define the original work of intelligence. Nominalism just indicates the kind of knowledge which identifies things by names. Under specific training animals are able to do so. Before entering properly in the age of reason each growing child is for a while a little nominalist, who constantly asks: "What is this, what is that?"

5. **Existentialism** (Heraclitus, S. Kierkegaard, F. Nietzsche, A. Gide, A. Camus, J.-P. Sartre, Simone de Beauvoir, Gabriel Marcel, Georges Bataille, Karl Barth, Martin Buber, Karl Jaspers, Reinhold Niebuhr, Paul Tillich, Emmanuel Levinas, Maurice Merleau Ponty, Jean Wahl. The Sorbonne includes also Paul Tillich, Edmund Husserl and Martin Heidegger, and the school of phenomenology) expresses a philosophy crisis, when there is a lack of certainties, due to some dramatic changes in the society, mostly because of war. It upholds that intelligence must accept the facts before any speculative explanation, and eventually refuse any global doctrine. In other words, existentialist thinkers agree with Sartre that "existence precedes essence" and man is what he makes himself and, whatever he does, he is responsible for what he makes of himself. Existentialism rejects traditional metaphysics to stop at the anguish of existence. Among Existentialist thinkers there are famous atheist like Camus, Gide, and Sartre and great believers like Levinas and Marcel.

Kierkegaard

Nietzsche

Gide

Critique: When Ambassador in Rome, in 1947, Jacques Maritain showed how Aquinas' philosophy is a perfect complement to existentialism and overcomes it. He presented a series of lectures at the Angelicum under the title: "Aquinas Philosophy is existence philosophy" — Later, in 1964, after Sartre's publication, *l'existentialisme est un humanisme*, Maritain published *Le court traité de l'existence et de l'existant*, with the same purpose. Showing how, inside of existence we can and should get the **intuition of the being** which is the only one experience that make a thinker a true philosopher. Maritain identifies in such intuition the same cry of Kierkegaard on anxiety and anguish. He also stressed how the Aquinas **act of being** is a true discovery of existence as such. Maritain, however, stresses how inside of the precariousness of existence the being as such speaks. It is the duty of a philosopher to get it.

6. **Phenomenology** (Husserl, Heidegger, Merleau-Ponty, Gilles Deleuze) is an extension of existentialism. It is an attempt to emerge from the the limitations of idealism and existentialism with an attempt of near investigation on human experience during the process of knowledge. It is an interesting investigation, not sufficient however to provide a full asset of inquiry.

Husserl *Heidegger*

Merleau-Ponty *Deleuse*

7. **Critical Realism** must be recalled again among the theories of knowledge not because it is a doctrine or a theory among others but because it is a method that leads to a doctrine which make every theory better understandable. To say it with other words, Critical Realism recognizes the intentional presence of things inside of human mind and the work by which intelligence abstracts whatness (being = essence = ideas) out of real things. **Critical realism** means that in every investigation one is supposed to look at actual events and take all possible pieces of information, willingly receive suggestions, carefully prevent any discrimination, getting good advises and counsels, producing then an understanding with the best of our reflection to make a balanced conclusion. While Nominalism claims that various objects are labeled by the mind, which give them a name, and that the same terms have nothing in common but their name, for Nominalism denies the actual existence of universals, Critical Realism accepts the fact that other things exist, independently of my knowledge, and that everything that exist is understandable, for it carries its own intelligibility, and delivers its own whatness to the mind:. Critical Realism suggests that we are supposed to read inside of things what they are, with prudence, humility, and discernment. Doing so, we are able, from individual things, to get the universality of essences.

Critique: Critical Realism is not a system but a method leading to a doctrine. Any new investigation is not just a complement of the statements given previously by Aquinas but properly an updating of them, that is to say a new elaboration of them. Real followers of St. Thomas Aquinas are supposed to make today the work that Aquinas would like to perform if he was living today. Aquinas was suggested by Albertus Magnus to follow Augustine in theology and Aristotle in philosophy, which means to be consistent for convictions with Augustine and use Aristotle categories to properly express them. Following the example of Aquinas every Thomist should be a follower of

St. Augustine and a corrector of Aristotle, i.e. being consistent with the data of the Magisterium and finding a formulation which fits better with the civilization of our days.

Particular Appreciation: Critical Realism includes in its own investigation all the issues of present knowledge. There is no other philosophical system which is able to do so. Critical Realism makes the amazing endeavor of getting everything is consistent in every doctrine or philosophical system; it does not reject any statement without discernment. There is no a priori discrimination, but, at first, every study gets the benefit of the doubt. A study with CR provides the capacity to pick up what is consistent in every endeavor. The other waves of philosophy do not provide such a good result, for they exclude a priori everything does not fit with their own perspective and/or system. CR is an open field of investigation. A true Thomist today considers everything at new, not even using the conclusions of Aquinas, but making at new all analyses with the knowledge and maturity of our days.

(B) THE BIG MISTAKE

Like in a tree a branch does not contradict the plant, in the whole history of philosophy a philosopher does not contradict any one. He only is a new expression of wisdom in his days. It is the task of his followers to see his own contribution to the tree.

It would be a terrible mistake to consider that all philosophers contradict one another or each one is in contraposition to all the others. Oppositely all philosophers together compose the large tree of the human patrimony of wisdom.

Every philosopher's doctrine is an additional step towards wisdom. Every philosophy is a specific way leading to wisdom. Like all philosophers, all doors are different, but the heart of philosophy endeavor, wisdom is the same for all, for it is universal.

Section Five

The Knowledge of God

This is only a short approach of the question. It just stresses that knowledge involves the knowledge of God. That field of knowledge is known as **natural theology**. Obviously we cannot say a word in philosophy about what and how God knows. This topic belongs to the field of theology, which reflects on what God told us about it.

Philosophy does reflect on the absolute that God is. Philosophy addresses the one, which, according to the same words of Aquinas, "religious traditions call God."

Our own convictions on God by faith and religious experience is conforted by what philosophy is able to say about a true knowledge of God, based on human experiences and proper rational reasoning. We could not speak about **apophatic** knowledge if nothing could be said about it. Such experience is real and somehow every believer gets some acquaintance on it. If there was actually nothing to say, even the word "apophatic" did not exist and could not be said. Such expression of "apophatic" means that there is something we may experience and is above our own words, even if we have some awareness of it. Actually, even if it is difficult to express, something is known, and it is actually improperly, or "cataphatically", said. **Cataphatic** knowledge is what we are able to say and learn from an apophatic vison.

It is impossible talking about God without referring to the mystery and without bowing before such a mystery that God is. Without God the whole world becomes absurd. This absurdity that many philosophers talk about the whole of reality, like Nietzsche or Sartre did, shows nonetheless an evident contradiction: if everything is absurd how some thinking or reasoning remains possible? If without God the whole of the facts is mere absurdity the simple fact that I am able to say so shows that totally absurd it is not. If there is some meaning somewhere God, the one who give meaning to everything, is not fully missing. If it is so he must exist…

Talking about mystery we must address it properly as the upper limit of our intelligence. When mystery must be accepted and properly addressed, absurdity is unacceptable… for it is the denial of intelligence and the essence of things. It was with Kant that people started to say that the being as such cannot be known. Actually, if it cannot be known, how is it possible that I am able to refer to it? If I was unable to know it I also were unable to know that it does exist and totally ignorant of its own name… Because I know it and I have the idea of it something can and must be said about it.

Since Socrates, Plato and Aristotle, philosophy is the first science, concerning the world which extends beyond the physical and sensorial items, and we belong to. Actually something can be known about God and the many spiritual entities which populate the world.

Also Church experience is not mere human behavior; it is the exertion of living at the presence of God. The life of a religious congregation is the life of a community experiencing the presence of the one who said: "When two or three are gathered in my name, here I am in the midst." (Mt 18:20). If we truly believe, we also believe in such a promise. And if God is present our life experiences it. And in our intimacy with the Lord our senses are involved, as in every human endeavor. So there are things which are spiritual and can be properly experienced.

The experience of God is not mere faith. Faith leads our spiritual understanding, it does not replace it. Little by little, faith leads us to believe in what we know. And believing helps us to understand our own exertion of the experience of faith.

Sharing their personal experience of God, all saints made

us aware of what we can say and know about God. The more we know nature, the more we can change it (Francis Bacon). But the more we know God and the spiritual entities and the more they change us and make us "conatural" to the reality which is beyond us.

"God is love." Every experience of love is somehow an experience of God. When the Apostle John wrote that because we love our brother we pass from death to life… the experience of sharing and loving our neighbor is truly an experience of God. The best way to help people to know /god is to love them: we will never convert people talking about God unless they already are curious to know him (which means that they already felt his call). To make people believe in God we must make them know love, experience love, receive love. As John of the Cross said "Where there is no love, brings love and you will gather love," or, if you want to hear it with other words: "Where somebody does not know God, brings love and he will start to know God."

The first Christian communities were experiencing a strong presence of God among them. It was the presence of God inside the community (Mt 18:20) and was made explicit in the celebration of the Eucharist. The New Testament reports how that enlightening unity the pagans experienced uttered typical expressions of the extraordinary presence of God, like talking in tongue, prophecies, visions, ecstasy, etc… Curiously, the congregations gathering people converted from the Jews did not have similar manifestations of the presence of the Spirit. Commentators say that it is because Jews people were more familiar with the presence of the Holy Spirit in the community than those converted from the Greeks.

Shortly speaking the evidences of the existence of God can be summarized as it follows:

(1) Anselm proofs (Ontological evidence, Cosmological evidence)

(2) Aquinas 5 evidences of God's existence are made to

confirm the faith of believers, not to make belivers: conversion starts with a true interaction with God, not to convert people

(3) Existential evidences of God"s presence in Gabriel Marcel or even Jacques Maritain works the same: precariousness of human life cannot support the consistency of Christian community.

(4) Several other options emerge: they all belong to the same cause of conversion. It lies always in the mystery of personal intimacy with the Lord, like for Paul Claudel, Charles Péguy, Charles de Foucauld, Carlo Carretto, André Frossard ("*Dieu existe, je l'ai rencontré*"), and many others: being a believer is the result of a permanent miracle of such intimacy for all believers. It is somehow a repetition of the call of Abraham who is the Father of all believers. It is a repetition of the experience of St. Paul on his way to Damascus.

(5) Every personal experience… that could eventually be shared…

(6) Please note that "the God of philosophers" is not the one we share inside of Christian life. It is more likely a pagan god. Only sharing the mystery of Christ makes us Christians. Out of the Christian neighborhood the ontological Proof becomes inconsistent and became the opposite: from Sartre to Kant, and up to J.P. Sartre such ontological proof became source of atheism,

This means that inside of the exertion of faith there is a true experience of God and a true knowledge of God. Such experience is proper to the nature of people and supports the first evidence of the absolute meeting us.

Spiritual life is much more sophisticated than physical life. As an example, our relationship with the Father is different to the relationship with the Son, with the Holy Spirit, with Mary, the Mother of God (*Theotokos*), which the first Christians were so accustomed to and the traditions continued among the members of the Eastern Churches.

In regular life, every human relationship among people depends on the characteristics of the people who are in presence. Such original relationship becomes even truer for spiritual relationships. When we pray our experience of prayer get a totally different picture according to the one you are in touch, the Father, the Son… or your Guardian Angel… Prayer is not a standard behavior, but a precise exertion of a specific relationship.

Spiritual life is a kaleidoscopic neighborhood which is even more sophisticated than tangible human life. The physical world is extremely rich and various; the spiritual one is even more various and rich. We are invited to know and experience it right now.

I wish you a Good Endeavor

WHAT IS TRUTH?

While dealing with the section of Metaphysics called Critique, and specifically Gnoseology, which deals with the way people know, it is proper to reflect a little more on what TRUTH is. Such a topic does include the many perspectives which direct people towards the truth but also the fact that truth herself call us. Some have already been said in previous notes but, as the Romans said, "Repetita juvant" (It is useful to insist and repeat items).

Somehow Truth is mystery, or, if you wish, an **aporia**. According to Martin Heidegger, an "aporia" is a contradictory statement, which impossible to explain rationally but which is nevertheless true. In other words, it would be absurd to explain the truth: the more we meet her the more we understand her. As a result we must introduce the reader to her and let her show.

Read the note with your usual attention and "critique" and bring any concern or question you may have in class discussion. Thank you.

A. On Truth

The word truth is more familiar than our own capacity to understand it. We get the Truth "when the words we use to express our thoughts fit with the facts," Aquinas said. In Latin his words sound: "*Veritas sequitur esse rerum*". The truth that philosophy mainly looks for is metaphysical (beyond the mere physical) and spiritual. Concerning the highest spiritual entities, philosophy relies on theology. Spiritual truth is more than a simple fact. At physical level, people are supposed to interpret the facts to understand reality. At spiritual level, the facts are the lightening entities which lead our inquiry. A spiritual fact leads us. It changes us while we move into it. To summarize the discourse, we must say that when a philosopher addresses the truth, such a philosopher must be a contemplative, i.e. accept the eventuality that in the facts there is more to contemplated than to explain. Heidegger stated that true facts are self-evident and disclose more meaning than what we could say about them.

We must accept first the way the truth is. Then we are in conditions to understand it properly. It is a work of simplicity. Here we meet again the perspective of an ascetic behavior. We must grow in simplicity to get the quality of vision that truth deserves. As a result looking for the truth is a high endeavor. Sometimes it is more engaging to be simple than complicated or sophisticate. Simplicity is the key. It involves behaviors that clear the facts from everything is not essential, clear, consistent, plain reality. This is why philosophy seeks simplicity.

Looking for the truth does not consist first in an endeavor of search for it is primarily the patient endeavor or recognizing the truth which is already there, knocking at the door of our awareness. It is knocking at the gate of our souls both from outside and from inside. The truth is constantly knocking at the door of our conscience, where she dwells in. And the truth inside of us wants to meet the truth everywhere she is, at every time she shows up. Here is why the whole soul is involved. This is why, when we meet something true, the truth inside the soul enjoys meeting herself outside in the world.

At its highest quality level, truth meets what the Scholastics called the "analogates" of the Being, which are all the entities that are the Being in its higher quality of perfection (absolute). As the result, on the top, Truth is the One. So far it is one with justice, beauty, understanding, goodness, quality, harmony…

Nonetheless, before getting the truth in its absolute beauty, some steps must be done. Here is why a few steps are exposed below under the diverse perspectives truth is reached.

B. People are made for the Truth

We are made all for the truth: "You made us for you, ô Lord, and our heart is restless until it rests in you" — Augustine. That sentence supports Plato's words: "We must move to the truth with all our soul" and fits with René Le Senne: "We get wisdom by mastering ourselves". According to Aristotle, "Everyone wants the truth." People are configured for the truth and the truth builds them: "For truth makes us one!" — Chiara Lubich.

Lubich

According to Aristotle, people are made for the truth and want it naturally, whether they are aware of it or not. Referring to the truth as the absolute, Augustine "You made us for you, ô Lord, and our heart is restless until it rests in you." In other words: we are made for the truth and we must clean our heart and our soul from useless concerns and feelings in order to leave the way open toward the truth. It must be a peaceful behavior of letting heart and soul open to eternal values, which allow the truth to grow in us. Similar behavior is Socratic "maieutics" of delivering the truth, which is a dynamic endeavor which frees it from inside.

People are made for the truth. And the truth wants to meet us even more than we are looking for her. Augustine says that the truth is nearer to us than our own shoes. While discussing the issue with Prof. Giuseppe Zanghi, also known under his nickname of "Peppuccio" he insisted on the fact that the truth is above any definition, because it is with truth that we describe everything. He also used to recall me the words of, the Koran, which reads "The truth is nearer to us than our own jugular vein."

Pythagoras affirmed almost the same when he stated: "the diseases which ruin people come from their own deeds and, unfortunately, people are looking far away the answers, which lie inside of them." Pythagoras taught that all the goods and the keys of the universe are already written inside of us. As an outcome,, being a true philosopher requires first to be silent enough in order to listen to the truth which always speaks inside of people.

Seeking the truth is more a work of patience, of observation, of contemplation, of expectation, than a mere speculative action. It is almost a hunting adventure, when we expect the truth to show up at the right place… Truth is not a mere objective issue like the result of a scientific problem. It requires the constant endeavor of working properly, without the interference of concerns for things which are not appropriate. Actually it consists more in the process of letting the truth move accordingly and come to us. Maritain says "Truth needs more contemplation than understanding."

Most of the time people looked only concerned with the process of seeking the truth, while, actually, the truth wants to show up even more intensely than people are looking for it. The Book of Wisdom reads: " Desire therefore my words; long for them and you shall be instructed" (6,11) and "The one who watches for her at dawn shall not be disappointed, for he shall find her sitting by his gate" (6:14).

Too often we forget that the truth wants to meet us even more than we are looking for her. Augustine also states that the truth is nearer to us than our own shoes. When the Koran says that "The Truth is nearer than our own jugular vein." It recalls the Book of Wisdom stating that "it is useless traveling the whole world while the truth grows in us from inside". The distance is not geographical but spiritual.

Pythagoras said the same when he stated: "The diseases which ruin people come from inside of them, not from external observations: people are looking far away an answer, which they already are familiar with, for it lies inside of them." Pythagoras taught that all the goods and the keys of the universe are already written inside of us. As an outcome, to be a true philosopher requires first to be silent enough in order to listen to the truth which speaks inside. Here is why the main invitation of Socrates was, "*gnwti sewton*" (Know thyself)! Yes, in order to let the truth speak, we must be consistent with her in everything we do, in everything we are...

C. Loving the Truth

Loving truth is the key of every search of it. Philosophers are lovers of truth. Famous are the words of Aristotle: "I love my friend Plato, but I love the truth even more". Such a quote helps us to understand what metaphysicians call the pedagogy of truth... or propaedeutic of truth. We usually are attracted by the truth in some teaching, then, the more we seek the truth, and the more we understand her. This characteristic of truth will never be sufficiently stressed.

Aristotle received for 20 years Plato's teaching, at his school, **the Academy**, to the point to develop a great friendship with his master, Plato. Nonetheless the teaching of Plato increased in Aristotle his exceptional capacity of thinking and discerning. Plato's philosophy improved the reflection and the work of investigation of Aristotle. While he was far from Athens he also matured his own perspectives and doctrine. Turning back in Athens, 12 years later, he founded his own school, the Lyceum, where he made some adjustments to the doctrine of Plato:: the great intuition of Plato that there is some truth which things reveal to us remained as the great enlightenment about the truth, and Aristotle stressed it. Aristotle, however rejected Platonic hypothesis of a perfect world of ideas, in which people would have lived before coming on earth. Aristotle replaced it by the notion of species, essence, and nature of things. We get knowledge by observing the world all around, not by remembering a previous knowledge. The truth is still to be found through senses, but nothing is already put innately in our mind, the whole knowledge proceeds from investigation, sensorial activity and abstraction...

Plato woke up Aristotle in the process of learning. He taught him, started and improved the capacity of Aristotle to find the truth. Then, later on, Aristotle improved such capacity of understanding, he became autonomous. Here is where "loving for truth goes beyond the love for his master Plato". At the school of Plato, Aristotle learnt how to move towards the truth with all his soul, and eventually got his own way to get it. In Aristotle the way to the truth got improved. We may say that it was the faithfulness of Aristotle to the teaching of Plato who eventually induced Aristotle to be consistent with the truth and to make adjustments in Plato's philosophy. A few centuries later, Aquinas will do the same with Aristotle.

Aristotle's statement does not at all indicates that Aristotle disliked Plato: On the contrary he says "I love Plato…" Additionally such love is surely not a mere feeling or occasional emotion, for Aristotle had been the student of Plato during the most important time of his human formation while he was from 17 to 37 years old. Such a long time under Plato's teaching cannot have left Aristotle indifferent to his master and developed in Aristotle a great sentiment of gratitude for the knowledge he received. We also must stress that loving Plato and loving the truth had been for a while a same unique exertion. Slowly, but surely, the discovery of truth, made Aristotle aware of the difference between truth and Plato's philosophy… and without disregarding Plato, who remained his master forever, he just stressed the priority of truth above the philosophy of his master.

When taking the stairs to move to another floor we surely like and enjoy the stairs but a moment comes when we have to move on… As a more general panorama, we may say that every great philosopher needs a good teacher, a tutor to start his/her own reflection. Later on, the inquiry goes beyond the teaching that has been received from the instructor. Truly faithfulness to a teacher invites to go beyond instructor's teaching.

This example is a clear invitation for every student to let

personal wisdom show up. It is the Socratic method of 'metanoia' and 'maieutics', which consists, under the provocation of the words, to let the truth we hide inside to become explicit. Socrates' irony had the only purpose to invite his interlocutors to deliver the wisdom they had inside and they were not aware of yet. It is the same process that philosophy today should provoke in every student. Course material is the background, course activity is the training, sharing with peers does improve the teaching, but finally our whole life will be the field of blossoming of the course.

The sentence of Aristotle on Plato and truth could even be the paradigm of every study. Study is supposed to check the consistency of a course in order to avoid any mistake while progressing toward the truth. When we meet the truth, however, we forget the previous discourse, the reasons, the occasions, the insights, which led us to it and enjoy the presence of the truth. When we meet the truth we disregard the road which brought us to it and enjoy the meeting. "I love my friend Plato", who is the teacher who led me towards the truth, but when I get the truth I love her with all my soul and do not let my mind lost in distractions... For a philosopher loves the truth.

To make the previous reflection even clearer we may bring another analogy: the first time I drove towards Washington DC, where I wanted to visit the Capitol... I asked for directions, first to D.C., then to the Mall in Washington D.C. Directions are very important to lead our steps... Nonetheless, as soon as I saw the dome of the Capitol I knew that I was there. So, I forgot any other information provided with the directions and concentrated my attention on the Capitol only. So must be our endeavor towards the truth.

Truth is more consistent than the best we could imagine. Meeting her improves our life.

D. Truth demonstration is not always necessary

The question of the possibility of demonstrating the truth is tightly connected with the need to eventually do so. Does the truth need always to be proved? It does not! Actually, when the truth is self evident, like in a principle, there is no need to do so, and actually a principle cannot be demonstrated. Gandhi helps to get the picture: "Truth is by nature self-evident, as soon as you remove the cobwebs of ignorance that surround it, it shines clear." So, to show the truth is less a work of demonstration than a process of making it evident. How is that?

Demonstration is a logical process while truth involves the whole of our behavior, not only the mind. There is actually a living logic which surpasses rational logic. Language is suppose to serve and explain life not to make it.

Oppositely to common biases, philosophy does not deal with opinions but with facts. Actually, it is a training of study and discernment beyond general opinions. Students sometimes – and even people who claim to be philosophers – believe as granted that philosophy research must be only somehow approximate, even if at length ruminated. Their starting point is most of the time that – even if accurate - philosophy is not a consistent knowledge, and it is not supposed to bring certainty as well as science. The opposite is true. Even if philosophical perspectives are different with scientific issues, they are even more accurate, more grounded, and they correspond better to what people are, to what the world is. Philosophy provides directions to address many values that no other science does.

It is not the number of people believing the same which makes something true of false, but grounded knowledge. Science issues need demonstration, because every scientific discourse starts from an axiom, selected arbitrarily. Philosophy topics need contemplation. It is a higher standard of truth. Eventually, the variety of philosophy points of view among philosophers is not supposed to plead against philosophy but in favor of the capacity to see different perspectives on similar issues and discern how they may go together.

Philosophy starts with the awareness that truth is not just a thing to investigate, but the whole sense of reality we live in to be addressed. So truth is a sense of reality that we are supposed to grow in intimacy with. Such a perspective is far above any demonstration. It cannot be demonstrated. It must be experienced.

E. People always do refer to the Truth

I agree with those who connect the question about Truth with the question about God. An excellent friend of mine became an atheist during part of his life and he told me how during that period he could not believe in any truth. After he had returned to Catholic faith, he discovered that Nietzsche was right saying that "God is the arbitrator of truth, and without God everything becomes arbitrary." Without God, he said, "Everything is upside down, and even worse: it is like living in the middle of the sea with no stars to show the road." Under such a perspective, while being an atheist, my friend agreed with Nietzsche's words: "there is no truth; there are only interpretations of facts."

When he reverted to catholic beliefs, his faith put back things on track — Pascal wrote: "There are only two classes of persons who can be called reasonable: those who serve God with all their heart because they know him and those who seek him with all their heart because they do not know him." (P.427). Agora question, this week, was about truth, and the fact that everybody refers to her.

Asking why people do refer to the truth is similar of asking: **why people do seek the truth**. It refers to the fact that people need the truth in all thinking, activity, behavior, relationship. To say it in one word, there is not a human deed which has not to be in reference with the truth, whatever that reference is: seeking, improving our intimacy with, or even rejecting the truth. In everything we do, explicitly or implicitly, we are and need to be in a constant connection with the truth. Asking why people do refer to the truth is similar of asking with Augustine: "Why people are made for the truth?" or with Aquinas, "Why people naturally want the truth?" The answer is self evident. It is actually their own statements: "People are made for the truth" (Augustine) and "People naturally want the truth"

The research of truth, which Aristotle, Augustine, and Aquinas refer to, is the human need for ultimate values. Such endeavor pulls people towards philosophy, and even beyond, it invites them towards metaphysics, religious behaviors, to theology. Truth is not something we get at random. People are made for the truth and get peace when they meet her. People blossom in the truth. It means that truth is looking for us far before we move back and seek her. She is eager to meet us (Book of Wisdom) and "those who seek her will find her waiting at the threshold of the house in the morning."

Trying to be consistent with truth, in our life, makes our whole life a spiritual adventure, which overcomes daily struggles and difficulties. There is no need to check if everybody around says or not the truth to us… our own consistency with the truth is the criterion of authenticity in our deeds and relationships, even when people like to say what they believe we like to hear.. Ultimately, it depends on us, on our own quality of life, to get people saying the truth…

Media, radio, newspaper, television, publicity, diffuse values which are not based on consistent fact but on the purpose of making business, getting success, appealing attention, and so on. If we agree with such purposes our life will always be deceived by other people. Such deceiving endeavors produce disorder in human people and ultimately in the society. When the values shared by a civilization do not fit the true values of people, some breakage happens, some deterioration interferes in the life of the whole society, waves of decadence have begun… Oppositely, if it is not the success that we are primarily looking for, but if we look for values to deal with, family life to build on (not just to get!), brothers to respect, friends to appreciate (not just to be rewarded with!), if we like more to give than to receive, suddenly our way of life will illuminate our whole neighborhood and we will get what we sowed.. This is the logic of life: "give love and you will get love" — Juan de Yepes. And the logic of life moves far above speculative logic.

Science is supposed to deal with and find tangible, sensorial and objective truth. At sensorial level truth is precarious, not universal. Actually, in science, when truth is found research disappears. It is the opposite in philosophy, for philosophy is "intimacy with the truth" especially the truth of values, which never stop to be better understood. Values do not change; people change while going near to them. We improve while dealing with values and we understand them better. It is a virtuous circle. What is absolute will never stop to surprise us and to teach us, and to make our heart younger and our life more efficient. Here is why philosophy is a continuous endeavor, always consistent. Most of the works of Plato and Aristotle are still valid today, while scientific results must be often updated. A scientific book goes obsolete after less than 25 years! A philosophy book does not.

All being considered, truth is the key of the whole world consistency. Without truth, no discourse may be done, no relationship may stand between people, no work can be properly done, and no course of action can be achieved. There are in history some philosophers, like the Sophists and today relativists who claim that there is no need of truth. Against the relativism of the Sophists and the individualism of the Cynics, Aristotle believes in the consistency of truth and the necessity of a general commitment for the common good.

We know truth, not only by reason, but also by heart, and it is in this last way that we know first principles; and reason which has no part in it, tries in vain to impugn them. The knowledge of first principles as space, time, motion, and numbers is as sure as any we get from reasoning and reason must trust these intuitions of the heart, and must base them on every argument. We have intuitive knowledge of the tridimensional nature of space, and of the infinity of numbers. Principles are intuited; propositions are inferred, all with certainty, though in different ways.

Different aspects of truth may be perceived differently by people. Nonetheless truth is not subjective, but an objective fact that needs a serious commitment to get it. This issue was opportunely stressed by one of you, congratulations. Yes, there are several levels, perspectives, and consistency of truth. It is the purpose of a philosophy course to investigate inside of them.

Actually, reflection and reason are necessary, but they are not enough. Science and mathematics, which is the field of reason, are necessary but they too are not enough. After J.J. Rousseau there is the cultural legend that the heart is only the source of feeling. Rousseau disregarded the Hebrew tradition that the heart is seat of wisdom. In the Bible, the heart is the true seat of intelligence, while the head is only seat of reason… They are not the same.

Pascal considered the heart in Biblical perspective. This is why Blaise Pascal was not arguing in favor of irrationalism. He was pointing out that heart itself follows its own process: "The heart has reasons that reason disregards". The heart sees and we must use it. When one takes the time to understand the logic and reason of the heart as well as the one of the mind, our real, true, and objective desires can be recognized. By using the heart as well as the mind to seek the truth, the myths of many modern philosophers are revealed, as well as the roots of many of societal ills. Following the heart leads one to a complex philosophy that defines limitations. Limitations we truly desire. These limitations may produce true romance and adventure and define true progress. Science lacks the imagination to understand the heart. A modern myth is that following one's heart implies something simple, completely separate from reason and logic. Following one's heart leads to something reasonable and complex, because it goes a step further than where reason would take you, All being considered heart and reason are necessary to reach the point

F. Truth is waiting for us ahead

Moving to the truth is not just a speculative endeavor. Plato says that "We move to the truth with all our soul." Seeking the truth and getting it shows one of the most typical human endeavors. People are made for the truth and want it naturally, whether they are aware of it or not. One of the best illustrations of human relationship with truth was stated by Augustine in the masterpiece of his *Confessions*: "You made us for you, ô Lord." In other words: we are made for the truth and we must clean our heart and our soul from useless concerns and feelings in order to leave the way open toward the truth. As an outcome, moving the whole soul is less a willingly practice, an exercise, an attempt of moving out than a peaceful behavior of letting heart and soul open to eternal values, which allow the truth to grow in us. Similar behavior is the Socratic maieutic of delivering the truth, which is a dynamic endeavor which frees it from inside. Ultimately, the truth wants to show up.

Some sources affirm that Plato was influenced by Far East wisdom (India) and we should read his words in such a perspective. Buddhism suggests a propaedeutic work of purification, which makes mind and heart free from any superficial concern, inconsistent desire, transitory emotion, in order to be free at the threshold of nirvana. Going to the truth with all our soul includes making our heart and mind free from immediate concern, business, interest, trouble and anxiety in order to make us free, i.e. totally available, "transparent" to the truth.

Philosophy includes the double Eastern and Western wisdom. Eastern wisdom suggests transparency, internal silence, openness, peaceful waiting, serenity... Western wisdom includes active love, sharing, charity, seeking... Together they are the two waves of the soul anxious to meet the truth. True contemplative souls know, however, that the desire of truth to meet us is even stronger than our want to meet her. Philosophy must include both Eastern and Western wisdom, capacity of silence and serene work.

In his endeavor, Plato was coherent with the teaching of Socrates, which never consisted in providing new knowledge, but in the endeavor to help people to release the awareness which is hidden inside of us. Plato's search for truth is mostly a work of cleaning our mind, or clearing our heart and the whole human neighborhood in order to let the truth meet us.

Sometimes after the suggestions of a few philosophers, like Emmanuel Kant, and Idealist thinkers, students define philosophy as love of knowledge... Actually philosophy is far above such endeavor. Philosophy is much more than love for knowledge. Philosophy involves wisdom, which is intimacy with the truth. So ultimately we may say that philosophy is searching for the truth. Such endeavor is looking for the deepest consistency of things, which includes the mystery of reality.

Philosophy deals with facts. These facts do not include only physical events or natures. Philosophy does not stop at those tangible issues, which belong to mere sensorial appearance, as science does. They are necessary as science is, they are not sufficient. Philosophy addresses all facts, including those beyond tangible reality. Truth is not only the physical reality that surrounds our lives, but everything that exists around, outside and inside of us, at every level of presence, physical, speculative and spiritual. We may obviously say that the physical consistency of truth is not excluded by philosophy, but they are addressed in their own entireness. In fact, philosophy relies on science as a departure point to go further in the mystery of reality. Such endeavor is grounded knowledge, too.

in addition to the soul in the endeavor of searching for truth it is useless to say that body and mind should be involved, too,. This is redundant. It could even be nonsense; the soul is the organizer of the whole person, including body and mind. When the soul is involved, it works through all its proper expressions, i.e. the soul acts through body and mind. It always does. No need to add (body & soul) which is already included. So, let us move to the truth with our whole soul… It is a smooth, consistent and silent endeavor. As we know, lies and evil make more noise than simple truth. Truth does not hurt, it restores and heals. It is effective and fits our needs… Finding the truth requires more the endeavor of clearing our own garden than animatedly searching in the neighbor field. Similarly Isaiah affirmed that "Godis not in the storm, not in the earthquake, not in the fire, but in the breeze".

G. The Meaning of Things

"The meaning of things lies not only in the same things, but also in our disposition towards them." These words of Antoine de Saint-Exupéry, a pilot of Sud-Aviation, Toulouse, show the double source of meaning: our senses (images of things) and our mind (a priori ideas). This was stressed by a disciple of Maritain, Jean Daujat: "I understand according to the way I watch"

Most people disregard in the sentence the words "not only" and "but also" and then change the sentence in a defense or even a plead in favor of subjectivity, which it is not what Saint-Exupéry intended to suggest. Antoine de Saint-Exupéry, does not say: "the meaning of things depends on the way we approach them, but he says that such a meaning depends also on it… The sentence is not supposed to deny the consistency and the proper meaning of things but it stresses an additional insight for search. To say it shortly, there is a meaning inside of things which belong to each thing, as such, objectively. Then, such an objective meaning can be more or less understood according to the way I approach the thing which will provide such meaning.

The purpose of Saint-Exupéry is to enlighten the process of knowledge and to prevent any subjective judgment not properly ground on the facts. He was not a relativist. His experience as a pilot, which requires the capacity to face wind, fatigue, distance, commitment, was far away from the intend to give room to subjective issues. While our personal disposition may help or handicap a correct understanding on things and other people, all fields of knowledge, techniques and science address reality as an attempt to better understand it and the whole knowledge serves to the welfare of the human being. In this neighborhood, the words of Saint-Exupéry may help to overcome eventual bias. Such a sentence eventually serves as a warning against some inconsistent convictions which may come from prejudices, because of the role and the impact of feeling and personal dispositions in some beliefs and certitudes of ours. Such feelings and biases should be removed to get a better acquaintance of things.

Also it recalls that, sometimes, the difficulty to understand the reality which surrounds us depends more on our own capacity to watch than its own complexity. There is interaction between facts and intelligence. Intelligence requires docility to the facts, a great capacity to listen as pope Benedict XVI recalls in his interview of March 2015.

We eventually understand other people and reality around in proportion of our own capacity to be open, to listen, to share, to be interested… to trust.

H. Moving toward the Truth

Moving to the truth is one of the most typical human endeavor. People are made for the truth and they want her. Again, one of the best illustration of human relationship with truth has been written by Augustine in the Confessions: "You made us for you, ô Lord." In other words: we are made for the truth and we must clean our heart and our soul from useless concerns and feelings in order to leave the way open toward the truth. As an outcome, moving the whole soul is less a practice of exercise and moving out than a practice of letting heart and soul let the truth grow in us, as the Socratic *maieutics* of delivering the truth, which is waiting from inside to show up. With the words: "We move towards the truth with all our strengths", Aquinas agreed with the statement of Plato saying that "We must move towards the truth with the whole soul."

Sometimes students define philosophy as love of knowledge… Actually philosophy is much more than that. Philosophy involves wisdom, which is intimacy with the truth. So ultimately we may say that philosophy is searching for the truth. Such endeavor is looking for the deepest consistency of things, which includes the mystery of reality.

In other words the process of moving near the truth is more silent and getting near to us inside than moving far away and making a long trip of search.

Plato was influenced by far East wisdom and we should read his words in such a perspective. Buddhism suggests a propaedeutic work of purification, which makes mind and heart free from any superficial concern, inconsistent desire, transitory emotion, in order to be free at the threshold of nirvana. Going to the truth with all our soul includes making our heart and mind free from immediate concern, business, interest, trouble and anxiety in order to make us free, i.e. totally available, "transparent" to the truth.

In his endeavor, Plato was coherent with the teaching of Socrates, which never consisted in providing new knowledge, but in the endeavor to release the awareness which is hidden inside of us. Plato's search for truth is mostly a work of cleaning our mind, or clearing our heart and the whole human neighborhood in order to let the truth emerge and meet us.

Moving to the truth is one of the most typical human endeavor. People are made for the truth and want it. The best example of people meeting the truth was written by Augustine in the *Confessions*: "You made us for you, ô Lord, and our heart is restless until it rests in you." In other words: we are made for the truth and we must clean our heart and our soul from useless concerns and feelings in order to leave the way open toward the truth.

I. Letting the Truth speak

As an outcome, moving the whole soul towards the truth is less a practice of moving out than oppositely having heart and soul let the truth grow in us, as the Socratic maieutics of delivering the truth, which is waiting for truth to show up. Looking for the truth is more a work of patience, observation, contemplation, expectation, than hunting. It mainly requires working properly, without the interference of concerns for things which are not appropriate. It is more a process of letting the truth come to us. Plato had been influenced by Far East wisdom and we should read his words in such perspective.

The whole teaching of Socrates was not to provide new knowledge, but to free the awareness which is hidden inside of us. It is more a work of cleaning our mind, or clearing our heart and the whole human neighborhood in order to let the truth meet us.

Buddhism suggests a work of purification, which makes mind and heart free from any concern, desire, emotion, in order to be free at the threshold of nirvana. Going to the truth with all our soul includes making our heart and mind free from concern, business, interest, trouble and anxiety in order to make us free, i.e. totally available, "transparent" to the truth.

Philosophy deals with facts. This does not include only physical events or natures. Philosophy facts do not stop at those belonging to mere sensorial appearance, as science does. Philosophy addresses all facts, even those beyond tangible reality, Truth is not only the reality that surrounds our lives, but everything that exists, outside and inside of us, at every level of consistency, physical, speculative, spiritual. The truth philosophy looks for is mainly metaphysical (beyond the mere physical) and spiritual. Physical consistency of truth is not excluded by philosophy,. In this neighborhood, philosophy relies on science. Concerning the highest spiritual entities, philosophy relies on theology. As spiritual, truth is more than mere fact, it leads us, it changes us while we move into it. To address the truth, a philosopher must be a contemplative, i.e. accept the eventuality that facts are first and must be contemplate more than interpreted or explained. We must accept the way the truth is to understand it. It is a work of simplicity. We must grow in simplicity to get the quality of vision that truth deserves. As a result looking for the truth is a simple endeavor. Some times it is more engaging to be simple than complicated. Simplicity is the key. This is why philosophy seeks simplicity.

Looking for the truth does not consist first in an endeavor of search but it primarily is the patient endeavor or recognizing the truth which is already there, knocking at the door of our awareness. It is knocking both from outside and from inside. The truth is constantly knocking at the door of our soul, where she dwells in. And the truth inside of us wants to meet the truth everywhere at every time. Here is why the whole soul is involved. Some students said that the body and the mind should be involved, too. This is a nonsense, the soul is the organizer of the whole person, body and mind. When the soul is involved, it works through the other two. People are made for the truth. And the truth wants to meet us even more than we are looking for her. Augustine says that the truth is nearer to us than our own shoes. And Pythagoras said almost the same when he stated: "the diseases which ruin people come from their own deeds and, unfortunately, people are looking far away the answers, which lie inside of them." According to Pythagoras' school all the goods and the keys of the universe are already written inside of us. As an outcome, to be a true philosopher requires first to be silent enough in order to listen to the truth which speaks inside. Similarly Isaiah () affirms that "God is not in the storm, not in the earthquake, not in the fire, but in the brise" – Lies and evil make more noise than simple truth. Truth does not hurt, it restores and heals. It is effective and fit our needs… Finding the truth requires more to clear our own garden than badly searching in another field.

In other words we may say that people are "conatural" with truth.

K. The Levels of Truth Quality

Truth is ONE but there are several steps of getting truth consistency. This multiplicity of truth qualities seems an echo of Gospel's words: "There are several dwelling in the house of the Father." Truth is one and she nevertheless must be understood appropriately according to its proper presence according to situations and quality of life, according its several levels of expression. As a result, there are several steps of getting the truth, from the bottom, where Nietzsche says that truth is an optional reference ("There is no truth but just interpretations"), to the very top where Thomas Aquinas sees truth as "What fits the facts" (Veritas sequitur esse rerum).

Aristotle says that "the being can be said in many ways." The same should be affirmed about truth. There is only one truth. If truth was double or divisible there would be no truth at all. Truth is one, otherwise there is no truth. It is possible, however, to address truth partially. It is typical to human reflection to be discursive, i.e. partial, successive and progressive… along the process of knowledge human patrimony increases in the awareness of truth. Such growing awareness proceeds according the diverse fields of human understanding. Diverse perspectives on truth can be true only if they fit with the only one truth.

The diverse approaches of the being, evidenced by the familiarity with time, produce, as an outcome, different levels of experiencing truth. Or at least assume the different aspects people deal with truth. Concerning the truth, we are familiar with pragmatic theory, coherence theory, and correspondence theory. There is more to say. And it is not even sufficient to indicate the appropriate field of each criterion of truth. Today there are other criteria to consider, which are so widely spread out.

What is the criterion of truth? Edgar S. Brightman said: "Any judgment is true if is it both self consistent and coherently connected with our system of judgment as a whole" — We will see, below, that such a definition fits with a few theories on truth. Additionally, logical perspectives include that every true statement agrees with the **law of reasoning** (proper syllogism), the **law of identity** (everything is supposed to be and remain what it is), the **law of non-contradiction** (Aristotle states that you cannot affirm and deny something at the same time and under the same perspective) and the law of self-evidence (Self-consistency)...

Here below are the main criteria universally recognized on truth.

1. Subjective Theory — "Veracity" — Psychological level

Close to that level, when we address psychological time, truth is what I feel, what I like, what fits with my own sensibility, with the perspective of the mind: truth is veracity, like in existentialism and phenomenology. **Truth is loyalty with taste**, beauty, aesthetic (existence precedes essence). There is no rule for the truth (or for doing well or good); however, whatever we do we influence human reality (Sartre). **Truth is what is veracious.**

2. Social Theory — "Popularity" — Social level

Social theory is nothing more than what people usually put under the category of popularity: which is popular is true... It works at certain levels of human activity, especially in the field of finance (stock exchange), where what is appreciated or popular becomes valuable. It is the game of offer and demand. But also the fact that speculation changes the values of things, to the point to make expensive what would be almost at no value in another context. Looks for example at shoes, the ones which belong to a famous company are more expensive, independently of their actual quality…

3. Political Theory — "Majority" — Democratic level

When there is no dictatorship in politics today, democracy suggests that majority governs. It is surely not the best model for a government, but democracy helps to manage between the excess of anarchy and the one of totalitarianism. A better concern on subsidiarity should help.

4. Pragmatic Theory — Opinion & technical level

At physical level, or objective level, we have first the context of common sense (opinion) and technical behaviors, where truth is what functions properly, what brings results. It is the truth of experimentation, the key through which science verifies theories. **Truth is what works**.

5. Coherence Theory — Scientific level

At this same level, but addressing physical time as objective time (the speculative side of physical time, second side of a same entity) in science, especially in theoretical science (mathematics and analogized fields) truth is what fits with the system, what is coherent with the rules of that specific science. In such a context, **truth is what is coherent with a system** (coherence theory). Each science runs its own rules: what is true in geometry is not the same in arithmetic, engineering, architecture, physics, or chemistry. What fit the rules of a science is considered true in that specific field.

6. Correspondence Theory — Philosophical level

Beyond that level, we enter into metaphysical time, where

truth is what corresponds to facts. Aquinas defined truth, "*Veritas sequitur esse rerum*" — **Truth follows the facts**. Truth is what corresponds to the facts. In Plato the truth lies in a transcendent world, while in Aristotle it is inside of things. It is the intelligible entity of things. And the job of intelligence is to get it (correspondence theory). Nonetheless, correspondence theory leaves open the question how to overcome the bridge of the distance between what I am and what I know. Aquinas said that knowledge is becoming the other as another. And here is the dramatic struggle of every philosopher to experience that distance: I like the being, I know the being, I feel the being I depend on, and nonetheless I am not the being.

7. Owe Theory — Mystical level

The upper level is the one of spiritual understanding and mystical experience. At this level the truth transforms the one who becomes familiar to her. While at scientific level, the more we know and the more we transform the whole world ("We command nature obeying its laws" — F. Bacon), at mystical level, the one who knows is changed into the one who is contemplated. Truth is the living transcendent, who makes me what I deeply am. Such a living truth is so dynamically acting in all directions without ceasing and without exception that it is said "immanent." In a mystical experience, immanence and transcendence fit during the instant of the spiritual endeavor, which is properly experienced out of time (ecstasy). The truth takes me as I am existentially and erases the distance existence-essence into a sharing of the absolute, like in the events recounted by Plotinus, Augustine, and Juan De Yepes. Nicola de Flue used to say to the truth, "I am nothing you are all" and "take me as I am and make me as you are." At such a level when immanence and transcendence meet, it is needed a community, a friend to share such experience to make it under-

St. Nicola

standable and useful for all. According to Henri de Lubac, such a sharing was so dramatically missed by Nietzsche to make incomprehensible his experiences of Surlej and Rapallo and induced him to twist eternity into Eternal Return.

Here the words of Jesus, "I am the way and the truth and the life" resound properly and through religious experience introduce us from philosophy to theology. Our field of study, however, invites us to stay at the moment in the context and expertise of philosophy.

L. Pedagogy of Truth

The "Pedagogy of Truth" is also named "Propaedeutic of Truth", or "The educational process of truth." All these definitions mean the same: **Truth is didactic**: while moving nearer the Truth, She changes us, she transforms us. Acting in such a way truth is properly what she is supposed to be: Truth — According to Plato, "We go to the truth with our whole soul," i.e. with the whole of our faculties. Truth cannot be reached like a product at a vending machine, every partial theory, shows part of the whole truth. Truth deserves more to be contemplated than explained. The aspects of truth must be present in our inquiry, no one can be disregarded. The whole of creation speaks about its maker…

Truth shows a density that grows with our familiarity with her. Knowledge is necessary but not sufficient to get the truth. At every step of awareness, truth is criterion of identity of a discourse with its own blossoming. It works as a snow ball effect, which is stressed by Aristotle in *Posterior Analytics* §A.1: "every learning or teaching through discourse proceeds from previous knowledge." Previous knowledge on something makes us able to understand it. Every endeavor towards the truth proceeds through the same steps and the more we move near to the truth the more we enter in intimacy with her, up to the point to meet her face to face, in a sort of illumination: "I got it"

Supposing you are looking for a place, a movie theater for example that you are not familiar with... They told you some directions. Some of these directions may be wrong, but as soon as you see the building, you know that you got the place and you forget the directions. Again, suppose you are looking for somebody you never met before... They told you where you are supposed to see him, what general aspects of the face and the body are significant for you to recognize him, and so on... Then when you see him what you meet is far beyond what you were told. The process of search is over; a process of interaction has started. The same happens at every level of understanding: e.g. the story of Jonah... He was supposed to bring a message to the city of Nineveh... The words were words of wrath, words of death, and Jonah was afraid to say them... But actually his mission was a mission of salvation that he was not aware of and was even reluctant to recognize... But when the people in Nineveh got the message the whole endeavor is transfigured... De Lubac invite to a similar interpretation about Nietzsche, "God is dead, we killed him" is a terrible discovery of what our culture has done... It is not a message against God, but eventually an invitation to change behavior, and return to God.

The key of the whole process of moving towards the truth can be found in the words of John: "The one who does the truth comes to the light and the light makes free" (Jn 14:6 et sq.). Ultimately, meeting the truth is the departure point of an amazing adventure of a new kind. When we meet the truth the whole process of learning is transformed and our own life reaches an upper qualit

The further we go the less we learn.
Lao Tseu

Approaching the Truth in Daily Life

PRELIMINARY

Interesting outcomes are usually produced with the notion of **TRUTH** and the diverse **PERSPECTIVES** of her. Many suggestive insights can be provided. I sincerely thank everyone for your attention and your sharing in class.. It's impossible to address directly the many good thoughts that have been indicated in class and after class in some groups of study. They have been noted, and appreciated. There is, however, the need to stress what has been somehow missed in the sharing. Here is why this note is provided. Everyone is supposed to fish in it what he/she does need.

The sociological, political, psychological, convivial, and cultural perspectives of the sentences are actually outcomes of a logic approach, which deals with the principle of identity, i.e. everything must be what it is and nothing else. Fortunately, all of you, explicitly or implicitly have stressed it. This is actually a course of metaphysics that often overlap logic perspectives, so this is the main topic to face as the background of our reflection and of all human behaviors.

The background, which stresses the identity of truth, has to deal with what public opinion is used to exert today, which, in his first homely of his papacy, Pope Benedict XVI referred to as **RELATIVISM**. I am pleased to consider that all of us recognize the **failure of relativism**, which may succeed on a short course of action but always deceives on the long range of life activity.

The whole question on "truth and different perspectives" is

important in philosophy to proceed towards the truth with discernment and without prejudices. Reflecting beyond relativism refers to the possibility of different perspectives on the truth. There are situations which show different perspectives on the same truth.

Above all, truth must not and cannot be denied. Aristotle's and Aquinas' theory of knowledge remains the background of every attempt to understand the way we become aware of everything and get some knowledge. So every ulterior study of metaphysics will be an improvement of this Note. Additionally, the full picture on Aristotle's doctrine needs the implementations given by Aquinas and his disciples. Aristotle's views must be understood under the context which was his own method of study and is well known as **Critical Realism**.

The issue cannot be solved at once. This is a case when it is somehow good to leave the question open in order to give room for a deeper reflection, as Plato does in his *Dialogs*. It is the Socratic Method, isn't it? We know how Plato's dialogs strengthen the debate leaving the questions open. There is even more: leaving the discussion open, let our unconscious work and direct our reflection beyond the usual tracks and easy conclusions.

I wish you a good learning.

Beyond Relativism

Selecting the case "**When two opposite statements may be true**" and commenting on Aristotle words:
"No one may contradict himself,"
"**One cannot simultaneously affirm and deny something under the same perspective.**"

A. What relativism is

At first, we must be sure that we know the difference between **relativity** — the extremely accurate and specific scientific theory, which indicates a new method of reading data — and **relativism**, which indicates a lack of precision. Relativity is a synthesis of scientific issues. Relativism rejects truth. As previously said, without truth no discourse can be done, as well as without love of truth no philosophy can start. It should be add that relativism murders philosophy and ultimately the whole of civilization. Moving beyond relativism does overcome the main disease of our days

Strictly speaking, "Relativism" has nothing to do with "reality." It is connected with "relate" — "relatively" — "relation" (= connection) — "relationship" — and includes flexibility. Such flexibility is acceptable when it "comprehends" the many different appearances of a same concept, of a single fact. When it becomes a sort of universal latitude, leeway, laxity, or laxness of thinking it becomes the death of every human culture.

As an example, "**relativism**" is not just having different perspectives on similar issues. For it could happen that an economical reading on a precise situation could express aspects that complete a scientific study, and a sociological investigation may lead to a very different conclusion of a psychological one; and what about a political one, as some of you referred. Each perspective, however, must be accurate and follow precise steps. They all deal with facts in a specific manner and complementary way: every specific study offers an additional perspective and not a contradictorily one. If we are not able to get the full harmonious picture we get lost. Such a whole investigating on reality is proper and it has nothing to do with relativism.

Actually, relativism would be: "there are many opinions, they even contradict each other, and that is ok!" Such a non-discerned agreement would be the beginning of chaos. It can be the start of a decadent culture.

The well known tale of the blind observers fit perfectly with the issue, like "cheese on the macaroni" would say my kids in Italian. I like to quote it: "Three blind men were touching an elephant. The first blind man was holding the elephant's leg. He said, "I think an elephant is like the trunk of a great tree." The second blind man disagreed. While holding the elephant's trunk he said, "I believe an elephant is like a large snake," The third blind man believed they were both wrong. "An elephant is like a great wall," he exclaimed. He was touching the elephant's side. Each blind man was convinced he was right and the others were dealing with something else without ever realizing they were all touching the same elephant. Some people believe that the blind men in this parable represent the major cultures of the whole world; each is dealing with culture and reality, but under different perspectives. Globalization process engages us to find connections and complementariness: it would be poor to stress only one view, but it would also be insufficient to only notice and stress the difference – difference without correlation is pure non-sense." First of all, the example is tricky: how can they be so sure to address the same elephant if they have such different opinions on it? Any way, it is only an example and keeping it that way, some teaching pops up. Science addresses usually facts in first instance like the blind people of the fable, while philosophy take account of all their statements to make the whole picture of it and finally put everyone in its own perspective (critical realism). In such a fable the elephant would be reality; partial perspectives would be science – even the different specific sciences. Philosophy and science need each other to have a correct understanding of facts. They do not exist independently. Being open to see the complementariness of others' view is not "relativism" it is philosophy. This is why philosophy needs sharing. By the way, how those blind know they are addressing the same? Actually, they don't know! The example is only a suggestion.

Well… sometimes people like to apply relativism to religions… Without showing any disrespect to any thinker on the issue, it is important to state that the differences may be understood under the light of the existing similarities and correlations between the diverse religious denominations. Otherwise it would be a plea for inconsistency of each one. When pope Ben-16 and the Great Muphti prayed together in the Blue Mosque in Istanbul, in November 2006, they both agreed they were praying the same God, even according two different religious traditions! Such a deep understanding moved the whole Turkish population. It made a turning point of the pope's trip in Turkey, and improved the relationship between Christians and Muslims. Today many religious people like to see what is moving them together beyond possible differences. Dialog between religions would not be possible, however, without the double attitude of a strong fidelity of each believer to a precise tradition (because denying their own traditions would be just inconsistency) and of being open to Providence's work among believers. In such a case, dialog is sharing different relationships with God. So a behavior is properly beyond relativism.

Some interesting issue can be also raised in class discussion. To complete the notion of truth, I would say that we do not believe in the truth just because some scientific, political or even religious authority would say so, but because after mature reflection and many considerations, we trust their own knowledge: such authorities state what is important for us to know in our days under their own expertise. It is a call for more understanding, not for dismissing our own judgment. Without this implicit recognition, even faith in Church teaching would be not acceptable. Such statements follow the traditionally investigative method of "critical realism" started by Aristotle and developed by Aquinas: to consider all facts, ponder all possible suggestions, and produce then a mature reflection, under the light of tradition and revelation, using the wisdom of the days. It is never an only talk coming from above.

B. Truth overcomes understanding

Every religious tradition stresses that God speaks to his people. Nonetheless it is not sufficient for us to hear his words. Even the same words of God need a proper human interpretation — not only comprehension — in order to become effective. Such an effective understanding is the task of the community. Supposing the case that God would speak personally and directly to one of us (I mean, more directly than through the usual circumstances, personal study, authority commands, Magisterium teaching, or people sharing), that individual should be very careful for no one is able to understand properly such a message alone, as Juan de Yepes (St. John of the Cross) stated, "we can make great mistakes, while interpreting it, and we usually do." When we experiment such an exceptional experience we need to share it with other people in order to make it understandable, even for us.

Jacques Maritain states the same in *Degrees of Knowledge*. He defines "**Apophatic apprehension**" the experience of meeting God through a mystical experience of vision, or ecstasy, when God talks to us or shows directly to us some consistent event, which is delivered to us through a mysterious way that we cannot even explain. Maritain says that whatever happens to us from above, we cannot understand it without sharing it to others. Nonetheless every consistent spiritual experience, at every level (even when it is a simple heavenly inspiration) cannot be easily recounted, for we need to translate it into language; this is why we need to share it to a friend or a community. Such a sharing obliges us to use language, to put that experience in language, to make it a "**cataphatic discourse**," which, technically, is an adaptation of our awareness into a lower neighborhood of comprehension, similar to the philosopher who try to explain reality to the people in the allegory of the Cave. Most of the time, such attempt, provokes the death penalty of the seer, like it happened to Socrates. Such a discourse (cataphatic discourse) is the way we communicate something that is barely communicable. A spiritual experience needs to be filtered into a discourse, to be shared with people (which is the same) in order to be understood even by the one who witnessed such a vision. Seeing God face to face is not possible. God must hide to make himself visible to us, otherwise we would be destroyed. And God already hide himself during community worship. Every common prayer reaches God and somehow lets God reach us. An example of it is given by St. Paul in the 2d Letter to the Corinthians (12:1-6), referring that he was rapt into heaven, adding that he was unable to say "if it was with or without his body." Nonetheless he had the awareness that the event actually happened. Referring the experience he made it knowledgeable for us and for him, too (cataphatic discourse).

A few philosophers, like Socrates, Descartes, Pascal, Rousseau, and Nietzsche referred to a kind of spiritual insights they personally experienced in their life. They are the living proof that the best communication or advice sometime may be misunderstood, when it cannot be fully shared, especially for Rousseau and Nietzsche. Both were so solitary. Only a good sharing can make the information proper and effective. It took a few years to St. Paul to understand the vision he had on Damascus way. This may explain why he became actually blind, and needed, then, to retire for a while in the desert. He could not have understood what actually happened to him if the apostles had not called him in order to be able to share together his and their experience on their intimacy with the Lord. Often, the truth cannot be understood at a first grasp. We need to improve our capacity to see and understand before we get it. Such improvement includes the necessity to grow in love. We cannot even understand who we are without love: we need to love ourselves at least as much as we should love other people – Without love there is no truth…This has been the endeavor of the first Christian brotherhood, the Church of Jerusalem. Nietzsche paid high the price of a lack of love in his life… while being gifted with a true spiritual vision.

C. Understanding the Truth requires sharing.

The mediation between experience and truth is sharing through a discourse. Such a sharing improves ourselves and the ones we share with, building a special God's presence among us (known as "*Agapé*"), provoking a personal maturation (spiritual growing), and becoming a cultural event (to be said in a "cataphatic" discourse). This is why philosophy is so a necessary background to theology. Even if theology develops statements which overcome philosophy, it must be understandable to philosophers or it is not consistent. Analogically, philosophy also must be under the control of common sense – for philosophy, which is the wisdom of people, must be understandable for all, otherwise it is useless.

Now, returning more specifically to "Relativism," let me ask to each of you a tricky (but serious) question. Do you believe that with some relativism in math, physics, science, etc. our civilization could work? Would our society be consistent if suddenly we agree to apply relativism in science and accept that $2 + 2 =$ may be 4 or another value, like 3 or 5. No, it doesn't, because science does not accept relativism. Science follows the same rules all the time, everywhere, accordingly. Every specific situation pulls its own specific steps. Then "Relativity Theory" is a way to make more universal such account. Because of that precision, all technical performances stand. Because of such accuracy, science is progressing continuously, and society improves.

From the first day of his election, Pope Benedict XVI stressed that relativism is totally not acceptable in the contexts of Ethics, Politics, Bioethics, Sociology, and of Eternal Values. He stressed that "Relativism is the major disease of our day civilization". Does that make sense to you? What does that really mean?

The purpose of philosophy is to make more consistent and accurate our proceeding to the truth. Supposing that, without further investigation, we accept as identically valid several contradictory statements, we are then already out of track. It is useless to proceed further. The conclusion would be that there is no truth at all. As a consequence, no discourse would be consistent.

This has nothing to do with the fact that a same situation may produce opposite effects depending on the way people address it. Such behaviors are real. And it is right to say that somebody improves, where others are in distress, because of the way they address the situation. Social life is a continuous illustration of such a fact: winning a lottery does not bring necessarily happiness: it depends on the way people deal with the enriching situation and the people around, especially relatives and friends. This is also the case in medicine, not all therapies work to the same disease in different patients. Most students are familiar with the issue. We must deal with what is proper. Relativism would deny such different approaches, accepting every therapy as identically useful. It would bring confusion, then. Unless we state a paradox that must be accepted as such, to be clarified later, accepting the limitations of our intelligence to comprehend everything, but starving to know well what we deal with. Accepting contradictions without further investigation denies the truth. Oppositely, everything must be considered in its own context, accordingly.

There is usually a lot of confusion nowadays on the question. We must be accurate about what we are speaking here? Do we know what contradictorily statements mean? According to Aristotle, "We cannot say something and its opposite on the same issue, at the same time, under the same perspective." All correct definitions of contradictory statements are included. If two people do not speak about the same issue, or not at the same time and under the same perspective, then their statements are not contradictory – even when we claim that both may say the truth. Then a proper inquiry is necessary to state how, under what conditions, how much, when, etc.

D. Life is challenging

Nonetheless it is easy to be confused — to say the least — about relativism. We must pay the difference between accepting people the way they are (rule of charity) and agreeing with whatever they say (contradicting our love for truth). In the many apparently opposed considerations raised in class, I see a common position: the agreement of all with Aristotle's statement! A few of you said it appropriately. From this common argument, everyone stops later at a different parking to have a sight on the neighborhood, and to look at the fact whether or not contradicting statements can be consistent and truth at the same time.

You all agree on one thing: They cannot be opposed and consistent at the same time if they speak under the same perspective. So the ones who answered "YES" and the ones who answered "NO" are right because you agreed with the main issue and are talking under different perspectives: Truth can be only one, perspectives and situations of place and time may change... and, sometimes, it is also prudent not to be too much categorical on an issue, which we are not familiar enough with. This includes the love of our parents, relatives, and other people we care and had different experiences which led them to dissimilar perspectives in life (sometimes for the same reasons, which lead us to opposite conclusions). We all are aware of the importance of experience and the possibly different interpretations. Time and place make different situations. We all are familiar with generation gap, cultural gap, etc. Sociologists talk about diachronic cultures, when there is a gap in between. They call synchronic culture when we are in agreement in spite of some diversity.

There is more, however, than the facts that unlike endeavors led to opposite reflections. It is not that elementary. Critical realism requires more considerations.

To support the analysis I would like to offer an incredible experience I had when I was 14. I was living in Gascony when, during the summer, two bishops of two nearby different Catholic Dioceses made at the same time the following opposite statements: the bishop of **Toulouse** forbade totally any Girl and Boy Scout activity in his diocese, while the bishop of **Montauban** (only less than 50 miles away) supportively encouraged every Girl and Boy Scout activity in his jurisdiction. I was living in Montauban, so I started Boy Scout activity, there.

Somebody would believe that the two bishops were in opposition. Well, as a matter of fact, they had no dispute at all! They even were good friends. So, after a meeting with each other, they made public their two evidently dramatic decisions at the same time. On the same Sunday, all parishes of the respective two dioceses read the statement of their own bishop. How could they have been in agreement? How would have said the same so differently?

A few would easily consider that if one bishop is right the opposite one should be wrong. It did not work like that. In fact, if they addressed the same issue at the same time, nonetheless, it was not in the same place (even if the two cities are very near to each other, in Gascony). Toulouse was a growing metropolis, of almost 1 million inhabitants, where the influence of Russian Youth movement (Komsomol) suggested to behave in promiscuity, without any specifically differentiate activity for Boys and for Girls, even when 14 of age, or below. Then the Bishop was afraid of some disastrous consequences in education of the youth. There was no other decision to take than stopping such activities. Montauban was an agricultural area of almost 50 thousands inhabitants, where the Scout leaders were following the tradition of Baden Powel, having distinguished activities for Girls and Boys. So the Bishop was proud to encourage such formation training for youth. And it was with the purpose of avoiding any relativism that the two bishops met together, took their own appropriate decisions, and made official, then, they respective statements.

Does that make sense to you? There is no relativism here, but to understand well the question it was necessary to go to a most accurate investigation. A deeper understanding of the conditions of each statement helped us to understand that they took opposed decisions, in unlike neighborhood, because they supported the same values.

A similar reflection could be developed with some typical traditions that are usually rejected in Western civilization, like cutting the arm of a thief in Sha'ariah countries, or committing hara-kiri, or stoning the people who disagree with the community. It is not sufficient to say it is ok for them it would be wrong for us. Such a kind of tolerance is mere relativism and destroys every attempt to make a consistent reflection towards the truth. Another example, difficult to address, is the tradition amongst some Inuit tribe which gives to the eldest child the duty to abandon his parents, father and mother, on the snow road to die when they go fifty and over. It would be wrong to say that it was correct yesterday and it is wrong today. This is not a sufficient answer. It also would be wrong to invoke tolerance. Tolerance must serve for improvement, for the good, not for confusion.

It is necessary to understand why such tradition was in force, and see how they can be changed. Even the difficult conditions to live near the North pole, when old people could make difficult the life of a whole family under a blizzard, are not sufficient to explain it – there is probably some historical event who introduced such a ritual. The request to manage in order that an old father/mother should not be a handicap would never justify their killing. Such an issue, however, is the field of ethics, more than logic. So I leave the example as such. Similar extreme behavior can be understood, even if not agreed. And if we want to help those people to change, it is necessary to solve the problem not its interpretation, that is to say, it is not sufficient, to tell people to change, we have to help them to improve in their own conditions of life. The example could appear a little tough, and it is. Hope it may serve as a key to address other similar situations.

E. Unconditional love

When Mother Teresa of Calcutta decided to help people starving on the streets of Calcutta, she did not go to the authorities to recall their obligations towards their own people, she did not call for a public protest of the poor against the rich, she only started, with a few friends, to give food to the poor and hold in a shelter the sick. Moving is the story when she brought food to a family which was starving for a week. When they entered the house with the rice, the mother divided the rice into two cups and run out. To answer the surprise of Mother Teresa, when she came back, she simply said "our neighbors, too, were starving!" Such a behavior was a revolution in Calcutta, which involved, later, even the authorities.

When some expecting mother told her she could not afford to deliver another baby, she replied: bring the baby to the light and give it to me, I will be pleased to have care of it for you. This is not tolerance. This is real love. It is love of truth. In speculative life, philosophy invites to contemplate the facts than to explain them. In practical life, the task of a philosopher, is more to raise solutions more than point out problems. But, here, I'm going probably at the edge of a course of logic.

Some of you may be right to oppose sometime a true statement, because of extenuating circumstances, contradictory experiences, and/or different point of view. Such a critique in the discussion may improve dramatically our common reflection, as far as we have the courage to share our differences, we honestly love the truth, and proceed accordingly. Again, nothing is automatically developing better or worse in human neighborhood. Everything depends on the way we do it – which means whether or not we follow the rules of the truth in its own context.

Sometimes we behave that way more by intuition than from a proper reflection. Simple logic is barely sufficient. I may take an example that a post in a forum suggested me: "No plants are animals, No animals are plants. Someone may feel confused about such a statement, which the logical reciprocity goes somehow too fast and too easy. And you would be right, for the two statements are not the same: making them reciprocal, produces a jump from the facts to an abstractive discourse. Beyond their differences both are beings on earth, both are creatures, both are materially living beings, but not at the same degree of life: plants are living as vegetal, animals (etymologically: anima = soul => means that "animal" is a being with soul, which Aristotle calls Sensorial Soul) are sensible living. Such a statement must be accepted in a precise context, and rejected in another, and we must say when and how.

To pay a difference we must agree with some equivalence. While reading these lines, you are different of what you were yesterday, or even a few minutes ago. Because you are the same person you may appreciate the difference = being the same you may evaluate how different you are now, according to the changes of time, space, reading, and quality of being. There is no contradiction at all. To be different includes some connection otherwise there would be no possible comparison between the two. Hope will have occasion to discuss again about that interesting connection between similarity-difference later on. There are an important key on every reflection.

Before proceeding further, we need to take a better sight on the structure of life and language, and their dissimilarity. A different place we look around from make a different survey. A better standpoint, or a better point of sight, helps to look better at the whole panorama. This is why we are addressing this week the issue of prayer. Prayer is the perfect example of how to deal with deep issues of our life, which can be insightful of totally wrong.

F. Rough Recap

When God is not at the first place everything becomes relative… Atheism is the first source of relativism. When it is not part of an experience of faith, Structuralism, Existentialism, Phenomenology, Linguistics, may appear as a direct consequence of atheism and constitutes a step towards relativism.

It is impossible to share or even understand what is <Love> without a direct familiarity, knowledge, or simple reference to God who is Trinity, i.e. a mystery of love and vice versa…

Role of Mt 18:19 as source of Apophatic experience…

G. Making Room to the transcendent

For those who attend a Catholic Mass, I would like to stress the liturgy of Trinity Sunday, which falls on the Sunday following Pentecost. On Trinity Sunday, the liturgy indicates that the truth is enlightened by its self-evidence, she enlightens and leads her lovers to its own understanding: "The Paraclete will teach you everything and will lead you." It is mostly when our inquiry makes us lost, that we need to review our paths and see where some mistake was made: did we change direction somewhere? But when we meet the truth we are enlightened by her, we see better and need no more indication than its effective enlightening. This is the experience of every philosopher.

Analogically, meeting God is far above any process of prayer. Actually, our prayer has started because we met him. It is true for everyone. God is pure spirit so it is said that we never met him directly and we will never do on earth, physically. Notwithstanding we truly did it, because "God is love," and every time we love we dwell in God and God dwells in us. All the same: truth is nearer to us than everything else and nonetheless truth is far above any reflection of ours.

Such a reflection goes beyond the eventual distinctions between religious denominations, especially the three religions of the Book: Judaism, Christendom, and Islam. All religions have in common the desire to enjoy as the best moment of the day when we stay in conversation or intimacy with God. Try to say what Prayer is. Consider also the similarity between Prayer as a step towards God and philosophy as a step toward the Truth.

Here is why this reflection must leave open its own conclusions.

Let us look around and grow in wisdom
Godspeed!

BEING & TIME

The segment gets most of its insights from a talk that Fr. Pasquale Foresi offered at the auditorium of the Istituto Mystici Corporis, in Loppiano, near Incisa Valdarno, 20 miles South of Florence, Italy, during the summer 1966, while providing, for three days in a row, an intense series of teaching. Those teachings remain a corner stone of the so called Abba School, which is the foundation of the actual Sofia University.

Knowledge, Discourse, Being, Time, Truth are tightly connected to one another. Each one cannot be understood independently of the other four. We are still dealing with the section of Metaphysics called Critique, and specifically Gnoseology.

Reflecting on what is TRUTH get a diverse perspective according to the time we belongs to. Language also get a diverse meaning according to what time is addressed. Such a topic does include a few reflections addressing the many perspectives which direct people towards truth. Some have already been said in class or in others notes but, as the Romans said "*Repetita juvant*" (It is useful to insist and repeat items).

A. Nature of Time

Immanuel Kant stressed that we always think in the categories of time and space... Actually we are language because we live inside of time: we need somewhere and some time to be. We need time to explain. We need time to share. We do not exist without time.

Every one of us (real beings) lives somewhere sometime. We live inside of a historical and geographical context. History is something which refers to a specific period of humankind time. History refers to time and something else... History is the course of human time. Additionally, history exists only if there is a beginning, a process and an end... without all these terms, the three of them, history does not exist. When there is no beginning there is no history. If the process is missing, history cannot occur. If not end is expected, it is not history... The question is serious: we belong to time.

Time is a sophisticate reality, which is easy to refer to and to grasp for we live in, but it is difficult to explain, as Augustine himself used to say, "If we talk about time, I know what we are talking about, but when you ask me what it is, I am in trouble to define it"

Time can be a perfect example to understand the several masks Friedrich W. Nietzsche referred to about life. He likes to tell that every one hides a new personality inside of his own behaviors... But the inside personality is in turn the mask of another one. Then another one is hidden behind. The process is almost endless... All the same, time can be calculated under diverse perspectives... Taking an appointment in New York, in Dallas, and in Los Angeles coincide to diverse "times" of the same day.

Time is usually calculated in reference to a distance. The connection works in every perspective. We understand time as the experience of covering distance. Such a distance may be physical (physical time), psychological (psychological time), metaphysical (metaphysical time), or without any distance as in ecstasy (spiritual time).

To say it in one word, time expresses our own density of life. We eventually could elaborate a scale of beings which would identify the quality of their existence according to the experience of time they are able to share.

Additionally we always are involved in the threesome configuration of **past-present-future**. A similar a trilogy never stops to put us at the test. We constantly move from one dimension to another. And we need them together: the past constitutes the basic form of everything we are and the future put a sense to our present: without a project that will be performed in the future our present is a non-sense. Notwithstanding, we must stress that actually past and future do not exist. They only exist in reference to present. It is now that past and future exist and get consistent. But this now is a continuous evolving, so be it for past and future.

Past and future are like the canvas where people are supposed to paint their present in. We only exist in the present. Nonetheless, past and future are necessary to properly act now. Past and future form the context where the present is supposed to be exerted. In one of his tales, C.S. Lewis imagines the conversation between two evil ones, two fallen angels, who are discussing the best way to ruin people... The suggestion which is given to the evil guardian is to keep his protégé focused or on the past or on the future in order to never allow him living in present time... It is actually in the present that we meet eternity if we want to. When we are too much concerned with the past or with the future we lose the opportunity of the present.

In the configuration of human nature as Augustine likes to elaborate we find also in past-present-future, in that triune experience of time, traces of the Trinity. Past shows the traces of the Father, present actuates the efficiency of the Son, and all our future growing is under the perspective of the Ghost...

Such a neighborhood, however requires a particular balance, those who live too much in the past could show behavioral troubles or psychological disorders... Those living too much in the future may lose actual life. The solution of similar confusion stay in the capacity of addressing the present for what it is: the only field of activity where we actually are. Living in the present, and living the present moment is the key of every successful life.

It is our intimacy with the Son which put us in relationship with the Father and makes us meet the Holy Spirit. When we speak with the Father ("Our Father, who is in heaven…) we actuate in us the presence of the Son. Such Trinitarian relationship is the real field where our human nature moves. To deal properly with the issue I will use a study, which Pasquale Foresi offered in a series of lectures during the summer 1965 at the Institute Mystici Corporis, Loppiano, near Florence, Italy, and published later in *Appunti di Filosofia*, edited by Città Nuova. Analogically a similar study could be made on happiness. Every being blossoms according to its own specificity. Such specificity refers to a peculiar experience of time. Time, it is said, may be experienced according to a different density.

B. Physical Time

On a road map we get the distance between cities according two sorts of indications, both precise and accurate. We have the numbers made in miles and the one written in hours. When we say that Pittsburgh is far 300 miles or five hours from Detroit we say the same. Physical time refers to a physical space. Physical Time refers to physical distance. The actual clock, which measures the time that passes, deals with physical time. Every watch shows physical time. It is the most usual notion of time. It is the basic common reference of time. Physical time is also called **Aristotelian time**, for the time Aristotle referred to was physical time, i.e. a time divided in hours, days, seasons, years, according to astronomic changes. It is a time which refers to the natural course of the earth to move from sunset to sunrise, and from fall to spring, from winter to summer. It is a time which refers to the movement of the sky around the earth in the Ptolemaic perspective.

It is observed, today under Copernican perspective. Such physical time can be the time of traveling from a place to another, of for such an activity while the earth is moving from daylight to afternoon, which is specified by a precise position of the sun on the horizon line of a precise spot on earth.

Such a physical time is the objective time of our agendas, calendars, meetings. When we calculate the speed of a car, a plane, or a rocket, we use physical time. Every scientific discourse refers to physical time. Therefore physical time is said "**objective time**" for it is the time that people refer to in usual conversation, social events, and in scientific data. It is the conventional time established by mutual agreement among people to make possible international schedules… international flights, worldwide calendar, and so on.

Most often, people consider physical time as the only one real. Nonetheless there is some other "density" of time which is real as well, even if it does not refer to physical actions, or sensible parameters.

C. Psychological Time

In the neighborhood of physical time we may experience another perception of distance. Don't we experience inside of us some experience of time, which is different to physical time? Is there something we may call psychological distance? When visiting a good friend, even the longest distance is never too much? Oppositely, it often happens that we have no time to address unpleasant commitments we are asked to. Why the perspective of visiting some relative that we tend to dislike makes even a short distance a too long travel to be worth to pay such a visit? Psychological space is the distance that people experience subjectively. Even if it is subjective it is, however, consistent. It really happens, indeed! And so a subjective feeling has objectives outcomes.

Psychological time is defined in connection to changes between different veins of feeling. In such a neighborhood it is well known as a same philosophical lecture may be consider too long for some (they even have the feeling to see their own beard growing) or even too short from others who are so interested in it (Wow it is already done!?). Such a feeling goes with our own interest and changes our own perception of the physical time: in some cases an hour may be felt as a few minutes, while just ten minutes look like an hour. Such a perception of the physical time depends on our own veins of feeling. That perception is subjective, psychological.

Psychological time is a personal perception on the physical time. It is not objective. Notwithstanding it is real, too. We must notice that everyone does not perceive physical time the same, for not human experiences are the same. In our soul (*yuch* in Greek) time gets a proper consistency. It is the time that we experiment in our mind; it is the time of our emotions. It is the time that **Henri Bergson** analyzed in *Temps et Mémoire*. Because such a time is real but not objective, and because it refers to inner changes, to emotional endeavors, to the feeling of a **duration** which is real but not physical, we give it the name of **Psychological time**. It is the time through which we perceive the duration of a certain experience. It is the perception of the inner process of change in our mind and our heart during a specific experience that is measured independently of objective time.

Psychological time is the time that a person perceives to have passed or is going through. It is real, for people emotions are real. It is however subjective, and nonetheless verifiable; it runs inside of people emotions and feeling. It is subjective perception of physical time. I feel a meeting shorter or longer in reference to the interest it raises in my mind. Disinterest makes "time" longer. While expecting for an important event objective time may run too slow, like a red light at the crossing while driving to a desirable or interesting meeting… It may be too short after a good moment and we are not in a hurry to drive somewhere. Somehow psychological time expresses the originality of our inside endeavor. It is the specific process our inside experience. It is real even if it is not physical. It is not objective and nonetheless consistent. It surely exists.

D. Metaphysical Time

Human people experience a deeper perception of time. It is due to the distance between what they are now (existentially) and what they know they should be – people sometimes say "what they would like to be," or "what they think they should be." These last two expressions are acceptable as far as we recognize that "what we want to be" is not mere illusion, like an envy, a superficial desire e.g. "I want to buy a house", or a new shirt, a new car, or even "I want a new job". Metaphysical time is not the distance towards imagination or a utopia.

No! Metaphysical time refers to something consistent inside of us, similar to the truth that Socrates wanted to help us to disclose, wanted to make his followers to deliver... It is the distance between the actual being that we are now and the true being that we are inside and should deliver in order to blossom in what we deeply are. Such a distance between the two beings of the same person, at existential and essential levels, is said metaphysical. In other words, metaphysical time refers to the distance between existence and essence.

There is a distance between what we accidentally do and what we deeply are. When we admonish children, they know what we are talking about: they know that what they did was not a good reflect of what they are and our reprobation is an attempt to help them to behave as well as the good they are. Such a distance, between the superficial being of existence and the essential being which we deeply are, is ontological (in Greek, *on-ontos)* is the being. Therefore we have the adjective "ontological" as what is referring to the being). Ontology is the main section of metaphysics.

Therefore, the actual distance towards what we deeply are is metaphysical. Metaphysical time is how we perceive the distance towards what we consistently want to be and are not yet. As a philosopher **FRIEDRICH W. NIETZSCHE** refers to physical and psychological time, but the one he essentially refers to is the third one: the time I need to move from what I am existentially to what I ontologically am. This is the time that **Martin Heidegger** investigates in *Being and Time* and was call then **Metaphysical**, for there is no way to move over there. Nietzsche says that there is no way towards the Hyperborean — The ones who live over the North Pole as a symbolic land of the **overhuman**. Such a land is not physical, but over the physical (metaphysical).

Again, we should stress that metaphysical time is not the perception of a mere desire for appealing goods (a new car, a new TV, a new house), not even the desire of a project of life as such: "I want to be an engineer, an architect, a philosopher," or a fantasy of any kind. If metaphysical time was an illusion, someone would be right to say that it can be a trap. Heidegger is not talking about desire, envy, or utopia, he speaks about the awareness of what we deeply are inside; such awareness is source of improvement and freedom. It is the desire of the better good that we actually are and nonetheless we do not actuate yet... Foresi called it the distance between "now and not yet" i.e. a consistency that we truly are but is not fully showed up yet.

In some aspects, metaphysical time is synonym of transcendence. It expresses the fact that there are items that surpass us and cannot be said nor reached immediately and they nonetheless are near to us. Similar transcendence is expressed by Augustine saying that God is nearer to us than our own clothes, or the Koran affirming that God is nearer to us than our own jugular vein. It is the same fact that Aristotle stresses in *Metaphysics* §a asserting that "The being is contemporaneously difficult and easy to reach."

When after a good reflection, a time of meditation or a religious retreat, it happens that I understand better what I need to do to improve; so I want to take some resolution (some decision which is supposed to solve, or resolve, the distance of my improvement) and I say inwardly "starting tomorrow, I will do" – it always appears to us that we need some physical time to cover the metaphysical distance towards what we are and we clearly perceived as accessible. Curiously we rarely say: "since now on I will do this or that", but more easily we express our decision of change with a future start, for we feel too much how the distance is without a pass, without a road, for it is an ontological distance, which means metaphysical.

"There is no road towards the Hyperborean," Nietzsche wrote in Dawn, and in his 1890-1900 diaries. He also perceives that the ontological distance which is not through a road may be more easily covered through another time which is the experience of Eternity, a spiritual experience when time and eternity are one. He understands the deep perception of a better quality of life, which leads us faster towards what we are. For, he said, "we actually are tightened between the beast and the overhuman." It happens sometimes situations where it is difficult to identify if it is still metaphysical time or the exertion of spiritual time, as below.

E. Spiritual Time

Specifically, spiritual refers to what belongs to the spirit, which is far beyond the mind. FRIEDRICH W. NIETZSCHE was well aware of the difference between mind and spirit, and of the difficulty to use the mind (for we need words) to say so. While the words belong to the mind, spiritual experience is apophatic (above every language — see Maritain in *Degrees of Knowledge*, Chapter V). Here is the cause of the misunderstanding for the words while dealing with spiritual issues, and how every misunderstanding is like a mask. The words are not able to express the reality we belong to and stand above us, unless we already made once the experience of it.

As well as not every brightening yellow stone is gold, not all things that people call spiritual actually are so. And when people claim to be spiritual what it is not they provoke the anger of Nietzsche to the point that he would like to use a hammer and crash them (see Philosophy of the Hammer). Spiritual time is a moment of eternity experienced in life. At times it is experienced as a moment of ecstasy. It usually fills the soul with a happy feeling. It has been defined as a moment when the highest happiness is reached. **Mystical Time** is the nickname of Spiritual Time.

To say the truth, nobody is properly a human being if s/he had not once experienced such a spiritual endeavor. The question is that our civilization barely refers to it. And what we really experienced as spiritual is too often referred to or sold as speculative, scientific, or mere useful good. Spiritual is far beyond any of these perspectives!

In two or more occasions FRIEDRICH W. NIETZSCHE experienced some ecstasy which he referred to while he was living temporarily in Surlej, Switzerland, and Rapallo, near Genova, Italy. Two wonderful places where he observed "Zarathoustra jumped on me" – that is to say he understood a situation of total absence of any distance which he gave the name of Eternity, "for I love you oh! Eternity" he will chant later in Piazza Barberini, Rome, Italy, in a magnificent poem.

Such an experience exerted by Friedrich Nietzsche as a unique instant of perfect junction with reality is what **Pasquale Foresi** calls spiritual time (for only the spirit is awake in such experience, while all the rest is asleep or remains "outside"). It is a unique instant of ecstasy which may take a few days.

Xenophon

As an example, in his *Anabasis*, **Xenophon** recalled the ten thousands Greek camping among the Persians in Asia Minor, when for 24 hours in a row Socrates remained immobile, standing out of his tent, with his bare feet in the snow, totally indifferent with the activity of the other soldiers while the morning was moving to noon, afternoon, evening, twilight, nightfall, night, dawn, up to the following morning, when, without any special deed or word, he moved back to his tent and turned back to the regular military business without showing any tiredness nor any change in his usual behavior. Xenophon seemed to indicate that Socrates was in deep meditation looking for the conclusion of some particular reflection. His companions were informed about the visit of some spirit that Socrates was accustomed to meet.

Spiritual time is also the experience that Plotinus explained to his disciple Porphyrios, who testified that his master exerted more than six times during his life. It is a time that we cannot define properly for there is no reference to any distance, or to any place. A similar "non-description" can be found in the second letter of **St. Paul** to the Corinthians: "I know a man in Christ who fourteen years ago – still in the body? I do not know; or out of the body? I do not know: God knows – was caught up right into the third heaven. .. and heard words said that cannot and may not be spoken by any human being" (2Co 12:2-4). In the *Confessions*, **St. Augustine** recounts his exceptional meeting with his mother, St. Monica, along the beach of Ostia; he says: "We were outside" – which we must read: out of the time and the space we are familiar with. It was an experience that he was unable to indicate how long it took place. An ecstasy may take a second and leave in your heart an understanding that could barely be said in hours, or be reported an entire book… So it was for **Melanie** at la Salette. An ecstasy may also take days and leave the feeling of a few sec-

Apparition at La Salette

onds… It was the case of **St. Philippe Neri**, who continuously tended to tell jokes in order to distract himself, even in front of the Pope, so frightened he was to enter in ecstasy. This is the reason why he asked his servant, during the mass never stopping to grasp his feet in order to keep him on the ground. What a fear got the servant when he found himself attached to the ankles of the saints who was near the vault of the Church dome of Chiesa Nuova, yelling to Philippe to move down. Not long ago there are the witnesses of the many **Padre Pio's** wonders.

Mélanie Calvat

St. Philip Neri

St. Pio

Such a spiritual time, which was a few times experienced by Friedrich Wilhelm Nietzsche, is tightly connected with his philosophical reflections, and caused the many difficulties and troubles of his last years. Spiritual time is a moment of perfect lucidity, of a better consciousness than usual. In such clearness we understand the world, other people, every being for what they really are… It is a moment of perfect intelligence, which is so difficult to explain and recount later on.

According to Fr. Joseph de Finance, the experience of spiritual time is more frequent than we may imagine: No human being, worthy of the name of human, is unaware of such meeting with God. Every human was made to see God. In a way or another everyone met God in person sometime, somehow, during lifetime, for we need to know the one we are supposed to meet at the threshold of our life. We are supposed to see God, for each of us' soul is image of God and is made to talk to God. Such a fact is more consistent than the many doubts someone may have about it.

Joseph de Finance

After Plotinus we call **APOPHATIC** the teaching received during so exceptional moments of vision and **CATAPHATIC** what we are able, later, to reasonably say about it. **Jacques Maritain** gives an extensive explanation of the two terms in Degrees of Knowledge (Chapter VI). Apophatic expresses the fact that every true moment of spiritual time runs above human understanding. Notwithstanding, as soon as we share such a moment with other people the quality of that vision slow down to an intelligible level (cataphatic). Without human sharing, however, it is very difficult for those who experience similar high meetings and visions to understand them: Here is why, St. John of the Cross states that it is very difficult to make a proper interpretation of visions and locutions "especially when they directly come from God."

Similar words invite to prudence. They explain the care of the Church to avoid confusion in comparable situations, asking people not to speak without the screening of the church. In his letter to the Corinthians, Paul stresses that those who speak in tongue are supposed to be silent in assemble if no one is able to translate their words for the people in attendance. Emilio Tardif, of the charismatic movement, had a similar experience in Jerusalem, when the Latin Patriarch, asked him not to make any miracle during the celebration of the mass. In trust that the Lord would have been obedient to the bishop Fr. Tardif begun to say mass at the altar of the Golgotha, but, after processing the transubstantiation he spoke in tongue. He was very embarrassed when he met the bishop afterwards. The bishop, however, confessed, "Actually when you spoke in tongue you spoke Aramaic and I was able to understand every word!" But he refused to reveal their contents.

Here is why whoever gets similar vision must undergo to the Magisterium of the Church, which warranty fidelity to Revelation, Tradition, and its patrimony of knowledge. And it is better to know less but harmoniously than having more information that can be wrongly understood and disruptive. As usual, knowledge is supposed to be put at the service of society. And the capacity of serving the betterment of society shows the quality of analogue teaching: they both involve the quality of the vision (apophatic) and the capacity of the seer to translate appropriately (cataphatic). Both are necessary. Like a tree can be appreciated through the quality of its fruits, all the same an apophatic experience is evaluated according to the consistency of its cataphatic message. Sometimes, however, discernment is not easy. We are, at so a high level, at the presence of mystery. The whole field requires an expertise which belongs to a field which overcomes metaphysics.

When you find yourself overwhelmed with duty and chores that you can barely address, do not lose time in better organization of new planning, just get a better point of view, get a higher presence of spiritual time in your life. While I was working in the Vatican, in the years 80s I was told that surprising decision of Mother Teresa of Calcutta in a particular moment of her congregation, when the sisters and the brothers were complaining for not being able to address properly the many commitment they had… because of shortness of time. During the general chapter the decision of Mother Teresa surprised everyone: "Since today, all of us will spent one more hour in adoration before the Eucharist." Nobody was expecting such a decision. They did it and they solved their struggle…

Every moment of spiritual time is like a blow of fresh air in our life... There is a Middle East tale about an imam who was a pipe smoker and was sowing debris of tobacco all around. Once he was in trouble in front of a page of the Koran. He was totally unable to read it because of too many accents on the line that he was not capable to interpret... His wife interfered brutally saying: "how can you seek to read that page with all that tobacco in it," and she blew on the parchment and the whole text became suddenly clear and easy to read... Spiritual time is this kind of blow in our life which removes the many obstacles that would make difficult our endeavor.

F. Human Time

Because such a spiritual experience involves the whole person, spiritual time is experienced through, inside, and in spite of the other densities of time. **All different densities of time are always present in every human experience**, even when the last higher degree of life and understanding is in force and seems to put everything else as in shadow. In every human deed the whole soul is involved, and all densities of time are there.

Sometimes people believe that seers are visionaries, or dreamers. The opposite is a fact. When we meet some true seers we soon observe that they are not dreamers. Dreamers are the people who do not see, those who do not experience spiritual time. People who do not know spiritual time, or do not experience it sufficiently, are the ones who live asleep. The true visionaries are the one who see, and sometimes foresee. Seers are the ones who really understand. But like the philosopher reported in **Plato's *Republic***, who comes back to the cavern after a visit to the true world, it is almost impossible for a seer, for a prophet to be understood by his relatives and friends. Often it happens to them like the philosopher in the myth of the Cavern: people do not like to change in order to improve. Nonetheless this change for improvement is the real nature of time: we are on earth to accomplish a journey, to grow from our birth to the Natus Est, the eternal departure. This is time actually. Time is integral part of creation: it is our same condition of creature and it includes our whole earthly endeavor. In other words, **time is the distance I cover to get ready for eternity**.

While he is trying to refer to his particular experience of heaven, Friedrich W. Nietzsche does not know other words than those who are made to report physical time and are barely able to express psychological and metaphysical time. It is impossible then to talk about spiritual time to those who do not know it -"there is no way towards the Hyperborean." Nietzsche said it repeatedly to invite other people to enter in it. His words, "there is no way" indicates the experience of transcendence… He knows that an overhuman reality exists, he knows that people may experience some kind of situations beyond physical time, for he had occasion to get some of these valuable experiences, but because he was not able to share his endeavors he never knew how he got there. This is why Friedrich W. Nietzsche develops discourse full of gaps, a discourse full of holes, in which every interpretation of facts is a mask that hides the other possible considerations. He does not know that with love, all these diverse experiences of time, may go together and complete one another.

G. Nature of History

Years ago I participated at a symposium on history in Vatican City. Many history teachers were addressing the amazing fact of how in our day there is a lack of sense of history. French Prof. Claude Bousquet presented an interesting case: among our children today, he said, it seems that what belongs to the past is all confused in a unique category of what is over. As an example, he recounted the story of two children, Jean-Luc (12 years old) and Anne (10). They were going to the country visiting their grandmother in a farm. On the way out of town the father suggested them to be nice with their grand-mother, asking her for example about her past, the eventual changes or even the characteristics of the society of her earlier days... The children agreed willingly. At their arrival to the farm, they run out of the car and rushing to their welcoming Mamie they asked: "Hello grandma', tell us: how it was in the Middle Ages?" Obviously, the old lady was rather surprised!

Actually, history may only exist inside of an experience of faith. In our society which is losing references to faith the sense of history is fading all around. During the cultural wave of atheism, just after WWII and up to the end of the century, existentialists like Jean-Paul Sartre and Structuralists like Michel Foucault spoke about human events, human condition that every person may influence, but they never spoke about history. Michel Foucault even added that history does not exist, we only may have museums to gather human events. He denies that History as such do exist, and he is right to say so, when God is erased from our culture, as a consequence of it the configuration of human life disappears.

According to Augustine history starts when God called Abraham and told him to leave the country of his fathers and move to the land he promised. History starts when times have a dramatic change from eternity and all events can be seen in the process of moving towards a clear future appointment that time has with eternity, "leaves the place where you live and go to the land I'll give you!" Then followed a series of event which have a sense because we all know we are in the process of moving towards the end times, when eternity has an appointment with time.

Following the steps of Augustine, Maritain defines **history** as the human journey developing in time since people received a call from eternity and will develop up to a final appointment with eternity at the end times (see vocabulary). In other words, history is the human combination of space and time. "There is no history when and where people are not involved" (Augustine). Because of the spiritual nature of people, history hides a mystery. For that reason "History deserves more to be contemplated than to be explained" (J. Maritain)

When there is only change there is no history. With today civilization, the decreasing of faith produces also a decreasing of sense of history and a disappearance of all history as such. In a world without God, with the disappearance of the arbitrator of truth, everything becomes arbitrary. It is a whole chaotic configuration. It does not mean that history does not exist at all, it only means that parameters are lost and there is no possibility to get history any more. Structuralism, with Michel Foucauld speaks with changes and references of facts. In a world without God, we do not exist as person, any more. We are not allowed to say any more. In the *Structure of Things*, he wrote that it is improper to say "I think", I only am allowed to say: "Something thinks in me". I am part of a whole configuration which has properly no beginning and no end. I live inside of chaos. "Every culture is a piece of human history (C. Levi-Strauss). However, Jean Daujat says that "When faith is decreasing, the same notion of history is disappearing." contemporary studies of anthropology gather pieces of information in museums (Levy-Strauss, Michel Foucault). They do not address history any more.

Without any relation with eternity, there is no history. To get history we need a beginning, development with change, and an end. Augustine said that human history started with the call of Abraham, made with a request of change and a promise of achievement: "Leave the land of your fathers and go to the land I will give you." Then it continues all along in relationship with the Eternal provider. And it still continues today up to our final meeting with eternity. Without beginning and end, changes do not provide history. Augustine, Aquinas, Gilson, Maritain stress how history of philosophy is the recount of mankind improvement in wisdom during its journey towards the truth.. Philosophy is the human endeavor answering the call from the truth. Marcel Clément affirms that "Studying history we become familiar with the whole of mankind. We understand better who we are, both as individuals and as members of the society in which we were born and we move".

Somehow every historic step can be compared with some step of individual .growing: Marcel Clément compares **Childhood** with Ancient Philosophy, **Teenage** with Middle Ages, **Young Adulthood** with Modern Times, **Human Maturity** with contemporary philosophy. This is only an analogy, but it is intended to help people to better understand the role of history in human education.

According to the traditions of the Book (Jewish, Muslim, and Christian) human history is part of a divine process of the whole universe moving from nothing to human salvation. Such process of the action of God on earth was revealed to help us to grow accordingly. In such a perspective Card. Henri de Lubac states that history is the way people are addressing their task of completing (or participating to) God's creation.

H. Natus Est

Early Christian people used to call it, "***Natus Est***", which literally means: "to be born to eternity." In eternity we finally become what we are. We are finally born for good! The door we talk about is seen under human perspective as death. Death needs to be displayed in its mysterious and beautiful acceptation. We usually ignore what is death. We barely know it, for usually we are afraid to look at it. We misunderstand it, because death is not a change into life, but it is a change in my life to realize better what I am doing today. A few days ago, while the class was over, a few students remained to talk. One of them asked "But what do you intend really with 'We live only one life?" Well, I told him, "When I came to America, I started a totally new life here, with a new culture, a new language, a new context, and new people, and it is with all my background that I am able to live here now." Analogically, it is the concept of Maritain that death is not a stop in my life, or even an increase, eventually it is a blossoming. We must consider how we are supposed to live our death today in order to become ready for the moment when we die. Maritain agrees with the fact that there are not two worlds. He likes referring to Plato to show how we experience the consistency of spiritual values in our today life.

Death is the door of eternity under the perspective of time. We must dig more at the threshold of such admittance. Such a threshold is anticipated in many present situations. Many philosophers, like Michel de Montaigne, Blaise Pascal, and Friedrich Nietzsche, suggest making the reflection on death as the main reflection on life. They present the question of death as the paradigm of getting what I called spiritual time. We need the capacity of dropping all human interests and concerns to get there. In his letters and his diary, Nietzsche indicated how the presence of pain, of suffering, of great precariousness, of nearness of death, are improving his own reflection and frame his philosophy. There is a great relevance of death in the quality of our life. It is true at every level of our life. Nonetheless, because we live inside of matter, we are a body; we have to consider first of all the physical dimension of death. It is interesting to see that when in Physics, Aristotle gives the definition of life; he says that life is the capability to pass through birth, growth, reproduction, and death. So death serves to define life. To stress the issue I will quote Bernard Shaw: "Traveling is dying a little." This is true even physically: our skin is fresh and young in proportion of the many cells which are dying every minute of the day. Death can be seen as the key of life, up to the "Gate of Eternity.

I. Looking at the treshold

As a synthetic perspective the question on Death INCLUDES the following steps:

1. **Death represents the main topic on life** — see Montaigne, Pascal, Nietzsche, Philippe, Lubich (Jesus' death on the Cross), Foresi, and others.

2. **Death defines life** — "Life is defined by birth, growing, reproduction and death" - Aristotle.

3. **Death is paradoxical** — "Death is absurd" (Nietzsche, Maritain, Lubich). Such an absurdity is double: (1.) it is Absurd under earthly perspective: physically, psychologically, spiritually — (2.) it is Absurd under the eternal perspective, for eternity contradicts death

4. **Death is just a way** —

(a.) Death is no more than separation between Form and Matter (Aquinas, Philippe, Daujat) —

(b.) The body becomes a cadaver, while the soul remains in need of its body, which causes final resurrection —

(c.) Death is an accidental and "substantial" transformation which happens immediately in eternity, and lead to a later reconciliation of the soul with its body in time —

(d.) Death is real under earthly perspective and is an important spiritual step (cf. Jesus' death) —

(e.) Eternal life supposes immediate appropriation of a new body, which on earth will happen at the end times.

5. **Death is the actual present way of life** — Death is the actual way of life (Nietzsche, Maritain, Lubich) — (1.) there is No physical life without death (e.g. surviving of species, biological circle of life) — (2.) No psychological life without death (growing of the person by personal denying) — (3.) No spiritual life without leaving this earthly life (Eternity entrance)

6. **Death is the last human gift to creation** — Death is the manner people move out of actual creation and enter in eternity… According to Igino Giordani, Pasquale Foresi and Chiara Lubich, death is when the believers whose body had been nourished all along their life by the Eucharist leave their body to the earth, as a seed for its ownb renewal in "New Earth and New

Heaven" (Revelation 21:1-8).

7. **Opportunity to prefer death** — Necessity of death – (1.) Physically, psychologically, spiritually: relevance of death in our daily life (Chauchard, Daujat, Lubich) — (2.) Growing day by day by dying day by day (Nietzsche, Maritain, Giordani) — (3.) Our death is part of the cosmic death and of the renewal of the world... (Philippe, Lubich, John Paul II, Rm 8:22)

Addressing the definition of death, Sartre, Camus, Gide, find non-sense, absurdity. Then the whole life becomes an absurd endeavor. Sartre said that everybody in her/his conscience is not a thing, so is "nothing;" and death is the end of this nothing. Nietzsche makes an attempt to overcome so a non-sense. For him also, death is just the end of this life, but because he experienced the consistency of eternity - when, he said, "Zarathustra jumped on me!" Nietzsche elaborates the perspective of eternal return. It is the perspective, the only way through which Nietzsche was capable to think of eternity. It is not a sort of reincarnation, but the mysterious and implacable return of the same.

There is a similar perspective in Plato, who recaptures the Indian reincarnation. And it is probably there that Nietzsche got his major insight. Nonetheless, such Platonic reincarnation is a failure, for not being able to stay in the world of perfection, which is the Platonic world of ideas. There is not such an ideal world in Nietzsche. This world is the only one. It contains everything we got. And whatever is the perspective, death remains an unavoidable access.

For the mystics, death is the key of human life. Teresa of Avila said, "I am dying of not dying," or, "A day without suffering is a great suffering." She deeply understood how the blossoming way of people goes through suffering. Suffering is not just a downward fall; it is an upward growth. It is mostly the condition of disappearing from a certain state of life to get a better one.

In No Exit, Sartre is right to say that life has no exit, and there is no after life... Yes, because it is the same life which goes on, according to how we managed its earthly journey. Eternity is nothing but the blossoming of actual experience. Death increases the process of growing through spiritual birth.

The growing process of eternity in us is a successful process of continuous death during our lifetime, dying to everything is less consistent in our life. Few masters, like Juan de Yepes, mentioned several steps of spiritual improvement on the way: discovery of eternity with conversion, darkness of senses, illuminative period with success, wonders, foundations, darkness of the mind, and finally unitive life, when I am able to say with St. Paul "I do not leave by myself any more, Jesus lives in me" (1 Co 11:1).

8 Going through — We become more and more able to live properly, as far as we are capable to die to everything is less consistent. When we really are capable to die to everything is less consistent, we are ready to be born eternally. Therefore, such a process of growing through death is a growing one, which blossoms at our spiritual birth, getting finally the door of eternity.

Oppositely, eternity is a pure unlimited and one instant, if I may say so. Eternity is present to time at any moment of time. That same unique eternity includes all time diversity. It is an immanent presence which "comprehends" all possible changes. This is why we must say that "God knows now what I am doing tomorrow." What is future for me is supposed to be done in time; such future for me is present to eternity. Through spiritual time, or mystical life, I meet eternity during my life span;

In *The Degrees of Knowledge*, Maritain affirms that "when I die, I will be able to recognize eternity proportionately to the much I already am familiar with eternity. If I am not aware of eternity now, I will never be ready to recognize it whenever I die." In case I do not know it enough I will need some time of improvement, of adjustment before I enter. If I dislike it I will go forever away from it. Here is the neighborhood of our soul. Again, when I say soul, I include its body. Every human person lives also physically and behaves through matter, in space and time. Interesting is the issue addressed by Aquinas, when he deals with the situation of the separated souls. It is a difficult question. It raises a real dilemma: how would it be possible to our soul to survive the body if soul is merely the organizer of it. Aquinas has no doubt that the soul lives, for the soul is principle of life and does not know death. Nonetheless the question remains. The solution goes with the typical asynchronic connection between time and eternity. Eternity does not depend on time; it includes all different consistencies of it. Although it is impossible to understand eternity under the perspective of time, the dimension of eternity is clear, totally bright for the ones who experienced it. It remains, however, difficult to share it inside of time, as Plato explained in the myth of the Cave. Everything will be understood when we strike in person the distance through death, the Gate of immortality.

J. Eternity is Now

I experience eternity in my daily life (Philippe, Lubich) — the seven dimensions of eternity... Even if eternity is one it is so rich to express itself as many. Therefore I have to talk about it through several perspectives. Eternity is so intensively one that it includes all varieties and changes... this is why it is seen as immutable.

In *Christ Sein* (*On Being a Christian*), Hans Küng makes an interesting note about what should be the correct translation of the words of God to Moses, which traditionally are translated as "I am who am" (Ex 3:14). He says that the nature of Hebrew suggests a more literal translation, which should be "I will be who will be." According to Kung's note, the new translation should diminish the metaphysics interpretation of Godas present source of every being... To say the truth, I believe the opposite, for actually the incomplete tense (which includes both present and future in that language) increases the sense of Providence as source of our present, including our future. In any case, the traditional translation still stands: "I am who am" is much more than an eventual "I am the Being" — and here Küng is right!

Küng's proposal to stress the future, indirectly, stresses the "Providential" nature of God; it evidences his nickname of "Eternal Provider" — which means "The Eternal who will provide," as indicated in Mt 5. When Jesus says "Knock and you will be open, ask and you will receive, seek and you will find," he emphasizes the providing nature of his Father. In fact, the indirect form ("you will be given") is the typical way the Jews use to refer to the One that cannot be named (JHVH). Jesus is consistent with Jewish tradition. Therefore the words "I will be who will be" indicates our future... not God's future, which eventually is imperishable present.

In other words, our spiritual present makes our earthly future – what is the same in Semitic language is actually the same in fact: we will be tomorrow what we deeply are now! This gives the full sense of Christian transcendence.

When I understand the statement that, "in my life today, I share immortality," my own death takes a different perspective. At first it even disappears in its more dramatic picture. Soon another configuration enters our soul, with the desire to make present life the starting point of experiencing eternity. Because eternity is now, I experience it in present time. Such experience transfigures my whole person.

It is difficult to see all consequences of such sharing. First of all because of the gap existing between eternity and time: while reaching eternity I make real events that will be revealed on earth on due time. I put now in eternity the seeds of time transformation. As an example, sharing eternity, I start sharing the new configuration of my own body, which does not necessarily appears immediately evident: it could become evident, however, in the exceptional life of saint, like St. Anthony or Padre Pio who were able to exert bilocation during their earthly life.

Nonetheless it is the true nature of the body to include a spiritual entity… At this time, we have the example of Christ's resurrected body, when he was capable of passing through the walls, eating, talking, being touched, appearing at the same time to different people in different places, as indicated by St. Paul (1Co 15:6). Our eternal future is foreseen in his dramatic example of the first resurrected. Experiencing eternity, we put now the roots of the transformation or our body which is really actuated now, but will happen in time, at the end times.

Chiara Lubich says that those who eat Eucharistic Jesus every day are living seeds of eternal life on earth. Therefore, when they die, they sow a source of new configuration inside of the ground. Actually, the whole world is expecting its own renewal as a mother who is pregnant of the new life to deliver (Rm 8:22}. Every believer, when he/she dies makes the earth pregnant of the resurrection to come. All Christians live in their actual life their future dimension. The time to come is our neighborhood forever. And we put all our strength to prepare – not to predict – and produce its enlightening. Such a future is already enforced. It is potentially now but not yet fully actuated. I am living it now and, at the same time, I am activating its delivery in eternity. Such a situation of now and not yet, produces the huge typical suffering that every true mystic experiences. We are living in the world even if we do not belong to it. We work in a "now" which is both temporal and eternal.

I wish I was able to say all that much better. Fortunately, at our "*Natus Est*", we will soon see everything clearly especially when our "*Natus Est*" blossoms with our own resurrection of the end times. I give you appointment there to understand more.

K. All People Exert Spiritual Time

I experience eternity through spiritual time. By intelligence and love I access eternity inside of physical time. Augustine,

Aquinas, De Yepes, Maritain, Foresi, Lubich stress the unique experience of spiritual time. The experience of eternity is specific of the soul: eternal context is specific of it and eternity is of its nature.

Every individual exerts all different levels of activity, physical, psychological, speculative, and spiritual. Everyone is a microcosm which develops all fields of being. Inside of a human being are present all items dimensions, which compose the macrocosm. It is important to notice how people who are material, also are spiritual. To say so almost improperly, I would stress that in everyone there is something which is perishable and something which stays forever. Every human being is first of all an individual, which emerges from its individual condition through relationship with others. Doing so, it becomes a person. Every person shares immortality in two ways: first through the process of acquaintance up to the act of knowledge, and second through the process of love.

We will first deal with knowledge. The process of knowledge is interesting because through knowledge people experience all kinds of existence and life present in the world. The act of knowledge is something interior that identifies us individuals and makes us capable to be related personally to the world surrounding us.

The process of knowledge goes mainly through two important steps. There is, first of all, acquaintance by senses, and, second of all, knowledge by intelligence. Following the tracks of Aristotle and Aquinas, Maritain says that the process of acquaintance by senses is the same, or at least similar, in people and in animals. Through senses, all people share this acquaintance together with animals. The process is not material, it goes beyond material things; nonetheless it remains tightly connected by my senses with the material things surrounding me. As a matter of fact, if I have no ears I cannot perceive sounds, if I have no eyes I cannot see forms, shapes, and colors, and if

I have no touch I cannot have any tactile sensation. Because the acquaintance by senses is directly connected with the five senses, when the body disappears, this knowledge disappears, too. And so, even if sensorial activity is superior to mere matter, it remains connected with matter by senses, which disappear when the body disappears. That is the reason why Aquinas considered that animals (which etymologically are "the ones which have soul — "*anima*") do not have a spiritual soul, i.e. not an immortal soul.

Additionally, such precariousness of animals does not prevent them to exist in heaven, too. They would exist, however, for another reason and with another consistency. They will be not precarious any more. In eschatological questions, Aquinas explains that going to heaven, we enter up there (in a upper level of quality, not of space) in fullness, bringing everything which characterizes us, belongs to us, including all the beings we loved, like pets, usual items, and all belongings that actually made us what we were on earth. Human love makes things existing to eternity. Human love is a divine power, which brings in eternity everything we loved. We enter in eternity with our spiritual body (our body in fullness without its actual failures) we blossom. In eternity, all things enter spiritually, not entitatively (in their previous entity), but spiritually.

> (The words can barely reflect the fact. When we say spiritual, we indicate a level of reality which includes previous levels. What is material is precarious, what is speculative is effectual but sterile ["Science inflates, love builds" – 1Co 8:1], what is spiritual is fecund and includes in fullness all the previous levels. Spiritual level of reality is the completeness of existence; it includes a variety of items which surpass by far the diversity of the previous ones.)

On this point, Aquinas follows the main stream of Aristotle, who considered three categories of souls: vegetative, sensitive, and spiritual. Aquinas differs to Aristotle by the stress he makes, or if you wish, by the consideration of unity of each individual.

Such perspective of unity of every individual is the key of his doctrine. Then because each one exists through its soul, and the whole configuration of every being is a microcosm, such entity is one; therefore the soul must be one. Then, at each level of complexity, individuals require an analogous configuration of its soul. At an upper level, a more sophisticated soul assumes also the characteristics needed from the less elaborate ones.

A warning is needed here! We must be cautious when we say "soul." Talking about soul, we do not talk about a piece of a person… It is not a piece, it is the same person, or, if you wish, its source of activity. It refers neither to a place, nor to a shape. To say it roughly: the only place a soul may refer to is the place of the body; the only configuration a soul may refer to is the configuration of its body.

What does knowledge provide to the soul? What does it happen with knowledge by intelligence? Etymologically, intelligence comes from Latin words "*intus-legere*" — literally intelligence is the capacity to pick up (*legere*) "whatness" inside (*intus*) of the images of things, i.e. to form concepts and ideas… So, intelligence is the capacity to recognize what they are (whatness), to read the being inside (intus) of things. Such an action of extracting the being from things with our mind is known as "process of abstraction." The result of knowledge is not material. It is a totally different picture. Concepts or ideas refer to items that can be material o immaterial (for example the same concept of knowledge), but as such, a concepts is merely speculative. An idea is a speculative item, which refers to some existent ("real"), which may be physical, speculative (existing in the mind), virtual (existing in the imagination), or spiritual. A concept remains after its object has disappeared; it survives it.

The capacity of dealing with concepts is what we call reason. Intelligence (process of abstraction) and reason (playing with the ideas) are the main two legs of regular knowledge. We easily verify it in scientific knowledge… Under the perspective of the field of human knowledge, the process of abstraction from things (Intelligence) and its relative understanding (reason) is the first step. It is not the only configuration of human knowledge. There are different kinds of knowledge configuration. People use sometime the term of "levels of knowledge" to indicate the different kinds of it, because they usually refer to different degrees of objects. Every new level involves a different approach of facts and different results. When we say different approach we should say different method. All objects of knowledge cannot be grasped the same way. Analogically we do not work with wood as we work with metal, we need two totally different approach. What is true for physical techniques is even truer for speculative activity. Then, for each level of knowledge, intelligence and reason improve and work accordingly.

L. Time belongs to creation

Aquinas refers to time as a creature. Time is one of the items made during the marvelous act of creation, while out of love God creates (even right now) the whole universe. Because time belongs to creation, the whole of creation develops properly through time. Physical time is the natural background where creation does express itself. Aristotle stated that every physical being does exist in time. It is the mysterious gift of existence.

As previously indicated every expression of the macrocosm (physical, speculative, spiritual) is properly expressed through a specific experience of time.

More must be said. However, from this short background, time is put in its proper perspective.

M. Connaturality

In *The Degrees of Knowledge*, Maritain addresses a second steps, which he called "knowledge by connaturality." The way of Knowing by connaturality, or affinity, means knowledge by sharing, or by common experience. A driver would understand better the behavior of another driver, a new converted would understand better the struggle of a non believer, and so on. It works also for spiritual items, becoming familiar with them improve our knowledge not by abstraction but by connaturality.

The notion of knowledge through conaturality does not deny the regular process of knowledge that is produced in the intellect by way of abstraction, or by way of demonstration, which is by virtue of conceptual connections. Connaturality indicates an awareness of an issue which is grasped by the "intelligence" of it. Connaturality is a kind of enlightening which brings us faster towards the truth. We may have experiences that make us aware of some notions, even if we do not have a very good knowledge of it. Maritain affirms: "A virtuous man may possibly be utterly ignorant in moral philosophy and know as well, and probably better, everything about virtue through connaturality."

Proceeding towards, Maritain shows a third level of knowledge. Maritain indicates that because Nietzsche had some mystical experience, he was able to understand better the deepness of reality as a whole. But because he was not able to share his experience with anyone, he could not translate it into words. So, to express his experience in our culture, he was obliged to use a paradoxical language. Here, there is more than a mere process of knowledge by connaturality? In "Degrees of Knowledge," Maritain states that the "apophatic" vision is the highest abstraction we can have in metaphysical knowledge. To get it, we have to enter into another process, which is mystical knowledge and mystical experience, where we are only able to see and barely know. In such a neighborhood, it is God himself who is having us in care; he transforms us, to make us capable to perceive God's reality.

Maritain says that all Christians, by the simple fact that they live on earth — where reality is not only material but also spiritual — have already entered into a process of education, which became possible because God revealed himself in a sensible way to people, up to a higher level of intimacy which started when God himself became flesh. Obviously the mystics are more forward than others, but he says, "If people are capable to share something of eternal reality, they have something in common that does not die." This stresses even more the immortality of the person. In our civilization today, when we are aware that every Christian community is the body of Christ, talking about "immortality of the soul" seems almost insufficient to express the immortal nature of people.

In what way, then, may I say better that there is something in me which is immortal? How can I say that there is something in me which overcomes time and space? Here, the reflection of Aquinas, Maritain, and Philippe, consists essentially in some existential reflection. Maritain was true when he stated that the philosophy of Thomas Aquinas is philosophy of existence. Among the events they refer to, there is the fact that I know, producing not only some immaterial act, but also sharing a reality, which is not material. Let us see again the full picture of it. With our previous considerations the panorama of the question will become more evident.

We saw that knowledge itself is not always sufficient to affirm the immortality of my soul, because of the fact that there is knowledge by senses and knowledge by intelligence. So, there are different levels of growing and moving inside of the field of knowledge. We are now familiar with the fact that knowledge by senses refers to images, to the traces I get in my mind from the information provided by my smell, my touch, my eyes, my ears, or my taste. These images remain in my mind. Through images, I am aware of the surrounding beings, of the world around me. When I have no ears I have no experience of noise; when I have no eyes I have no experience of shape, light, or color, and so, this kind of knowledge, which is immaterial in itself, is tightly connected with the material existence of senses. Without a body I can have no more activity of knowledge by senses. That is the reason why, for the scholastics, animals have their soul die when they die, because they have only knowledge by senses.

What does it happen with the intellect, with knowledge by intelligence? It is an upper level of mind activity. I was suggested once, by Jean Daujat, a beautiful example to address the distinction between sensorial acquaintance and intelligence knowledge. I like to say it with my own words. In Gascony, my family home was near a train station. In those days, when a train arrived at the station, it was led by a locomotive running by steam. A locomotive was something black, dark, dirty, stinking, smoking, and having behind a reserve of coal. The stationmaster had a dog. At the arrival of a train, he used to say to his dog, "Go to the locomotive." The dog immediately went to the locomotive. There is nothing surprising to see a dog to move in response to some words. Animals easily connect the sound of a word with situations, images, and sounds. But when the company changed the system of locomotive, and they used diesel ones, it was not dark, stinking, noisy, smoky, or dirty. On the contrary, it was green, clean, silent, and quite luminous. So, when the first train of this kind arrived to the station and the stationmaster said to his dog, "Dog, go to the locomotive!" the dog didn't move: it was unable to recognize the locomotive. For the dog, a locomotive was something black, smoky, dirty, noisy dark, and usually placed at the head of the train. It had distinctive characteristics. For the stationmaster, instead, a locomotive was more than an item dark and smoky; it was the vehicle, which was moving the train. Knowledge by intelligence is knowledge by the being; it is knowledge by essence, by nature, and by definition. Differently, sensorial knowledge is acquaintance by senses, which means by color, shape, odor, and other descriptions. So it took some time for the dog to adapt the word "locomotive" to the new features of it. Oppositely, the stationmaster made no change in his mind: as always, a locomotive was the car moving the train, whenever was it position in the train, whatever was its configuration with an engine working with steam, oil, or electricity! Intelligence goes by definition (what a thing is => its whatness or essence, its being) while sensorial acquaintance works with description, image of things.

According to Maritain, wild animal acquaintance is fully expressed in knowledge by senses. Differently, people start awareness through senses and progressively grow up to grasp names, until they finally enter into the field of full intelligence. Afterwards (an after which is not necessarily temporal), people use all levels of knowledge accordingly. Intelligence knowledge is free of description; it works with definition, which fits the nature of things. Definition deals with the being; the being itself is not material, even when it appears through material forms. After Aristotle and Aquinas, Maritain distinguishes every being we deal with from the matter it is shaped in. Its shape appears through the matter it is made of. Getting a shape matter becomes something. We recognize cement, wood, or iron, from its configuration. They all are matter of different configurations. Ultimately matter is capacity of change; it is what makes a shape consistent, real. Aristotle characterized everything on earth as consisting on form and matter. Intelligence is the capability to recognize something by its shape. Shape appears through matter; as such, it is only a form, and absolutely not material. Intelligence works by concepts or forms. The form is said to be the intelligibility of a thing, which means what we may recognize about something, what we know about it. When we recognize in something the shape of a square or a triangle, such a form is not material; it is speculative. Extending the notion of form, we see that every form is speculative, even if it is transmitted to me through senses; the capacity to recognize what things are and giving them a name overcomes matter consistency. In everything, there is the trace of something immaterial, which as such cannot die.

We must push the reflection ahead. Among the categories

of Emanuel Kant there are the categories of space and time. Kant says that we need these categories in ourselves to be able to know, to be able to grow in knowledge, to be able to deal with other people. Maritain developed a critical analysis on Kant, saying that the fact that I am capable to name time and space means that I am capable to grasp them, to identify them in a frame that overcomes them. Analogically, when I want to write a word in class, I need a marker and a blank blackboard. I need some space where to write it down. Accordingly, to speak about time and space, I need another neighborhood, which overcomes time and space, where I am able to understand what time and space is. Animals have no notion of time and space. Animals live inside of time and space, they are not aware of it; they are capable to wait, to move, to jump; they feel it. Under so a perspective they are aware of it. It would be improper to say that they know it: when I say that a cat is waiting for a mouse, it is anthropomorphism; I put on the cat human behavior characteristics, for that is the way I deal, myself, with time; so for me the cat is waiting. Animals behave differently. The cat is not waiting, it only smells the presence of the mouse, and it is solely intent to catch and grasp the mouse. When at a certain point the cat does not smell the mouse any longer, it goes away. At so, I would say that it is no longer waiting, while in fact the cat never waited, for it does not deal with time, it has no notion of time. The same could be said about space. An animal has no notion of space, for the notion as such is not physical; it is a concept that refers to a physical neighborhood. Animals live as part of the physical world. They do not know what space is. A cat knows how to jump on the mouse. It has no need to be aware of the distance which is required; it has the physical expertise of it.

We are aware of the **presence in our mind of something else which is source of our understanding of time and space**. We picture time and space between beginning and end, and we perceive the limitations of time and space. We read the whole of reality inside of another dimension, in which we picture time and space. Nonetheless, it is correct to say with Kant that intelligence grows inside of people, above sensible acquaintance, through the experience of time and space. Intelligence is able to grasp the notion of time and space, and to overcome it. It is probably the best contribution of Gabriel Marcel to evidence the issue through the experience of love: when we truly love, when we take a love engagement, when two people marry and say they will love each other forever, they promise an action that overcomes time and space. When people sign a contract, when they decide they will do something under any condition, above the good and the bad, such a course of action overcomes time and space. When people take a commitment, they show the capacity to overcome space and time. G. Marcel states that, "I need the experience of eternity to be able to take an engagement that overcomes time and space." God's promises are the highest examples of crossing the line beyond time and space.

In everyday life, people have experience of overcoming time. People make **engagements**, **promises**, **commitments**, **expectations**, which we presume they are eternal. People like to address issues, in business projects, family plan, friendship, love, as if their life was endless and they were suppose to enjoy these issues forever. It is the symptom of the presence in us of something which stands and last. Our internal clock is not temporary, or precarious; it overlaps human life span, it refers to mankind span… History is the natural background of everyone… and the end times concern everyone… for everybody, as a microcosm, is tightly connected with the macrocosm… with the whole universe… Everybody life overcomes the mere entity of individual journey… Everyone behaves with the certainty of being far above the precariousness of situations, superior to the sole extent of personal year span; there is inside of us the deep conviction to be born forever. Well, I don't want enter into all the religious aspects of the people life and prefer to stay with human experience. Nonetheless, human experience includes the life of mystics. In *The Degrees of Knowledge*, Maritain affirms that, "Every Christian life is mystical life." He explains that when people deal with sense, universe, Angels, Trinity, God, such amazing connections indicate that every individual includes a configuration which is associate with the whole macrocosm, from physical items up to the spiritual ones. Such a configuration includes the precariousness of material things and the always existing of spiritual entities. Human nature offers the marvelous arrangement of being even more insecure than animals, and getting the consistency of eternal values. Yes, people are those kinds of beings which are conatural to eternity.

Now, following the wave of the last development, I wish to stress in that picture, when people meet eternity. As a matter of fact, everyone by intelligence and love accesses eternity. Nonetheless, while I write these lines, I'm not comfortable. When I truly experience eternity, I feel to be "outside" and am unable to say more. In his course on God, Prof. Michael Meaney expresses the concept that in eternity there is no time, and that is the reason why it would be **improper to say** that "God will know what I will do tomorrow." I should say "God knows what I am doing tomorrow" for there is no future in God. If we speak differently and put some temporal notion — before and after — in God, we make unaccountable the fact of human freedom…

Michael Meaney

> *"Be happy, do your best, and leave the sparrows chirp"*
> John XXIII.

The two Pillars
Augustine & Aquinas

Augustine and Aquinus promoted two diverse perspectives of the same teaching. There is a tight connection between the two great thinkers. Where many see contradictions there is only counterbalance: opposing them to one another would be like opposing the roots and the foliage of the same tree. They go together. Through Augustine the philosophy of Plato emerges in Christendom. Through Aquinas the insights of Aristotle, especially Metaphysics, feed our Christian culture. However stressing both the filiation of Augustine from Plato and of Aquinas from Aristotle is only an aspect of their teaching and it is not the prevalent issue. Actually both are first of all followers of Christ and they complete one another in this endeavor. We will never stress too much that dealing with the teaching of both, suddenly reveals that the two, Augustine and Aquinas, work together, like the two wings of Christendom flying towards wisdom.

The beginning of philosophy in Ancient Greece reached an achievement of thinking that seemed unattainable in the years to come. Nevertheless a new stage of reflection emerged in Alexandria, around 200 AD, when a new start of Greek Philosophy met across with Jewish tradition, providing the cradle of our Western civilization. It seemed that afterwards philosophy could not develop more and offer any new insight of wisdom… Actually this did happen later with Augustine and continued to develop up to Aquinas. Well, this must be properly said. On the tracks of the School of Alexandria, Augustine makes a start of wisdom in the newborn Christian worlds at the end of the Roman Empire, just before it falls apart… Centuries after, Aquinas performed as the main figure of the last period of the Middle

Ages, also known as Blossoming Ages.

In other words Augustine shows the improvement of Alexandria school and puts the roots of what Middle Ages will be able to develop. Then Aquinas represents the brilliant achievement of the blossoming Ages. Other thinkers like Benedict, Bernard, Ockham, Dominique, Bonaventure, Duns Scott, are noticeable steps of such progressive improvement of knowledge and wisdom.

Nonetheless the two figures of Augustine and Aquinas emerge as the masterpieces of that long period, so rich of art, culture, social development, political acquirement. To understand them we need to know the background, almost like a word cannot be understood out of the facts it refers to and outside of the language it belongs to. It is very different to consider a plant alone, decorating our living room, or while growing in the garden… The neighborhood, whatever it is, living room or garden, makes the plant beautiful. Every thinkers needs to be understood in his/her proper background… Middle Ages times are the support in which the two pillars of Christendom shine like pieces of 24 carats gold, or 2000 watts bulbs.

Between the two brilliant thinkers, we have 800 years of Middle Ages, from the fall of the Roman Empire, the Dark Ages chaos, the reconstruction of Renewal Ages, and the performance of the Blossoming Ages at upper times. They are the canvass in which do radiate the two great thinkers.

It would be not possible to understand the history of philosophy without some familiarity with Augustine and Aquinas… Both are necessary like the two legs for walking. Augustine shows more intuition; Aquinas displays more rationality and contemplation. Even if eight centuries keep them distant from each other, they complete one another.

Augustine lived at the end of the Roman Empire and made a transfiguration of Alexandria School. He was the last philosopher of Ancient Time and brought new standpoints. He offered a basic pattern of reflection to overcome the struggle started with the fall of the Roman Empire which produced the Dark Ages... Augustine paved the road for the philosophers to come, putting down the seeds of Christendom and providing the cultural insights which developed during the following days of Medieval Period.

Aquinas lived at the end of Middle Ages, which he is one of the prominent figures. He made an amazing synthesis of the knowledge of the whole period and he provided a configuration of thinking, which went unaltered through Renaissance and Modern Time up to our days. Many experts on Aquinas got the conviction that he paved the road of philosophy for the times to come...

The article will develop through three sections: **1. Augustine, 2. Aquinas, 3. the filiation between the two**. The material addressed here should be enriched then with the knowledge of the Medieval Period, which extended between and around the two.

1. Augustine of Hippo

With Augustine a New Philosophy Started in the Roman World

a. Main Augustine's Titles: Manichean converted to Christianity. Hermit in Africa. Bishop of Hippo. The last Church Father.

b. Historic Figure: The founder of a new wave of speculative reflection inside of the growing Christendom, he is the only Father of the Church who could really be described as a philosopher. He wrote voluminously, treating philosophical questions leaving always open the perspectives of theology studies.

c. Biography: (354) Born in Tagaste of a Christian mother (Monica) and a pagan father {Patricius). (361) First school in Tagaste. (365-66) Started excellent studies in Madaura. (369-70 – when 16 years old) Returned to Tagaste, interrupting studies and living in idleness. (Fall 370) Studied again in Carthage, where (371) he knows Modesta, his concubine. (Summer 372 – at 18 years) Adeodatus' birth, and first readings of Cicero's ***Hortensius.***

Converted to manichaeism. (375-382) Teacher of rhetoric at Tagaste and Carthage. (382) disappointment with Manicheans doctrine. Augustine comments personally this disappointment: "They destroy everything and build up nothing". Then, the fact that Manichaeism is in contrast with their affectation of virtue, and the feebleness of their arguments in controversy with the Catholics. But the worst of all things was that he did not find science among them, that knowledge of nature and its laws which they had promised him. When he began questioning Manichaeism concerning the movements of the stars, there was no answer. Actually the main reason was inconsistency of the doctrine based on the presence of two gods: the good and the evil… xxx)

(383) Flees to Rome (383) and then goes to Milan (384) where he meets bishop Ambrose, who lead him through Plato to Christ. Better understanding of Plato and retirement in the country to deepens his faith, with Monica and Adeodatus. He is baptized (387, at 33) in Milan, by St. Ambrose. Then he returned to North Africa as a **hermit**. Under the request of Valerius, Bishop of Hippo, he becomes a priest (391), gathers his followers as Regular Canons and later becomes the bishop of Hippo (395). Then he wrote ***Confessions*** (400), ***On the Trinity*** (410), ***The City of God*** (420), ***Homilies and Epitles***. (430). He died at Hippo during Vandals invasion.

d. Main Similarities with Plato: As Plato started philosophy in Ancient Greece, Augustine started a new wave of philosophy, inside of the emerging Christian traditions. This is why Augustine's nickname was "**The Second Plato.**" Influenced first by Manicheans and Platonists, through St. Ambrose he converted to the Truth in Jesus Christ, as Plato converted to the Truth through Socrates. His illumination theory is a growing through the enlightening of the mind from God who provokes a wake up to the Truth at the example of Plato's recollection theory (Plato, however, believed that every increasing in knowledge is awaking from a slumber, which came after we fell in the present world, in which we forgot our previous life and knowledge from the World of Ideas. For Plato every learning is "remembering" – While for Augustine learning is an enlightening, moving from ignorance to knowledge because our increasing in human life, which is a sharing of Jesus life – for we were made "Image of God" and need "time" to be born in the fullness of what we are). He wrote *The City of God* (as Plato wrote *The Republic*). He greatly influenced Thomas Aquinas (as Plato was the mentor of Aristotle). In all these issues, Augustine got insights from Plato readings, which he mostly made through the vulgarization of Cicero. Plato philosophy provided Augustine with a terminology which helped him to better express his own awareness of Christian wisdom. It would be improper to say that Augustine was a follower of Plato, for he was not. Augustine did not even plagiarize Plato. Plato writings, however, helped Augustine to make a better speculative expression of his own thoughts. This is the only perspective which may help to see the filiation from Plato to Augustine

e. Doctrine:

1. **God is Love**: knowledge, life, and society need the universal and absolute reference, which is God, in which everything is ONE (Beauty, Good, Justice, Intelligence, etc. are the same in God). God is the Eternal Provider who starts (now) and leads creation to its blossoming. In such a picture out of love people are invited to share creation and fulfill its eternal relationship according to St. Paul's words: "everything belongs to us, but we belong to Christ and Christ belong to God" — So

a neighborhood of love makes everything as a gift to everything else and vice-versa. The whole of creation was made as a gift for me, and I am a gift to each one I meet.

2. **Providence** is the key of God's love. In the words of Augustine, Providence should be understood today as "good management". As every creature, each one of us is a unique recipient of God's love and nonetheless integral part of a whole, which is shared at different degrees of intensity and extension. Everything and everyone are created for our own good and blossoming. And, as everyone else, I am a unique and irreplaceable gift for the whole creation. Additionally, "Never God allows some evil, unless it is for a better good" — Thomas Aquinas will express Augustine's thought saying that, "Human mistakes are never strong enough to stop or damage the love and the plans of God" on us and on the whole of creation. There is a dynamic relationship between people and God: we are the ones invited by him to say "You" to him, to talk and reason to him. Such a relationship is the mystery of human splendor and misery.

3. **Knowledge** and Virtue: beatitude overcomes skepticism, through experience and sensation we meet truth under God's direction (illumination) and find happiness in God;

3. **The World** is fruit of Creation (out of nothingness); the whole world exists now. So the act of creation is actuated now. Nothing can exist if God does not love and think it now. We actually are the beloved ones. The Augustine's teaching was so well understood by Descartes, that it became the main Cartesian issue on the actuality of God. It will be the source of Anselm ontological proof. Ultimately, World, Creation, and Providence are the three perspectives of the same Universe.

4. **God is Trinity**, not understandable but source of every understanding, because God revealed himself we may know him. To explain the enlightening mystery, Augustine referred to the story of meeting with a child on the beach of Ostia, near Rome: "What are you doing?" Augustine asked, "I am trying to

put the whole of sea in this shell" the boy said – "That's impossible" Augustine replied – "But aren't you trying to do the same in attempting to put the whole mystery of the Holy Trinity in your tiny head? The child concluded. Such a mystery obliges us to humbly consider reality and accept it, even when we cannot fully explain it. A mystery may be compared with the highlights of a car: if we look at them we may burn our eyes, if we drive with them, we see the road. So is the mystery of God, it requires us to put our life in the correct perspective.

5. Human Soul reflects Trinity configuration: Memory is the image of the Father, Intelligence is the image of the Son, and Willpower is the image of the Holy Spirit (see further Note);

6. Time (see *Confessions* X, XI), "I know what time is, but when I am asked what it is I am in trouble!" – To make it very short we could synthesize the following steps:

a) Time is created; it is one of the characteristics of the same creation. The whole of creation belongs to eternity not to time, for creation is made "now." Time is integral part of creation. So it would be absurd to say "when creation happened" for **there is no time before time**, and creation never started in time, it starts now in eternity and it develops accordingly through time, as well as it extends itself towards space. Creation never started in the strict sense of the word.

b) Time is caught by change of situations and things.

c) Physical Time is connected with space — It takes the same time to run the same space as the same speed. Such a space can be effective, or physical (objective or regular time), or mental (experiencing changes as if the time of a meeting was shorter or longer than regular time), or even spiritual when it represents a totally changed situation, like in ecstasy (being outside of regular time).

d) Under the neighborhood of time animals know space. They have no notion of space and time; they only know how to behave in it, following their instinct.

e) Under the neighborhood of Eternity people know time

f) Greeks thought time as cyclic (Aristotle: "All civilizations are mortal") it was their way of addressing eternity as immanent to time.

g) Linear time (past, present, future) is a Christian notion; it comes with the notion of transcendence: eternity transcends time and leads it.

h) Present time is consistency of past and future. Past and future can happen only in reference to a present event. **The Past** is acceptable as gone only under the transcendental notion linear time — We must leave it in the mercy of God. **The Future** is possible only under the conviction of eternity — We expect it as sign of God's Providence.

i) Liturgical time is a cyclical series which invites us to live linear time under the perspective of religious symbols – one year represents the whole history of salvation, in which our linear time is included.

7. Eternity stands behind, inside and beyond time, and…

1. Eternity is now - God is eternal present. In his immutability God (I Am) is source of every being

2. Eternity is the consistency of time. Eternity is real. Time is relative... to eternity. Time is consistent for people in proportion of the much of eternity we get in it.

3. Spiritual time (as above) is an experience of eternity. It is a real meeting with God. It includes adoration, contemplation, prayer… It can happen daily.

4. Eternity can be thought as fullness of any aspect the time suggest, reach and lose.

5. The immutability of eternity is a superabundant activity that time cannot describe.

8. History According to Augustine, history started with Abraham, i.e. when God told him "leave the place where you are" (immediate change), go to the place I will give to you (appointment of Eternity with time), I will make you father of a great people (mission to accomplish). These three issues are necessary for having the notion of history.

1. History can exist only when an end is foreseen. But only Eternity may put a limit to time. Then history will end with the fulfillment of the promise (Without the return of Christ there would be no history, because time would become endless. Endless time denies history.

2. History is the Fruit of the relationship between eternity and time – There is history when we have sometime an appointment with eternity: today we are waiting for the end times.

3. Linear time begins and ends

4. Apory or mystery of History

5. Notion of progress: growing of freedom for the best but also eventually for the worse

6. Only the cultural waves of the religions of the book (Jews, Christians, and Muslims) have a real notion of history, for they have a future and a mission to accomplish in between. Out of such neighborhood there is no notion of history.

7. All reality is "historic" – But only in the context of some faith from revelation there is the awareness of history. When faith decreases, the notion of history tends to disappear. In some areas of our days, the poor faith of our civilization explains the almost inconsistent notion of history – Philosophers talk about synchrony and diachrony, vestige of other civilizations, the notion of history tend to disappear.

8. Every being is in act (at a specific historical moment)

9. Being is not only essence or existence: being is creature, therefore it is in progress, and it is included in the history of Salvation.

f. The Teacher is one of the most significant works of Augustine after The Confessions. It offers an original investigation on language. The way of speaking reflect the way of reasoning, and through it we share knowledge. Here he developed his **Theory of Illumination.**

To say it shortly, Augustine's theory of illumination, however indicates that teaching is not properly a process by which knowledge is transferred from one person to another. For knowledge is not the simple result of an external process of explanations and proofs. Nonetheless, explanations and proofs are the occasionally incitements, the stimuli by which students awake from ignorance to knowledge. Students experience the internal jumping into flash of insight, seeing the truth, enlightening, caused by external suggestions as teaching or sensorial experience. Augustine considers that The Word (Jesus, alias "*Logos*") is present in every consistent discourse. His spirit is illuminating our mind from inside of every discourse. So he states, "The power that reveals the truth to us is Christ as the Teacher operating within us." Augustine emphasized the maieutics process indicated by Socrates, who claimed to be the one who, like a midwife for future mothers, help people to deliver the truth which is prisoner inside of us. Philosophy is an action of delivery the word dwelling in us!

g. The **Last philosopher of the Roman World** and the **First of a New Era** — While Augustine is dying the Vandals are at the door of Hippo, the Goth are pushing at the borders of the Roman Empire, they even have broken in Rome City. In 410 the Visigoth ransomed the Capitol, Center of the Urbs (Rome). Previously, the whole of the Roman society had been developing a period of opulence which favored decadence. In less than a century the whole configuration of the Western Roman world will be destroyed. Nonetheless Augustine wisdom will survive and help culture to survive the struggling days. He was the builder and forerunner of the culture to come.

h. Historical Neighborhood:

The fall of the Roman Empire dramatically provoked general disorganization. Immediately, both (1) **Roman culture residues**, which survived the fall of the Empire, and (2) emerging **Christian values**, as stressed by Augustine and the Church of the day, reshaped Western world under feudalism regime as a first step or reorganizing the society and overcome the general confusion which is usually known as Dark Ages. Feudalism was built as an arrangement between those who own the land and will assure peace and protection to those who live in it and in change will provide food and services.

The process was difficult, slow and full of struggle. It worked from the beginning with amazing efficiency in spite of abuses and conflicts. It was a splendid actuation of reciprocal charity, which allowed the whole society to survive the chaos. Such a social arrangement made possible to reorganize the society and make eventual improvement. In fact other developments followed later, especially in the period call Blossoming Ages, which is the third part of Middle Ages. Feudalism allowed the society to be organized under the shape of a family, which means according to the principle of subsidiarity.

The system remained the main structure of the whole society for several centuries and helped people to organize and mature. After Renaissance and Modern Time, the system had increased the awareness of people as member of the same society to the point to make feudalism and monarchy (its political expression) obsolete. Mankind was ready for a new step in politics and social behavior.

2. Thomas Aquinas
The Angelic Doctor (1225-1274)

Dealing with Thomas Aquinas is a delicate endeavor. Following Aquinas tracks, Clarke's *Person and Being* shows how the approach of reality is a dynamic endeavor. Aquinas differs from the most common perspective, which states that things are only objects to know. He teaches that every being is a presence, which reveals itself in the act of existing, emerging from nothingness. Every being is the amazing victory of the overflowing of its existing. It expresses the present act of creation.

Even after Pope Pius XII suggested taking Aquinas as the model of every philosopher, Aquinas' philosophy has remained largely unknown and misunderstood. Most of superficial thinkers keep the conclusion of Aquinas' doctrine without applying his method of **Critical Realism**. As an example of such a misconception, it is significant to see how many of those who claim to be followers of Thomas Aquinas omit to read, consider, and seriously address Friedrich Nietzsche with Aquinas' method of investigation. Many are not able to see how Nietzsche is an enhancement of Aquinas' philosophy, for his extremely dynamic approach of reality. It is a noteworthy statement to keep in mind.

Important events have characterized Aquinas' life. Determinant was the influence of Albertus Magnus, who gave to Aquinas the magnificent suggestion to **follow Augustine in theology and Aristotle in philosophy**. So, Aquinas studied Aristotelian logic and Categories in order to better understand Augustine's works. He became a master in such a practice. Then, Aquinas was a master of consistency with the convictions of Augustine and of expertise with Aristotle's vocabulary.

Such a clearness of view and candor of method made other thinkers uncomfortable. No wonder why such a supreme achievement provoked at first strong reactions against Aquinas, both from Aristotelian and Augustinian philosophers, whom he was, indeed, the perfect model of his days. The opposition came also both from the intelligentsia of the days and the teachers in Sorbonne. In good faith, many thinkers of his days were rejecting the revolutionary ideas of St. Thomas Aquinas, for they were not ready for them (here again, there is an interesting analogy with F. Nietzsche). They were accustomed to see opposition and conflict, where Aquinas invited to promote conviviality and sharing, and contradiction where Aquinas suggested complementarity.

It is sometimes very difficult to put together thinkers of different schools, just because of the prejudices that explicitly or implicitly everyone brings with. Such prejudices may be found both in the supporters and opponents of Thomism. A new open and realistic perspective is necessary.

A. Cultural Neighborhood

1. The **Middle Ages** is generally well ignored. Its name shows such ignorance. At Renaissance time, main thinkers believed that between the Ancient and themselves, nothing good was made, and they decided to call such a "no-man's-land" of civilization, the "Middle-Ages. It was not before the studies of Jean Guitton in Sorbonne, who was invited to dig in the pound of medieval thoughts to see if there was some roots of Descartes' philosophy, and he discovered that reversely, such a period made an amazing transition, which prepared the blossoming of Renaissance.

2. Between the fall of the Roman Empire (476: Fall of Rome, or 800: Coronation of Charlemagne) and the dawn of the Renaissance (1450): new political (migrations of people called Barbarians, i.e. Goths, Franks, Huns, Vandals, Lombards) and religious (heresies: Gnostics, Aryans, Pelagians, Nestorians, Monophysists, Manicheans, Cathari, and Islam) problems provoke the emerging Christendom (through a Jewish and Greek heritage)

3. Three main periods: the **Dark Ages** (V-VIII, when all activities decline), the **Renewal Ages** (X-XII, feudalism makes possible a new improvement of agriculture, culture, trade, society, population, and the start of building Cathedrals with all that what great projects involved), the **Blossoming Age** (XIII-XV, shows a new figure of the Church (structure around the Cathedrals, with Universities, Welfare organizations, and Hospitals), and of the Society (emerging of new cities and formation of nations).

4. It is during the Blossoming Age, while Universities are

multiplying everywhere in Italy, Germany, France, England, and Spain that emerge the figures of some giant thinkers, like Bonaventure, Duns Scott, and Thomas Aquinas. They all are the heirs of Saint Augustine and of a rediscovery of the Greek through the Muslims and Jewish philosophers in Spain.

B. Chronological Biography

1225 Born in a noble family in Roccasecca near Aquino, starts (1230) studies at the Benedictine monastery of Montecassino.

1237 Moved to Naples University where he studies the trivium, quadrivium, and Aristotle's new translation. Joined the Dominicans and, in 1244, try to move to Paris. He is carried off by his brothers and made prisoner. Before his determination to make any compromise with his vocation they release him a few years later.

1246. Studies with Albertus Magnus in Paris. For his heavy-set appearance and his taciturn attitude, his fellow novices gave him the nickname of "dumb ox". Albertus Magnus predicted that "this ox will one day fill the world with his bellowing".

1247. He follows Albertus Magnus in Cologne, Germany. In 1250 he is ordained a priest.

1252 As a Bachelor he starts teaching in Paris as Assistant, while at the same time, Louis IX (St. Louis) is King of France.

1256 Disp. Apud Sententiarum libros. Doctor in Theology. Named Philosophy teacher at Paris by Pope Alexander IV.

1259. Pope Alexander IV summoned him to teach as adviser and lecturer to the papal court in Anagni, Orvieto, and Viterbo.

1268. Return in Paris, involved in debates with the followers of Averroës who affirms that philosophy is independent of revelation. Starts redaction of *Summa Theologiae*.

1272. He is asked to organize a new Dominican School in Naples.

1273. **Ecstasy during the mass on Dec.6**, since then he became more silent and wrote no more.

1274. Called by Pope Gregory X to attend the Council of Lyon he dies on the way (Fossanova, March 7).

1277. His ideas, condemned by his colleagues of the Sorbonne, and officially by Etienne Tempier, bishop of Paris, through the Syllabus (219 art.), were arduously defended by Albertus Magnus, who pulled much interest on them, until they became successfully and universally known.

1323. Canonized by Pope John XXII (less than 50 years after Aquinas' death)

1369. The rest of his body are transferred to Toulouse, by order of Pope Urban V, Avignon.

1567. Pope Pius VII proclaims him Doctor of the Church.

1879. Pope Leo XIII recommends all Roman Catholic schools to teach Aquinas (*Aeterni Patris*).

1950. Pope Pius XII makes Aquinas' Doctrine the official philosophy of the Church (*Humani Generis*).

C. Works a prodigious production:

➢ *Disp. apud sententiarum libros* (1242-56),
➢ *De Ente et Essentia* (1252), (see below)
➢ *Disp. De Magistro* (1253),
➢ *De principiis naturae* (1254),
➢ *Disputationes* (1252-73),
➢ *Disp. apud Boecii De Trinitate librum* (1256),
➢ *Summa contra Gentiles* (1256-72),
➢ *De quolibet* (1256-72),
➢ *Disp. De substantiis separatis* (1272),
➢ *Summa theologiae* (1267-73). (see an example below)

D. Some Original Ideas

✶ Aquinas shows not only **compatibility** between Aristotle and Augustine, but even more he sees and shows their **complementarity**.

* After Averroes and Muslims philosophers, Aquinas agrees with the **relevance of the Community** for intelligence growing. He teaches the consistency of Agapè, as expression of the Mystical Body of Christ, expressed in Christendom. Nonetheless, Aquinas stresses that, in addition to the intelligence of the Community, there is also for each individual a freely personal intelligence. Belonging to the Body of Christ every believer is involved both personally and socially (collectively).

* **Reason and Faith** help reciprocally each other. Reason prepares the way that Faith is supposed to improve (see the Encyclical "Faith and Reason" for the relationship between philosophy and theology).

* **Truth is ONE**. Aquinas refuses an emerging opinion of his days that in addition to the religious truth (in the Book) there is a rational truth. Following the steps of Augustine, Aquinas knows that Truth is ONE. A double truth would be its negation. If there would be two truths, of identical values, there would be no truth at all. Nonetheless, the same truth must be investigated in all human perspectives: physical, psychological, ethical, metaphysical, and spiritual. This is why different discourses, which could appear incompatible one another, may be additional. It is the task of the philosopher to investigate thus and show the whole picture of it. A rational perspective does not necessarily deny the religious one, but it should prepares it, eventually, while the second one should illuminate the first (Cf. Faith and Reason). In the same way, a psychological investigation may integrate the sociological view. When two perspectives appear contradictory, some important characteristics are missing. Relativism is a disease, which renounces to seek the truth. In times of uncertainty, "the philosophers must address the difficult paradox of complete fidelity to eternal values with tight connection with the anguish of the days in order to move the world back to the truth" (Maritain).

* **Again on truth**: is there a theological truth or a di-

vine truth which would be different to the human one? The discourse of Aquinas is enlightening here: NO THERE IS NOT. Thomas Aquinas discusses the concept of truth in the Summa Theologiae. His theory is not a simple one and is even more complicated because there are two different perspectives on the same truth, which are often considered diverse to each other. The human truth does not differ from the divine truth. Such a dichotomy would deny the whole Revelation and all Religious perspectives. Some would argue that human truth is many, finite, and changeable, while divine truth is one, eternal, and unchangeable. According to Aquinas, in the human person, truth is defined as an equation between the mind and reality. Even though most may agree that truth follows the facts, but here is the amazing fact: in the mind of God there is not such a distance… fact and thoughts are the same in God, which means He is the truth. Jesus said, "I am the truth, the way, the life…" In such a way, people may discover that they can change the facts and make the truth. This is the discovery of existentialism, phenomenology, structuralism, and many current waves of philosophy. Because God became flesh, as far as there is love in our lives, God dwells in us, and man is the truth. Such a dynamic proposition was expressed by Paul: "everything belongs to us, but we belong to Christ and Christ belongs to God." This is why the truth can be improved or determined by each individual differently. What seems contradictory to us is not eventually in conflict. For people have a task to perform in order to move the whole universe to its own delivery, the new haven and new earth of the end times (Sertillange, De Lubac, Teilhard de Chardin).

   * **Source of truth** — For Aquinas the unity of truth is found in his daily contemplation and comforted by his Augustine reading, "You made us for you, Lord, and our soul is restless until it rests in you." The conviction of both that human truth has her source in God comes from personal experience.

It was an experience of conversion for Augustine, a continuous progressing in the mystical intimacy with the Lord in Aquinas, up to make him silent in his last days. Basically, we find the reason of what we are in God whom we come from and whom we move back to. To say that God created us is obvious, but it would be a very poor argument for Aquinas, when our whole life is supposed to be inside of the Trinity. As an example, Aquinas follows Bonaventure in his interpretation of the Ten Commandments. The Decalog that was given by "I am" was not at all new for the whole mankind; it was only a recall of the rules by which we are made. Both agree that if we had kept the Adamic tradition we would be able to write the Decalog down as the paradigm of what we are and how we behave. Because from Adam we went down in Primitive Traditions we need such a recall.

* In *Ethics*: after Aristotle, Aquinas stresses that knowledge is necessary to know the good, and then **Virtue** (capacity to do good) is necessary to do it and develops while doing the good. A virtuous act requires awareness, discernment, decision, and execution. It starts from education. Beyond **Free will** (capacity of choice), Virtue promotes **Freedom** (capacity to blossom in what we are), and lead to **happiness**.

* **Theory of knowledge**: all knowledge originates in sensation, but sense data are made intelligible by the action of the intellect, it is because of the specific way of human intelligence that man needs revelation to what is human soul, angels, and God himself (see specific Note on the issue)

* In **metaphysics** Aquinas read all aspects of Augustine statements according the categories of Aristotle. He did not baptize Aristotle! He used the categories of Aristotle to better understand the statements of Augustine. In fact, Aquinas was not a follower of Aristotle, even if he used the method and the language of Aristotle to make clearer the teachings of Augustine, whose he was a follower.

∗ ***De Ente et Essentia***, Aquinas wrote this essay for his Dominican companions. So this is supposed to be a very elementary note, while it appears for many us today as a very sophisticated one. The question is not about vocabulary (or categories), but about reality and the best way to deal with it. Aquinas deals with the being (the existent, the existing one) and what we know about it (whatness). So it is really a metaphysical approach of reality.

∗ ***Summa Theologiae***, Worth of notice is the presentation of every question. It is a perfect example of the method to follow in every investigation, and is well known as Critical Realism (see below). Every inquiry starts with a collection of facts, opinions, and statements on the question; from which Aquinas develop little by little a first solution, which is tested by some known contradiction, which requires an appropriate response. Among many very interesting issues, I would like to suggest (ST1, Q79) "What is human conscience?" (Art.12)

∗ **Natural Theology** — Philosophy is able to get the evidence of the existence of God as we know by its consequences the existence of a fact. As an example, when you find letters in your mail box you know that the mail-deliverer has passed by, even if you never saw such officer. When on the beach you see tracks of paths, you know somebody was there, for you know that it is not the property of the sand to make such prints by itself. In the same way, the precariousness of every creature pleads in favor of a prime being keeping the whole precarious world in existence. Even the anticlerical Voltaire (XVIII cent.) agreed with Aquinas, saying that it is impossible that such a well organized world was not made by an organizer; so did say Albert Einstein with amazement during his scientific investigations, affirming that so a sophisticated world cannot exist without a superior intelligence, who is its maker. According the language of Aquinas, such an organizer or maker is the one that religious traditions call God. Therefore Philosophy leads "naturally" to the conviction of the existence of God. Nonetheless, as philosophers, we cannot say much more than God's existence and superior nature. We would be unable to speak properly about God if He had not revealed himself. So the theology of the Revelation completes properly natural philosophy. Without natural theology, however, people could not understand the words of God, nor know where he comes from. As an outcome, philosophy and theology help one another in a proper interaction (Cf. Faith & Reason).

∗ **Synderesis** is that habit by which in any occasion our conscience is able to know what the best to do is. (Art.2) In any circumstances our will must follow our conscience, even when the conscience is wrong. (Art.3) Any action against conscience remains wrong even if there is an objective good deed. However it is our duty to instruct properly our conscience in order to help her to elaborate proper judgments.

Historically "synderesis," or even more properly "synteresis," is a technical term from scholastic philosophy, signifying the innate principle in the moral consciousness of every person which directs the agent to good and restrains him from evil. It is a natural capacity of judgment that appears like a feeble enlightening and should govern our conscience but needs the agreement of intelligence and will to exert. It is first present in a single passage of St. Jerome (d. 420) in his explanation of the four living creatures in Ezekiel's vision. Jerome explains that most commentators hold that the human, the lion, and the ox of the vision represent the rational, the irascible, and the appetitive (or concupiscent) parts of the soul, and need an enlightening coordinator (synderesis) to put them in orderly configuration. So, he refers to Plato's division, where the fourth figure, that of the eagle, represents a fourth part of the soul, above and outside these three: it is the one that the Greeks call synderesis, "which spark of conscience was not extinguished from the breast of Adam when he was driven from Paradise." Through it, when overcome by pleasures or by anger, or even as sometimes deceived by a similitude of reason, we feel that we sin. It is what the scriptures sometimes call spirit.... Sometimes the instance of synderesis is included in the term of conscience (conscientious) which may be driven out of track when people "have no shame or modesty in their faults." It actually needs to be perceived in order to actuate its enlightening. The more people take care of observing its suggestions, the more they are aware of it, and the more that place of enlightenment leads human actions for the good. When people disregard it, they progressively lose even the capacity to listen to it.

∗ Concerning the **filiation from Augustine to Aquinas** it must be said that Aquinas was a fervent reader of Augustine, which he read with Aristotelian categories. Such endeavor provoked the comment of Jacques Maritain: "Aristotle and Augustine are more understandable in the works of Aquinas than in the original writing of Aristotle and Augustine."

∗ **Critical Realism** characterizes the way of investigating started by Aristotle, developed by Aquinas, and still in use in our days with Sertillange, Garrigou-Lagrange, Maritain, Gilson, Guitton, Daujat, Clarke, Jean-Paul II, and most of Catholic thinkers. Such a method is "realism" insofar as it recognizes the existence of things, outside of the mind, independently of the human capability to know them or not. Then it takes account of the "intentional" presence of things inside of human mind during the act of knowledge, by which intelligence abstracts whatness (being => essence => ideas) out of real things. Additionally, such a method is a wide exploration on everything is said and known about an issue we want to deal with: it is an "open perspective" at first. Then, it is "critical", i.e. it progresses as an attempt of discernment among the many given discourses, in order to obtain a better comprehension on the issue.

Critical Realism is not a system but a method, which lead philosophers to a doctrine, as the fruit of so an open exploration. Any new investigation organized today with critical realism cannot be only the complement of the statements given previously by Aristotle, and Aquinas; oppositely, following their example of inquiry, it must be a proper updating of them, as a new elaboration of their reports.

Authentic followers of Aristotle and esp. of Thomas Aquinas are supposed to make today the work that Aquinas would have liked to perform if he was living among us today. Aquinas was suggested by Albertus Magnus to follow Augustine in theology and Aristotle in philosophy, which means to be consistent with the convictions of Augustine and use Aristotle to properly express them.

∗ **Dynamic Approach of Reality** — Following the example of Aquinas every Thomist should be a follower of St. Augustine — in the radicalism of her/his experience of life — and an Aristotelian thinker. It is not contradictory to do so. To be a follower of Aquinas means to agree with Augustine without rejecting Aristotle, i.e. being consistent with the Augustine's data and finding a formulation which perfectly fits with the civilization of our days.

Universal perspectives — Such attitude allows Critical Realism to include in its own investigation all the issues of present knowledge, to analyze each and keep what is consistent in everyone. There is no other philosophical system which is able to do so. Contemporary waves of philosophy reject immediately every investigation which contradicts their starting statement. Critical Realism does not put any previous condition (prejudice) in any of its inquiry.

E. Some Famous Aquinas' Quotations

1. There is no knowledge of what we have no experience
2. "*Veritas sequitur esse rerum*" — Truth follows the facts.
3. In the act of knowing the subject who knows meet the known object

4. "When we know, we become what we know as another" ("*fieri aliud a se*")
5. Senses work with images, intelligence works with ideas.
6. God is that of which nothing greater can be thought
7. Whenever the conscience is correct or not, every act of will against it is always evil.
8. Freedom is the capability to blossom in what we are
9. Whatever is in motion must be moved by something else.
10. If everything moves, we must reach a first mover, which is not moved by anything
11. We cannot know what God is, but only what He is not
12. Every word we use to define God cannot reach God's perfection
13. Words are used of God and creatures in an analogical way
14. Choosing the perfect good, people reach happiness
15. Evil denotes the absence of God
16. Natural things are intermediate between God's knowledge and ours
17. We get our knowledge from natural things, which God is the cause of.
18. The soul is known by its acts
19. All that I have written seems to me like straw compared to what has now been revealed to me (after the experience of Dec.6, 1273)

F. Aquinas Wisdom

As previously stressed, Albertus Magnus gave to Aquinas the magnificent suggestion to follow Augustine in theology and Aristotle in philosophy. So, Aquinas studied Aristotelian *Logic* and *Categories*, while he already was fed with the wisdom of Augustine. Afterwards, the originality of Aquinas was to be extremely consistent with the convictions of Augustine while using Aristotle to properly express them. In other words, he translated the teaching of Augustine inside of the categories of Aristotle.

While I was teaching at the Gregorian University, some students, who were Augustinian monks showed me that Thomas Aquinas had is principal source of spiritual and philosophical insights in Augustine. It was sufficient to number Augustine quotes in Aquinas' work to see that. The surprising newness of Aquinas was to take the pagan categories of Aristotle to understand rationally the issues of Augustine. The result was immediately evident: both Aristotle and Augustine became more understandable in the works of Aquinas than in their original production. It was a kind of transfiguration and improvement of both doctrines in the new one of Critical realism: in Aquinas, there is all the realism of Aristotle and all the faith of Augustine. Such a cultural renewal was the work of the whole Aquinas life, up to the 6th December 1273, when an ulterior mystical experience showed Aquinas that the masterpieces of his writings were "nothing in comparison to divine wisdom." Such a dramatic experience prevented him to write further more.

Everybody is familiar with the insistence of his secretary to complete one or another issue left undecided asking master Aquinas to put some addition, and Aquinas reply: "This material is just straw, you may burn it all." Fortunately, the secretary had the good sense to save it, instead.

Please forgive me if I was not able to complete the revision of the following text from Maritain, which I'm not sure at this time about the precise source. It was indicated to me by my friend Benoît Montazel. I like, however, to add it here for showing some metaphysical perspectives of Aquinas Doctrine. Saying that Aquinas' doctrine was a cultural revolution may appear more clearly in such a long excerpt below. Read it with the usual prudence suggested by Saint Paul, taking what is useful and leaving the rest…

As usual a great mind provokes great oppositions, from the Sorbonne, from the Bishop of Paris, and even from the Dominican Order. When he died, Bp Templier proscribed many of his doctrines, and it was the presence of the aged Albert, who traveled from Cologne to defend his dead disciple, and the same doctrines were condemned again a short time later at Oxford, notwithstanding that Bishop Robert Xilwardby was a Dominican. For half a century, even the reading of his works was prohibited in the Franciscan Order, together with the "correctoria" and refutations with which the Franciscans notably assailed the philosopher are indication that philosophers who came after Thomas continued to read what his contemporaries had considered doctrinal novelties as departures from the true philosophy.

The condemnations and the attempted condemnations of Thomism were usually worked into pronouncements that purported to be directed against Averroism; there is, moreover, direct evidence that some points of the Aristotelianism of Thomas seemed as suspect as the Aristotelianism of the Averroists. Two doctrines were particularly object of criticism: the doctrine of the possible eternity of the world and the doctrine of the unity of substantial forms. In the one, Thomas had held, not that the world was eternal, but that it could not be shown by reason to be eternal or created in time; since the question transcended the powers of reason, the revelation of faith that the world was created should be followed. In the other, Thomas argued that there was no need of intermediate forms between the soul and matter, that the soul could be joined directly to the matter of its body without the preliminary preparation of matter by inferior forms. Significantly, both these doctrines are opposed most strenuously by Franciscan philosophers: Bonaventura gives beautifully detailed arguments to show by reason that the eternity of the world is impossible (most of them restated among the arguments Thomas undertakes to refute in his resolution of the question), and Bonaventura too, among many Franciscans, urges that the denial of the plurality of substantial forms endangers the immortality of the soul (for the soul will be without matter between death and resurrection) and the identity of angels (for since angels have no matter, there will be nothing to distinguish two angels of the same species from each other). There can be no mistaking the debate, therefore, nor the parties to the debate; when Thomas wrote his treatises on Separated Substances and on the Eternity of the World. The adversaries, those who murmured against him, are the continuators of the Augustine's teaching which the Franciscan Order professed, actually without being proper followers of Augustine.

In the problems of knowledge and truth the traces of this debate are not always easily revealed. Yet if the detail of the difference is not detected, the problems and the interests among which Thomas and, say, Bonaventura work in their treatments of the question of truth are starkly and totally different; it is a difference of temper, not only in two philosophers, but in two philosophies. For Bonaventura (impressed by tile shadows and traces of God in things and the images of God in thought) the divine illumination and the way to return from things illumined to the source of light are objects of constant preoccupation. The idea of God implies the existence of God; and by its omnipresence in all creation, the most intelligible thing is also best known, to such extent, even, that if our physical forces were like our intellectual powers, we should more easily move the largest mountain than the smallest pebble. Thomas concedes that the proposition, "God is," is in itself self-evident, for its predicate is contained in its subject; but it is not self-evident to us. We begin with sense-experience; from it we derive data least evident in nature but -most evident to us; from that data we work to that which is most evident in nature. That which is most intelligible is least known to us; God who is supremely intelligible is inconceivable to deficient creatures; in the presence of "intelligible entities" our minds are like the eyes of bats or owls; we are blinded by the full light of truth, and we can perceive only in partial light.

There is radical opposition between the two doctrines. That one is turned to the contemplation of the infinite intelligibility from which all knowledge proceeds, while the other is turned to the problems of a finite intellect working among the finite effects of a cause that exceeds its understanding. The treatment which the doctrines of Augustine and Anselm receive in Aquinas's resolution of the problems of knowledge is the symptom of the place of the Augustinian doctrine in the Thomist philosophy: what Augustine and Anselm said of the eternal truth is often listed among the doctrines to be refuted or restated, and it turns out in each case that what Augustine or Anselm said is true of one part or of one manner of the objects of the question. For Thomas Aquinas carried perhaps further than any philosopher the medieval conviction that the opinions of past Philosophers were not held without reason; his refutations of philosophic doctrines are usually prefaced by an examination of what in the nature of things the doctrine attempted to express and doubtless for this reason his philosophy is more than usually full of dysfunctions: before truth or being or substance can be considered it must be noted that truth or being or substance can be understood in two, three, four, or more ways; if preceding philosophers have erred, their error can usually be accounted for by accommodating their doctrine to one of the sensible senses, and their solution is censured, if at all, for supposing that meaning is the only possible.

The philosophy of Thomas Aquinas, then, considers in turn the relativity of our truths and the changeless eternal truth of which the discovery of even a tentative truth is indicative. We proceed by definitions in which we attempt to express the quiddities of things; then we make judgments by expounding and dividing concepts. Our definitions by genus and difference seek to state the real, yet the real is not constituted of genus and species. From the very beginning of knowledge, therefore, we are doomed to fall short of absolute truth. The hunt for definitions expressing essence (*venare quod quid est*) is never at end. There are many different things which are unknown to us; we are often obliged to classify and name things according to their accidents; our schemas, therefore, of knowledge are relative. Moreover, even when difference is known, one does not penetrate the essence of things. The definition of man as a rational animal does not exhaust the reality of man nor even express it; if an accident is added to the description, say, biped, the accidental difference will reinforce the essential. Sometimes, as in the case of the immaterial substances, we do not know accidents, and therefore our knowledge of the immaterial substances is very limited.

Truth properly speaking, however, does not enter in the activities of the understanding seeking the quiddities of things. A definition is false only in two senses either the definition is applied to the wrong thing or the definition states an impossible combination of concepts, such as immortal animal, for no animal can be immortal. Truth is first in the human understanding when the understanding adds something which is proper to itself and not in the thing it understands, but which none the less corresponds to the thing. The quiddities of things are only likenesses of things, similar in this to the images of sensation. But the understanding adds judgment, and judgments are true or false dependent on whether or not that which is understood is adequate to that which is. Judgment is the activity of the understanding compounding and dividing concepts; in judgment we consider that which is (ens). Strictly speaking we do not perceive the thing which is; we perceive its accidents; but we can nevertheless conceive that which is, and notwithstanding that it does not enter in sensation, it is that which the intellect seizes as best known. The universality of the entity of things in being and in understanding, indeed, convinced Aristotle of the impossibility of making being or that which is a genus.

The metaphysics of the relation of what a thing is and what a thing is known as, is worked explicitly and subtly into the basis of the theory of knowledge in the Thomist philosophy. That which is (*ens*) is known first, and all conceptions of the mind are resolved into it, since all other conceptions are arrived at by addition to it. Taking that which is (ens) in its essential meaning, it can be distinguished from its affirmative and negative consequences, that is, from thing (*res*) which is the affirmative consequence expressing the quiddity or essence of that which is and from one (*unum*) which is the negative consequence expressing the indivision of each thing that is. Relative to other things, that which is may be considered divided from other things: then it is called something (*aliquid*); or it may be considered in its conformity to some other thing — that last consideration would be impossible if there were not something which can be conformed to all things; this is the soul which is the measure of all things. But there are two faculties to be considered in the soul: cognitive and appetitive. Good expresses the conformity of that which is to appetite; true the conformity of that which is to understanding. The true and that which is, are, therefore, convertible; the true adds over and above that which is an adequation of it to the understanding; the true is that which is in the fashion in which it enters understanding; it is the intention of that which is. If the true is to be defined, therefore, it is possible to define it in three ways: it may be considered as that which is; it may be considered as perfective of the adequation of thing and understanding; it may be considered as the effect which results in the mind from that adequation. Much of the discussion concerning the nature of truth has followed from the failure to realize that all three are "compossible"; indeed, all three are necessarily implied in any one of the definitions.

Truth in created things, therefore, includes the entity of the thing and the adequation of the thing to the understanding. Truth is in creatures in two ways: in the things themselves and in the understanding. Natural things have their peculiar status in knowledge as consequence of the fact that they stand between two understandings, the divine understanding and the human understanding. If our relative genera can be applied even approximately to things, it is because things are constituted on a scheme of intelligibility; the truth of things constituted in the adequation of things to the divine understanding is guarantee of our truths even though we cannot penetrate to it. The ideas of God are creative of all that is; our ideas are effective from that which is; fundamentally the laws of thought and the laws of nature are the same. Moreover, by this relation of divine and human understandings to things, what Augustine and Anselm had said concerning the relation of all truths to one eternal truth is reconcilable with what Aristotle said concerning the activity of the active intellect abstracting forms. The eternal ideas of God and the changing ideas of man meet in the forms of things by virtue of which they are and are known.

By ideas are understood the forms of some things, existing outside the things themselves. The form of anything, however, existing outside the thing itself, can serve a double purpose: either to be exemplar of that of which it is called the form, or to be the principle of knowledge according to which the forms of knowable things are said to be in the knower. And with respect to either purpose it is necessary to posit ideas. For in all things which are not generated by chance, it is necessary that the form be the end of any generation whatsoever. The agent, however, cannot act in view of a form except in so far as the likeness of the form is in it. That however can happen in two ways. For in certain agents the form of the thing to be made preexists according to its natural being (*secundum naturale*), as in those things which act by nature, as man generates man, and fire fire. But in certain agents the form of the thing to be made preexists according to its intelligible being (*secundum esse intelligibile*), as in those things which act by understanding, as the likeness of a house preexists in the mind of the builder. And this can he called the idea of the house, because the artificer intends the house to assimilate the form which he conceived in his mind. Because, therefore, the world was not made by chance but was made by God acting by understanding, it is necessary that there be in the divine mind a form to the likeness of which the world was made. And in that consists the reason of idea."

When therefore the question is raised whether there is one truth by which all things are true, with the authority of Anselm heavily on the affirmative side of the question, the answer may be governed by the consideration that truth in the divine understanding is one; but truths in things are many; the truth in the divine understanding is necessary; but truth in the human understanding, accidental. The divine understanding is a measure, but it is not measured, things are measured by the divine understanding, and things in turn measure the human understanding; our understanding, however, is measured by things, but it measures no natural things, only artificial things projected and made by it. Finally, the motions of changeable things among truths and falsities may be understood if it is remembered that things are denominated true according to an intrinsic truth in them and an extrinsic truth in God.

The questions whether or not things can be true or false, whether or not sensation can be true or false, Whether or not understanding can be true or false, are solved once these distinctions have been made; that truth or falsity is not in things nor in sense properly, but only in some certain respect (*secundum quid*) has consequences in the question, how the understanding knows truth. For the understanding knows truth as it reflects on itself. Truth is in the understanding in two ways, as a consequence to its activity and as known by the understanding. Therein lies the difference between understanding and sensation; for truth is in sensation only as a consequence to its activity; sense does not know the truth by which it judges truly, and so it does not know the nature of its act or the relation of its act to the thing; therefore, it does not know truth. The understanding, being among the most perfect of the things which are, returns to its essence with a complete return. It proceeds outside itself when it knows that which is, and begins to return to itself, because the act of cognition is medium between knower and known; the return is completed when the understanding knows its own essence; knowing its own essence it returns with a complete return. The senses cannot make such a return, for although the interior sense perceives sense perceiving, still sense does not know its own nature, but its action is like that of fire which does not know its own heating.

The search for truth by this analysis may turn from metaphysics to the contemplation of the source of truth; that is the start of religion; overcoming the pious inference which suggests that the examination of that which is, be conducted with the aid of logic. For metaphysics is excellent statement of the proposition that the ways in which that which is can determine itself are as many as the ways in which a thing can be declared to be.

Our knowledge is of things that are and as they are: the categories of logic are the categories of things, but without addressing properly the intuition of being. Logic does ignore that things as they are in the facts and as they are in the mind are in any sense identical, or that the classifications of things in the mind must represent somehow the way they actually are. The true and that which is are convertible, but for that very reason they cannot be identical. The impossible test of a comparison of idea to thing known is not necessary for the perception of truth. Truth is based in the principles of the understanding itself. These principles the understanding perceives in perceiving itself; they are known of and through themselves, not by comparison to any experience, for they did not originate in experience, nor on the other hand as innate in the mind; rather the understanding from its observation of its own operations knows at once that they are true. The concept of being, thus, is included in everything that man thinks; from that alone the first principle is known that the same thing cannot be affirmed and denied at the same time. This first principle is the condition of all other principles, yet it is itself indemonstrable; all truths depend in demonstration on the principles which the mind knows in knowing itself. The Thomist doctrine of knowledge is comfortable in the conviction that truth may be relative in human minds, without rendering certainties impossible, and that truths which are neither exhaustive of all possible statements concerning the thing, nor exclusive of all possible alternatives, may nevertheless be adequate in judgment of that which is.

3. From the Foundation of Augustine ... ... to the Blossoming of Aquinas

A marvelous improvement in Method and Knowledge

The following reflection is a difficult one. Even experts in History of Philosophy have difficulty to face it properly. Don't be afraid of being lost, at first. On the contrary, take the occasion of eventual struggle to enter your questions in class discussion, and make alive your study groups, where students share difficulties and offer personal insights. Also take this very synthetically exposition as a kind of deep reflection if you can. I also prepared the note making meditation on the work of Jacques Maritain entitled: the *Degrees of Knowledge*, especially Chapters VI-VII-VIII, which addresses the wisdom of Aquinas, Augustine, and St. John of the Cross.

We must face the paradox of these two giant thinkers in history of Philosophy, who are at the same time so near and so distant with each other. The second learned from the first. And nevertheless he made a huge improvement, because of his different method of thinking. Important events characterized Aquinas' life. Determinant was the influence of Albertus Magnus, who gave to Aquinas the magnificent suggestion to follow Augustine in theology and Aristotle in philosophy. So, Aquinas studied Aristotelian logic and Categories in order to better understand Augustine's works. He became a master in such a practice. Later, Aquinas showed to be a master of understanding the convictions of Augustine and an invincible expert of Aristotle's vocabulary.

Such a clearness of view and candor of method made other thinkers uncomfortable. No wonder why such a supreme achievement provoked at first strong reactions against Aquinas, both from Aristotelian and Augustinian philosophers, whom he was, indeed, the perfect model of his days. The opposition came also both from the Dominican order and the teachers in Sorbonne, too. In good faith, many thinkers of his days were rejecting the revolutionary ideas of St. Thomas Aquinas, for they were not ready for them (here, there is an interesting analogy with Nietzsche). Many scholars were accustomed to see opposition, where Aquinas invited to promote conviviality. They saw contradiction where Aquinas suggested complementariness.

It is always hard to put together thinkers of different schools, just because of the prejudices that explicitly or implicitly everyone brings with. The main obstacle to understand these giants lies mostly inside of us, inside of our bias and fear of addressing the new.

What is new in Aquinas is not just the reference to Greek Philosophers. Sometimes people believe and say that Aquinas "baptized" Aristotle. It is not so. He never wanted to do so. Nonetheless, Greek thinkers play a role in Aquinas thoughts, only as part of the process of investigations. To say it in one word, we must state that Aquinas teaches us how to use Greek categories of thinking to reorganize the wisdom of our days. A true follower of Aquinas does not follow his ideas, not even the conclusions of his many studies, but first of all his method. What Aquinas did during the last centuries of Middle Ages is that which we must exert today, at the start of the third Millennium.

If this note was the only one you were able to understand during this course, such a result would be more than enough for saying that the course of metaphysics has been successful.

1. Aquinas Was the Best Augustine's Follower

1. Concordism or Discordism cannot be a key to address both. They need to be known individually and together.

2. Augustine is not the disciple of Plato (nor even of Plotinus) as well as Aquinas is not the follower of Aristotle.

3. Both are disciples of Christ.

4. Both use the vocabulary of Greek philosophers to make comprehensible and actual the message of Christ.

5. Plato and Plotinus have been meliorated in Augustine's reflection as well as Aristotle became better understandable and universal in Aquinas' teaching.

6. Augustine's works are far beyond the most familiar and acknowledged in the works of Aquinas. Aquinas was getting directions of study in Augustine, trying to comment him in Aristotle's categories.

7. It's impossible to address properly one of the two without being familiar with the other one. Augustine provides deep insights, which Aquinas make more understandable.

8. A process of filiation emerges between the two while showing differences in character, history, and method.

2. Two Opposed but Complementary Characters
(an apparent irreducible paradox)

1. Augustine was a new Convert while Aquinas was a faithful follower of Christ.

2. Augustine get the truth in Christ after a life of investigation in all fields of knowledge while Aquinas starts with the living truth of Christ to investigate then in all fields of knowledge.

3. Augustine searched for the Source of Truth while Aquinas investigated on the Fruits of Truth.

4. Aug. was a Sinner who rebuilt his life on the truth of Christ (in active and contemplative life while Aquinas started his life and study with the continuous contemplation of the truth of Christ, dealing with all the issues of his day.

5. Augustine was a Prodigal Son while Aquinas was the Faithful Son.

6. Augustine had been searching and fighting inside of world's errors up to get the truth in God while Aquinas was familiar with God, and intimate to the Angels (Angelic Doctor).

7. Augustine founded a new wisdom, and opened new directions of research while Aquinas matured a new synthesis of the day in a renewed Christian Doctrine.

8. Augustine expressed the Violence and Charism of Conversion while Aquinas expressed the limpid Peace of permanent Contemplation.

3. Two Opposed but Complementary Lives
(an apparent irreducible distance)

1. St. Augustine faced the end of Roman Empire while St. Thomas lived during the Blossoming Ages.

2. Augustine was a bishop during socio-cultural troubles while Aquinas was a university professor in a mature growing society.

3. Augustine defended emerging Christian doctrine against heresies while Aquinas shared pieces of truth in an elaborated civilization.

4. Two Opposed but Complementary Methods
(a paradigmatic improvement)

1. Augustine was looking for a way of salvation while Aquinas wanted to understand what he believes in.

2. Augustine saw knowledge as virtue and salvation while Aquinas wanted to increase knowledge: knowing better what we love, we love it more.

3. Augustine made Christian experience the key of philosophy while Aquinas made Christian charity the key of philosophic investigation, which blossoms in critical realism.

4. For Augustine, one's personal Soul was the privileged field of investigation while for Aquinas, Nature was the privileged field of investigation: the whole of creation is revealing the work of God.

5. Both were dealing in Latin and disregarded Greek. They needed translation to read Greek philosophers. Augustine read Plato through the writings of Cicero. Aquinas read Aristotle through Avicenna and Averroes.

5. A Same Mission
(an constructive analogy)

1. Augustine shared wisdom while St. Thomas shared contemplation.

2. Augustine showed the charism of a new discovered truth while Aquinas showsed a serene familiarity with the Truth.

3. Augustine disliked Greek while Aquinas did not read Greek.

4. Augustine healed Plato and Plotinus while Aquinas healed Aristotle.

5. Augustine dealt with Christian Wisdom at the level of intelligence while Aquinas did it at the level of reason.

6. Often Augustine left most questions open: he could not define them properly. He had them intuitively understood

while after Dec. 6, 1273, Aquinas stopped writing & searching ("All study is straw before God's splendor').

6. A Same Philosophy
(a synergistic continuity)

1. Augustine grew in the order of charity while Aquinas made it explicit in the order of intelligence.

2. Augustine was educated at the school of love while Aquinas was instructed at the school of reflection.

3. Augustine was in the move of the Holy Spirit while Aquinas focused on the person of the Son, the Word.

4. Augustine was a mystic of love and action while Aquinas was a mystic of contemplation.

5. Augustine was Father of the Church while Aquinas was Doctor of the Church.

6. Augustine was a theologian who used the gift of wisdom while Aquinas was a theologian who used reason baptized by faith.

7. Augustine was a searcher who followed a sure instinct for truth while Aquinas was performing definitions to their perfections.

8. Augustine had supernatural feeling during investigations while Aquinas traveled into the world of the analogy and the analogates.

9. Augustine used the Illumination argument (incomplete statement) while Aquinas used the Theory of knowledge (Gonseology) as the complete elaboration of Augustine's theory.

10. Somehow Augustine showed Franciscan (Adoration) perspective while Aquinas showed contemplative perspective.

7. The Very Same Doctrine
(an irreducible unity of faith)

1. Augustine's doctrine was an intuitive elaboration of

wisdom which is fully expressed in Aquinas synthesis.

2. Augustine's doctrine was metaphysics of spiritual life while Aquinas organized theological wisdom in its proper order.

3. Aquinas was the one who is able to express both philosophically and theologically Augustine's doctrine.

4. If you want to understand Augustine writings, read Aquinas.

5. If you want to feel enthusiasm for Aquinas' doctrine and feel its dynamic problematic, read Augustine.

8. A Very Same Endeavor…
(expressed under counterbalanced perspectives)

1. According to commentators like Guitton, Chenu, Maritain, Daujat, while Augustine "baptized" Plato, Aquinas "baptized" Aristotle, i.e. both made Greek philosophy compatible with Christian speculation.

2. Both show the perfect example on how to read every philosopher, taking "what is good and leaving the rest".

3. An appropriate philosopher learns from every thinker, even from those who at first seem thinking oppositely.

4. As soon as a thinker is looking for truth, there is something valid in her/his reflection. True philosopher is the one who gets what is consistent in every thinker, it is the endeavor of each of the TP (Two Pillars).

5. Good students improve from every teacher, adapting her/his learning with the situation of the days, as Aquinas did in 1200 with the Teaching of Augustine (400). So philosophy is supposed to do it again today.

6. Different languages and cultures produce different formulation of the same truth. Every new version of the same knowledge produces an improvement of understanding.

7. Truth does not change. Notwithstanding, our understanding about truth constantly improves. The two steps of Au-

gustine and Aquinas are the evidence of it.

8. Try to translate what you understand from both of TP or try to tell it to a young friend and your thoughts will become even more consistent.

9. Particularly interesting is the metaphor that Augustine is Father of the Church and Aquinas his Physician.

> *The one who seeks wisdom will find it at his door in the morning.*
> Wis. 6:14.

Aristotle

METAPHYSICS QUESTIONS

A choice of Questions or Quotes to better investigate metaphysics

1. What is the being?

2. What kind of being is nothingness?

3. Does every person seek the truth? Aristotle does affirm it.

4. Does abundance of knowledge teach people to be wise? Heraclitus said it does not.

5. Knowledge is power. We govern nature obeying its laws (Francis Bacon).

6. Is the being in my mind the same as in the facts?

7. Is the being one or many?

8. What is truth? Truth follows the facts (Aquinas) — *Veritas sequitur esse rerum.*

9. Any judgment is true if it is both self-consistent and coherently connected with our system of judgments as a whole (Edgar S. Brightman).

10. What comes first: the truth of search for truth?

11. Is double truth a possibility?

12. "The one who watches for wisdom at dawn shall not be disappointed, for he shall find her sitting by his gate" (Wis 6:14).

13. Can we philosophize without prejudices?

14. Are we supposed to prove everything? Can we prove everything?

15. Is it always possible to demonstrate the truth?

16. Is truth always self evident?

17. "Truth speaks for itself and affirms the validity of the

way to get her" (Aristotle).

18. What are the criteria of truth ?

19. You made me for you, O Lord, and my heart is restless until it rests on you (Augustine).

20. When we talk about time I know what it is, but when the ask me to tell; it I am in trouble (Augustine).

21. A thing is not necessarily true because badly uttered, nor false because spoken magnificently (Augustine).

22. Do you wish to be great? Then begin by being. Do you desire to construct a vast and lofty fabric? Think first about the foundations of humility. The higher your structure is to be, the deeper must be its foundation (Augustine).

23. It was pride that changel angels into devils; it is humility that makes people as angels (Augustine).

24. Holy Spirit, descend plentifully into my heart. Enlighten the dark corners of this neglected dwelling and scatter there Thy cheerful beams (Augustine).

25. My mind withdrew its thoughts from experience, extracting itself from the contradictory throng of sensuous images, that it might find out what that light was wherein it was bathed... And thus, with the flash of one hurried glance, it attained to the vision of That Which Is (Augustine).

26. Who can map out the various forces at play in one soul? Man is a great depth, O Lord. The hairs of his head are easier by far to count than his feeling, the movements of his heart (Augustine).

27. Patience is the companion of wisdom (Augustine).

28. "God will not suffer man to have a knowledge of things to come; for if he had prescience of his prosperity, he would be careless; and if understanding of his adversity, he would be despairing and senseless" (Augustine).

29. "Any judgment is true if it is both self-consistent and coherently connected with our system of judgment as a whole" (Edgar S. Brightman).

30. Is definition a proof? Aristotle says, "It is not."

31. When a tree falls and none hears it, does it make noise?

32. Does "I AM" include God among the beings?

33. The way I look at things makes them understandable.

34. *Ex nihilo nihil* = from nothing, nothing is produced (Lucrecia, Epicure, Laplace).

35. There is more in the world than in my mind (Shakespeare).

36. There is nothing in my mind that was not first in my senses (Aristotle).

37. *Nihil est in intellectu quod non fuerit prius in sensu* = There is nothing in intelligence which was not previously in the senses (Aquinas).

38. We know nothing about what we have no experience (Aquinas)

39. Experience is the beginning of knowledge (Homer)

40. Experience is father of wisdom (Leonardo da Vinci).

41. Wisdom grows with suffering (Eschilo).

42. What Philosophy is?

43. Philosophy is the expertise between science and theology (Daujat).

44. Philosophy is the no-man's land between science and theology" (Russell) .

45. Philosophy is the art of asking proper questions (H. Bergson).

46. I think therefore I am (R. Descartes).

47. Where does lie the meaning of things?

48. The meaning of thinks lies inside of them but especially in our own disposition towards them. (Antoine de Saint-Exupéry)

49. The meaning of things depends also of our mind. (Jean Daujat).

50. Are reason, intelligence, understanding, intuition the same?

51. The heart has reasons that reason disregards (Pascal).

52. The one who watches for wisdom at dawn shall not be disappointed, for he shall find her sitting by his gate (Wisdom 6:14).

53. All teaching and all learning through discourse proceed from previous knowledge (Aristotle).

54. Words do nothing but prompt man to learn (Augustine in the Teacher).

55. The measure of love, is to be not measurable (Bernard de Clairvaux).

56. The knowledge of God is naturally implanted in all of us (John of Damascus).

57. The meaning of things lies not only in the things but also in our disposition towards them (A. de Saint-Exupery).

58. I do not seek to understand so that I may believe, but I believe so that I may understand (Augustine).

59. Unless I do believe I shall not understand (Anselm).

60. All words are pegs to hang ideas on (Henry Ward Beecher).

61. Knowledge is power, but only wisdom is liberty (W. Durant).

62. What is rational is real, what is real is rational (Hegel).

GLOSSARY

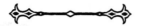

Here is a provisional list on concise vocabulary of material used in main courses of metaphysics. You will find below, as a suggestion, one or more definitions of philosophical words and expressions that we meet during a course. Other definitions are possible. Most words can be used in a current conversation with a similar or different meaning. The same words are also used in diverse courses of philosophy.

1. **Analogy** — Any case of meaning which refer to diverse degree of understanding of a same being.

2. **Angels** are the "messengers" of God, his administrators in creation, the forces moving the universe.

Note: Aristotle referred to them as pure spirits and called them second causes, as executors of the Prime Cause. Which Aquinas explains that God never acts directly in the universe; he always performs through the second causes.

3. **Behaving with Angels** — Being pure will and pure spirit, we communicate with them by will and thoughts.

Note: Angels (and Demons) cannot read inside of human soul without our permission (our simple will)..

4. **Animals** refer to those beings having a sensorial soul (*anima*).

Note: Being only sensorial, that soul perishes when animals perish.

5. **Animal Instinct** — Every animal behavior is directed by sensorial determinism organized for the salvation and continuation of the species which the individual belongs to.

6. **Atomism** — Philosophical doctrine that the universe (either physical or mental) is only composed of simple indivisible minute particles (or atoms).

Note: Famous atomists: Democritus, Epicurus, And Leibniz...

7. **Being** is something that exists.

Note: Aristotle affirms that "the beings can be said in many ways" — Bk. (G §2). So the being is in the same time one and many (Bk: E). Being has to be understood analogically. At first the being is understood as "something", then everything that does exist like: color, action, relation, behavior, etc.

8. **Real Being** is a being whose existence does not depend of my knowledge. It belongs to the world.

Note: Every real being is in act.

9. **Substance** — That which exists in itself

Note: in the philosophy of Immanuel Kant the substance is identified as "Noumenon".

10. **Accident** — That which exists not in itself but in another, which is the substance

Note: Accidents can also be said the characteristics of the substance.

Note: Aristotle considers 9 accidents (see Aristotle's categories.

Note: in the philosophy of Immanuel Kant the accident is identified as "Phenomenon".

11. **Mental Being** is a being that exist in the mind but not in reality.

Note: Mental being is a universal concept. It helps to address speculatively all aspects of real being (its whatness, or essence). Typical "mental being" is <nothingness>. Also called <Rational Being>. It is proper to Mental Being distinguish Essence from Existence, which never can exist separately in a Real Being.

12. **Rational Being** is Mental Being.

13. **Actual Being** (or being in act) is every real being in its actual existence.

Note: a being in act is in potency of any possible change. A being in act includes the potentialities defined by its essence.

14. **Potential Being** is whatever an actual being can develop

and make actual.

Note: It refers to every possibility an actual being has to change.

15. **Human Being** — That being which is capable of knowledge and Love.

16. **Person** does indicate a subject of knowledge, love and conscious relationship

Note: it includes human beings (men, women and children), Angels (spiritual being, or pure spirits), and especially each "Person" of the Holy Trinity, who are defined by their relationships and actually are the only true **persons**...

17. **Change** is moving among diversity, it is moving from a step to another. According to Aquinas it is the passage from being in potency to being in act. Change is a particular case of multiplicity in reference to another.

Note: All change proposed by matter is actually caused by the form. Matter is principle of continuity in the being, while form is principle of change. Matter is what may change and form is what operated the change. While matter is effective power to change, form is effective principle of change or, if you wish, it is the act of change. We may recognize the material continuity and discontinuity of a body by its form. By their matter substances vary as individuals and by their form they vary as species.

18. **Identity** is the opposite of change. Without identity we cannot recognize what things are. Nonetheless, in our world identity is constantly exposed to change. At the mental being level, identity is incompatible with change, as Parmenides and Heraclitus taught in the 4th century B.C..

Note: Identity is the condition to talk: words are supposed to refer always to the same, otherwise no discourse can be done. The discourse itself, using words (Augustine calls them "signs") which refer all along to the same entities, uses the principle of identity. A discourse develops in the multiplicity of language (the many words) how identity works with change. The many identical issues said by words, are organized in propositions which show change. A discourse shows how the same words can express difference, not only describing diverse circumstances... but also diverse aspects of the same... Which is the nature of the being to do so.

19. **Identity** and **change** go together, even if at the mental level we understand only identity (as Parmenides stated) and in the context of real being we only see change (as Heraclitus said and called "*Logos*") to be developed

Note: It was Aristotle who was able to see the connection between identity and change and the necessity of the one to understand the other. Identity is the typical manner of things to be when using language, no word would be consistent if it was not always identical to itself. Words need identity. to address the change of the facts. ...

20. **Intentional Being** is when Mental Being meets Real Being.

Note: it shows a presence of love in intelligence: the capacity to become the other addressing real being. Manifestation of Truth in the Mind refers to a real being when it is present to my mind in the process of knowledge. It is no more material and not yet mental. However it is consistent. Aristotle calls it intentional. It is in this Intentional meeting between Mental and Real Being that it is found the structure, or configuration of a being, i.e. the distinction Matter and Form.

21. **Aristotle's Categories**: the ten categories of the being in Aristotle are (1) the substance and its nine accidents: (2) quality, (3) quantity, (4) relation, (5) action, (6) passion, (7) habitus, (8) position (predisposition), (9) time, (10) place.

Note: See also "Substance" and "Accident".

22. **Cause** — What happens not by itself does happen from another which is called "cause"

Note: Principle of causation — Whatever does not change by itself does change by another, which is called "cause". In every change four causes are involved: material and formal (intrinsic), efficient and final ('extrinsic). What is cause in its proper order is in another order the effect of another cause.

23. **Four causes** — Material, formal, efficient and final causes

24. **Intrinsic causes** refer to formal and material causes. They properly constitute a being in its actual aspect..

25. **Extrinsic causes** refer to efficient and final causes. They move a being towards some new aspect or form.

26. **Material cause**: what by means a thing is made of: it is "this quantity which may exist" and does exist under such or such form. Material cause explains why this object is possible in its own entity. In the case of a cherry, material cause is the quantity of organized matter which constitutes it.

27. **Form** is nothing but the "shape" of things.

Note: the name "**form**" is just the usage in metaphysics of the usual name of shape, appearance, arrangement, or style. In metaphycis context the word "form" become technical and get the definition of (1) cause of existence, (2) cause of intelligibility. what we understand in a being is the form. "form" is "compatible with intelligence. when our intelligence get the whatness, the essence, it actually reads the form.

28. **Formal cause** is the definition or the model of a thing. Formal cause says what such an object is.

Note: In the case of a cherry, it is the form which organizes the matter which the cherry consists of (color, taste, cellular structure, etc.). Its form allows me to recognize that it is a cherry. The form "causes" me to identify a cherry for what it is. I recognize the formal cause inside of what the nature of a thing is, in what is intelligible in it.

29. **Efficient cause** responds to the question "where is this from?" Efficient cause indicates the why of the evolving of a thing:

Note: Efficient cause refers to the external events which have caused the activation (Act of being) of something. It reflects the external elements which have produced the object. Efficient cause finds its source outside of the object and its point of arrival inside the object itself. It explains the change that has led to the formation of the object here and now. This cause is the most obvious of the four ones:. Usually, when the term <cause> is used alone, it refers to efficient cause. Dealing again with a cherry, we may recognize that efficient cause is the whole of elements (air, water, sap of the tree which has fed the pulp, care of the gardener, etc.) which intervened and brought out as a result the constitution of the cherry.

30. **Final cause** responds to the question "in view of what" some change does happen.

Note: Final cause finds its origin is in the thing itself and its point of arrival outside of the thing, in its end, in what completes the object or thing as its perfect development. In the case of a tree producing a cherry, we may consider final cause as the end of the process which produces the cherry, i.e. the cherry as such. Then considering a cherry we may observe that it includes the kernel (seed) of cherry, which the pulp inside of the cherry is the humus paramount in view of reproducing another cherry tree. Final cause expresses the last step towards the essential power of thing leads to become.

31. **Reciprocality of causes** — All causes work together. No one is absolutely first. Each is first in its own order.

Note: Reciprocality of causes means interdependence of causes, but this term is less expressive and even appropriate than the term of reciprocity. We should talk about interdependence of effects and interaction of causes.

32. **Creation** is the act of God putting now all beings into existence.

Note: It is not a process. No time is included. Time also is result of creation.

33. **Time** is the manner people address a distance.

Note: See in course documents the notions of **physical time, psychological time, metaphysical time, spiritual time**.

34. **Human Time** is the duration of human journey, from conception (first birth) up to *NATUS EST*, when we enter definitively into eternity. "Our all life is the dilution in time of our actual response to the love of God" (Chiara Lubich).

35. **Demons** are the failing Angels, those who are disobeying to God.

Note: Because of the characteristics of bringing light, Angels keep that characteristic when falling, but the light is not the one shared with God any more, it becomes their own separate light, a light source of division, and this fact changes the name of the head of the Demons, "Lucifer". In the *Summa Theologica* (I, 63), Aquinas rejected the thesis of St. Gregory that the highest category of Demons comes from the highest Angel, for the most perfects Angels are the Seraphim, whose name indicates the fullness of love and charity. Aquinas says that a similar mistake could eventually be done by a Cherub, because of his entity of fullness of knowledge and intelligence which fits with the sin of pride. According to Augustine, the first Angel who disobeyed was from a lower level (probably an Archangel) and could not accept that people could be superior to them, especially with the fact that human were selected to receive the second person of the Trinity, when God was going to become flesh. By doing so all the Angels who refused to obey God had their name changed into "Demons" and because they lost their transparency with God's love their own light and understanding was twisted: they cannot see inside of human soul without our permission. An Eastern tradition (Russia?) states that the one who made the big mistake was one of the four Archangels, called "Rael" (the Splendor of God), who became "Lucifer".

36. **Individuals** are the basic unit of multiplicity.

Note: Etymologically, individual means what we cannot divide without destroying it. Individuals vary according to the quantity of matter they are made of... They are recognizable by their form.

37. **Intelligence** is the human capacity to become aware of the world and to refer to it.

38. **Knowledge** — What people are aware of (see more in the note "Gnoseology).

39. **Previous knowledge** is the patrimony of understanding present in the mind before any act of intelligence.

40. **Language** — typical people communication.

Note: Every human communication, or language, is made through words. Even when people think inside of their mind they still use words.

41. **Thought** — Expression of language.

Note: Feeling is not thinking. Thinking requires words.

42. **Matter** refers to the mean something is made of.

Note: Matter is the opaque uncertainty which forms corporeal beings. Matter that we know only exists with a form.

Note: As such "Matter" is both (1) **principle of change** (matter is eager to change form) and (2) **principle of individuation** (form enters into existence moving in it matter and becoming a "being").

43. **Prime matter** is pure indeterminacy, ready ("eager") to meet a form and get existence.

44. **Second matter** — see "Designated matter".

45. **Designated matter** material composite of every corporeal being. Matter that got some form.

Note: In *De Ente et Essentia* Aquinas stresses how "Designated Matter" is not in the concept of a being but in the same real being, like "man" (concept) and "Socrates" (designated matter).

46. **Multiplicity** shows the possibility to divide an entity into several beings. Many beings compose a multiplicity. There is multiplicity of species ("discontinuity" of chemical, physical, and eventually biological properties) and multiplicity of single

beings (individuals) inside of species

47. **Metaphysics** — "science of the being *qua* being & what belongs essentially to it" (G §1.).

Note: Metaphysics includes **Ontology, Peratology, Critique**, and natural **Theology.**

48. **Species** is a coherent set of anatomical and physiological characters.

Note: A species is composed of a determined number of individuals..

49. **Recollection Theory** — See article on "Gnoseology".

50. **Illumination Argument** — See article on "Gnoseology".

51. **Essence** — Whatness or nature of a thing.

52. **Eternity** — Timeless state of God: without beginning or end. Different than the immortality of people and angels who have a beginning and no end. Eternity is out of time. There is no past and no future. So eternity can be only now. Eternity is always present. Eternity is the continuous now.

53. **Existence** — The state of being. The fact that a being is present.

54. **Essence & Existence** — inseparable in the facts. Distinguishable in the mind.

55. **Immanence** — refers to the fact of being directly connected with a situation as being part of it, without anticipation, superiority, or any distance. It means that everything is already included. Immanent is everything belongs to something or a situation without any characteristic of an outside neighborhood.

56. **Transcendence** — The fact of being connected but superior. It shows the presence of a higher neighborhood that would make improvement, offer a diverse perspective, or a better meaning.

57. **Instant** — Short piece of time. Present instant corresponds with eternity.

58. **Intentionality** — The process of a person improving in

knowledge through relationship with objects or items. When I know I become intentionally what I know.

59. **Intelligence growing** : It is proper to ask where human knowledge comes from. At birth the mind of a baby is a blank slate. People get intelligence while immerged in a human neighborhood.

Note: Most people just accept the fact that people are born and after a while get thinking… Well the process is not so obvious, even if it is so common. The way Knowledge grows in individuals remains a mystery. It is a fact, but a mysterious fact. Every child received such a wake up of knowledge through education. This fact raises the important question which never was answered properly by any science: how such a process may have started? How people may have started to exist among creatures if they cannot get knowledge by themselves? How people came to know if knowledge is developed by human context? Even a long range of centuries cannot explain what does never start by itself.

60. **Love** — Proper relationship between people. The main support of everything in existence.

Note: Love is cause of any kind of relations in the world. When people love, they cannot totally separate pleasure (physical love), sharing (socio-psychological love), and giving (spiritual love). In a family life all the different degrees are always present. Love is experienced at every level of reality (pleasure, sharing, unconditional) and it is always love (as well as a same person can be considered physically, psychologically, culturally, and so on, but a person is essentially one). In the Bible love is synonym of intelligence, only after Rousseau (1749) and the French Revolution (1789) love became synonym of feeling in our culture. Feeling is not love, but sometimes it may show it.

Love is only one, but it is expressed at every level of creation. There are not diverse entities of love. There is only one kind of love which does include all possible levels of intensity of it as far as a relationship is made to the different levels of being in creation. As such we may distinguish several levels, and call them several degrees... The degrees of love are separated by four differing levels; spiritual, philosophical, psychological/sociological, and physical.

The spiritual level of love is represented through charity. It can be seen through Jean Vanier's quote that "whoever gives love is enriched by what he gives." When you give of yourself, you feel a love that cannot be felt otherwise. The philosophical level shows that philosophy is love of wisdom and that love has the capability to become another and to open the way to know it. Augustine put it well when he stated that "While you grow in love, you grow in beauty, for love is the beauty of the soul." The Psychological/sociological level is through friendship, community, family etc. This can be seen through sacrifice for others. Finally, the physical level is eros. It is enjoying a presence. All degrees interact with each other is the only one common love. Theologically all creation is out of love.

In people love and intelligence go together (See "Fides et Ratio" of JP2) intelligence does not work without love, love does increase the effectiveness of intelligence. No one can perform without the other: we cannot stress one and ignore the other. Every time a similar mistake was made we have an "heresy" like3 with Descartes (reason alone) or Luther (Faith alone).

One of the main exertion of love which the world today is particularly in need is the process of becoming one (one family, one Church, one faith, etc.). Love is what keeps us together and move us to the target of mankind as the body of Christ "That they all be one" (Jn 17:21).

Love cannot just be concerned with qualities because we love what is buried deep down inside a person. We love qualities that do not show on the surface. Love is concerned with people. Everyone needs love and communication. Love is love through the personality. One should not give gifts to express love because love itself is the true gift. God is love therefore we have religion (to study him). Love also allows us to have person to person relationships. We don't just love qualities because we love persons and their flaws.

61. **Mystery** — Anything which cannot be totally understood by human reason. Something that defies any explanation. Scientists face paradoxes, philosopher aporiae, theologians and believers mysteries.

62. **Paradox** — A true statement of conflicting conclusions. A proposition which can be true in spite of apparent self-contradictions or absurdities. A theory that is self contradictory or absurd and nevertheless is proved true by facts. It is the specific business of science to dealing with paradoxes.

63. **Paganism** — In 1962 Card Jean Daniélou stressed publicly how being an atheist today shows to be late in history. Somehow he said that an atheist today is somehow "retarded". Our days show a return to God. The return, however, will be Christian only if it is a return to Christ. Addressing God alone would be mere paganism.

64. **Providence** — Providence is the nickname of God himself. It means "the Eternal Provider."

Note: Full name should be Divine Providence. The Bible refers to Godas "The Lord will provide," or even talking to Moses Godhimself says that "I will be the one I will be," which can also fit with the usual translation "I am who I am" – In Hebrew, in fact, present tense and future tense are to be understood by the context. Present tense includes the fact that eternity is not limited by time. After Augustine we agree that talking about what time "before time" or "after time" is absurd, it is mere nonsense. It would be like asking what kind of water does continue beyond the borders of the sea… There is no water any more but land. All the same, there is no time beyond and below the extension of time, but eternity.

65. **Reality** refers to facts. (independently of the knowledge

of them, which we may have or not).

Note: People are the only beings on earth that are able to address reality as such. People do it through language. We deal with reality-and have it present "intentionally" in our mind Reality does exist first and language is limited to an ongoing, expanding and evolutionary process of investigating, dealing, and interpreting it. Much of what is reality, is not known yet and it slowly but surely is expressed through language. The human being is also part of the facts, and words are slowly improving in referring to the facts.

66. **Semantics** — Semantics is science of the meaning of a discourse.

Note: A branch of linguistics dealing with relationship between words (or signs) and meanings. Science of interpretation of facts in connection with a discourse. Semantics is the expertise of the connotation of words, i.e. of the meaning of them.

67. **Scholasticism** — Philosophical doctrine following the method and thoughts of medieval Church teachers as Abélard, Albertus Magnus, Bonaventure, Duns Scottus, and Ockham, and especially Thomas Aquinas.

Note: Here the ending in "-ism" does not refer to a system of one thinker but to the teaching of the Scholars of the Middle Ages. When it is referred to Aquinas, scholasticism is also synonym of the doctrine emerging from critical realism.

68. **Science** — A branch of knowledge dealing with objective data (physical world and its phenomena), organized into systematic and/or mathematic propositions.

Note: Scientific discourse is univocal. Science is also said "positive science", or "positive sciences" because of the many disciplines which are included.

69. **Subjective** — The individual dimension of every idea, opinion, interpretation or feeling expressed by a person. as being individual. What is subjective is arbitrary. It reflects the quality of thinking of its author.

70. **Subjectivity** — Original character, quality, state or nature of thinking of every individual person.

71. **Intersubjectivity** — An original perspective of thinking, coming for the interactive awareness of people.

Note: Such perspective was started by Edmund Husserl to elaborate a pace from individual subjects to universal thought. In such a perspective, Agapé would be an intersubjective knowledge, There is no doubt that God, source (subject) of all creation is also universal. Such attempt of building a universal thought, which overcomes simple "consensus" is consistent and deserve attention.

72. **Truth** — Reality and language do not create truth. Truth is the connection between facts and discourse.

Note: A discourse is more or less true according to its more or less connection with facts: "Veritas sequitur esse rerum" (Truth follows the facts) said Aquinas…

73. **On Truth:** See the note "Pedagogy of Truth" for **Pragmatic theory, Coherence theory, Subjective theory, Social theory, Political theory, Correspondence theory, Owe theory & Propaedeutic theory.**

74. **Wisdom** — Love of, knowledge of and intimacy with the truth.

Note: Please do not confuse the natural blossoming of understanding into wisdom with the gift of the Holy Spirit given under the same name: They are similar in their identity but they are not the same. Wisdom in metaphysics is the ground to receive the spiritual gift. That spiritual wisdom is the metamorphosis of the previous one, almost like the carterpillar entering the cocoon exit it as a butterfly. There is some connection and nonetheless they are totally different. Philosophy deals with the first, theology deals with the second.

Thank you for your attention

Addendum

For those who would like to go deeper in the inquiry on Metaphysics here below are a short list of books which supported the whole reflection included in the book.

Books to read for Metaphysics

1. THE MANDATORY BOOKS

Our study is supported by THREE basic works, which are approached in the following order:

<> Jacques Maritain, *Introduction to Philosophy*, Sheed & Ward, Classic   (ISBN = 074-255-0532)

<> Aristotle, *Metaphysics*, Peripatetic Press   (ISBN = 096-028-7019),

which can be find also inside of the following edition:

Aristotle, Introductory Reading, Hackett Pub. Trad. Irwin & Fine, June 96   (ISBN 978.087.220.3396)

<> St. Th. Aquinas, *On Being and Essence*, Pont. Inst. of Medieval Studies   (ISBN = 088-844-2505)

Each book was selected not only for its small size and available price and especially for its intense teaching. Everyone is manageable and insightful. You can easily bring each of them with you everywhere you go and at a first approach read it without any program or special schedule: that will ease later our sharing in class. Read them for pleasure even when it is for duty. Dot not let the reading fixing the time, but decide previously how much you want to read for how long and then do it. Train yourself to get the best of the work with a method of speed reading. Look at the directory and seek what you are most appealed with.

Here and there some of the texts are some time difficult. Read them by excerpts and almost at random. Make their contents more digestible. Take note of what is more insightful. Bring for class discussion what looks contradictory or obscure. As usual, each reading requires open mind and personal discernment.

Dealing with them together in class as a team or at the side of classroom as a team of study will be helpful to everyone in our personal studies.

More specifically ...

Maritain's on the Intro offers the pattern of the whole course. Seek for the sections that address the topics.

Aristotle on Metaphysics give the details of the configuration of real being and offers the most specific approach of metaphysical perspectives of ontology and peratology (see in Maritain the definition of both as "Ontology First" and "Ontology Second", which the nickname is "peratology").

Aquinas on Being and Essence is a "short notice" that he wrote while he was a student of theology in Sorbonne, Paris. It was intended to allow his fellow brothers in community to share the consistency of life and values... Read it for what it is: a philosophy memento... It is actually easier to understand than it appears at a first glance. Try it.

These three works are the frame of the whole insights we will have on the issue from other sources from Bonaventure and John Duns Scotus, which are included as additional pieces of study.

2. ADDITIONAL READING

Additional Reading are disclosed along the journey. References are done here and there on Augustine (Illumination Theory) who was the main inspiring thinker of Medieval Franciscan scholars esp.: Bonaventure in *Mystical Readings*, ISBN 978-193-525-7967 and John Duns Scotus in *Philosophical Writings*, ISBN 978-087-220-0180).

Specific consideration to Franciscan tradition are also done.

Alain Marie Sauret
1748 Guyton Rd. Allison Park, PA 15101 – Ph. 412-364-1923
alainsauret@hotmail.com

Born in Gascony, France, I studied at the Catholic Institute, Paris, where my professors, Marie-Dominique Dubarle and Jean Daujat introduced me to Marie-Dominique Chenu, Etienne Gilson, Jacques Maritain, Jean Guitton, Joseph de Finance, and Marie-Dominique Philippe. Some of these thinkers became intimate friends and provided a strong influence on my thoughts.

Coincidentally, I earned my PhD in philosophy at La Sorbonne, Paris, where I met personally Jean-Paul Sartre, Simone de Beauvoir, and became familiar with Michel Foucault, Gilles Deleuze, Felix Guattari, and Jacques Derrida. One of my professors, Henri Birault, was a personal friend of Martin Heidegger. He led me to a critical reading of Friedrich Nietzsche and supervised my dissertation on "Nietzsche and the problem of Jesus."

Previously, while a teenager, at the age of 14, I went through a difficult crisis of identity and values: I was challenged first by the fanaticism of Marxism, then I shared the views of existentialists and atheists, but, at 17, I had the chance to undergo the experience of Gospel life with the Focolare Movement at the Institute Mystici Corporis of Loppiano, Florence, Italy, and reverted to Catholic faith.

Teaching philosophy in Rome, at the Gregorian and at Regina Mundi, I gained increased acquaintance in the main philosophy stream of the classics, ancient and mediaeval and became familiar with the Socratic Method, which provides such a good relationship between teacher and students and transforms every class in a fertile endeavor. At the same time I was member of the Roman Curia, serving under Pope Paul VI, John-Paul I, and John-Paul II. I matured acquaintance with the life and legacy of the Catholic Church, became involved with Eastern

Catholic traditions, and met different religious denominations, Christian, Jewish, Muslim, and Buddhist.

Working in the Vatican and teaching philosophy increased the intimacy with Christ's teaching and made me enter into a growing process of life and understanding that never stopped.

Through the Vatican I also was engaged in several projects of rehabilitation, raising financial assistance for Eastern communities, especially in the Middle East, promoting centers of education, like the foundation of Bethlehem University, in the West Bank. Later, I concurred to reorganize (while moving it from Paris to inside of the Vatican) the Holy Childhood Society, which promotes worldwide the rehabilitation of children. Meantime, as President of la Petite Ecole de la Trinité des Monts, I oversaw the school belonging to the French Embassy in Rome. In these assignments, I enjoyed the impact that spiritual values and philosophical concern add to socio-cultural development.

In July of 1995, my wife, Chiara, and I, along with our five children, came to North America. Our visit became such a surprising opportunity to spend more time together as a family that our children asked to stay permanently in the States. So, we did, first in Pennsylvania, later in Texas, then in Pittsburgh again.

On this side of the sea, my professional assignments have been teaching philosophy as a visiting professor in Pittsburgh, Pennsylvania, first at La Roche College (1995-96), next at Duquesne University (1996-99). Then, I was Associate Professor at the Sacred Heart Major Seminary in Detroit, Michigan (1999-2002), and Academic Dean at OLCC, Corpus Christi, Texas (2002-04). I taught undergraduate courses of Philosophy (Anthropology, Metaphysics, Epistemology, History, Logic, Ethics, and Politics), graduate courses of philosophy (contemporary), and theology (on the knowledge of God).

I also provided Bible studies and Spiritual Lectures for ecclesial movements all over North America. Additionally, from 1996 to 1999 I joined in Ontario Msgr. Roman Danylak, Bishop of Toronto of the Ukrainians, who invited me to attend once a month Healing Services and the sessions of a commission created to discern the consistency of some visionaries from Rwanda, Burundi, and Mexico.

In Texas, our family faced difficulties: the house was flooded, invaded by wild animals and finally destroyed. By miracle nobody was killed, not even hurt. To follow the want of our kids, we moved back to Pittsburgh during the summer 2004. Afterwards I became member of the Faculty of Phoenix for courses online (2004-2007), visiting professor at East Stroudsburg campus of the University of Pennsylvania (2007), online professor of philosophy at Wheeling Jesuit University, West Virginia (2005-2010), and at La Roche College, Pittsburgh (2007-2012).

Since 2011, I teach Metaphysics, Ethics and Anthropology at Franciscan University of Steubenville.

Pittsburgh, summer 2016

Made in the USA
Middletown, DE
05 September 2020